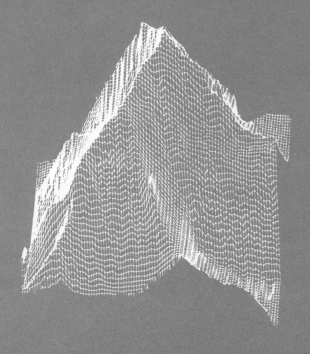

WHITE LIMBO

THE FIRST
AUSTRALIAN CLIMB OF MT EVEREST

Majesty of silence, casting
Shadows as long as life,
The mountain speaks in dimensions
I cannot hear.
I try to feel the power
Behind the wind and snow,
To know how the emptiness
Can pervade.
It is enough to feel that presence
Amongst these walls of ice,
In the sunset, catching pink,
The highest peaks.

To Swami Nirmalratna Saraswati

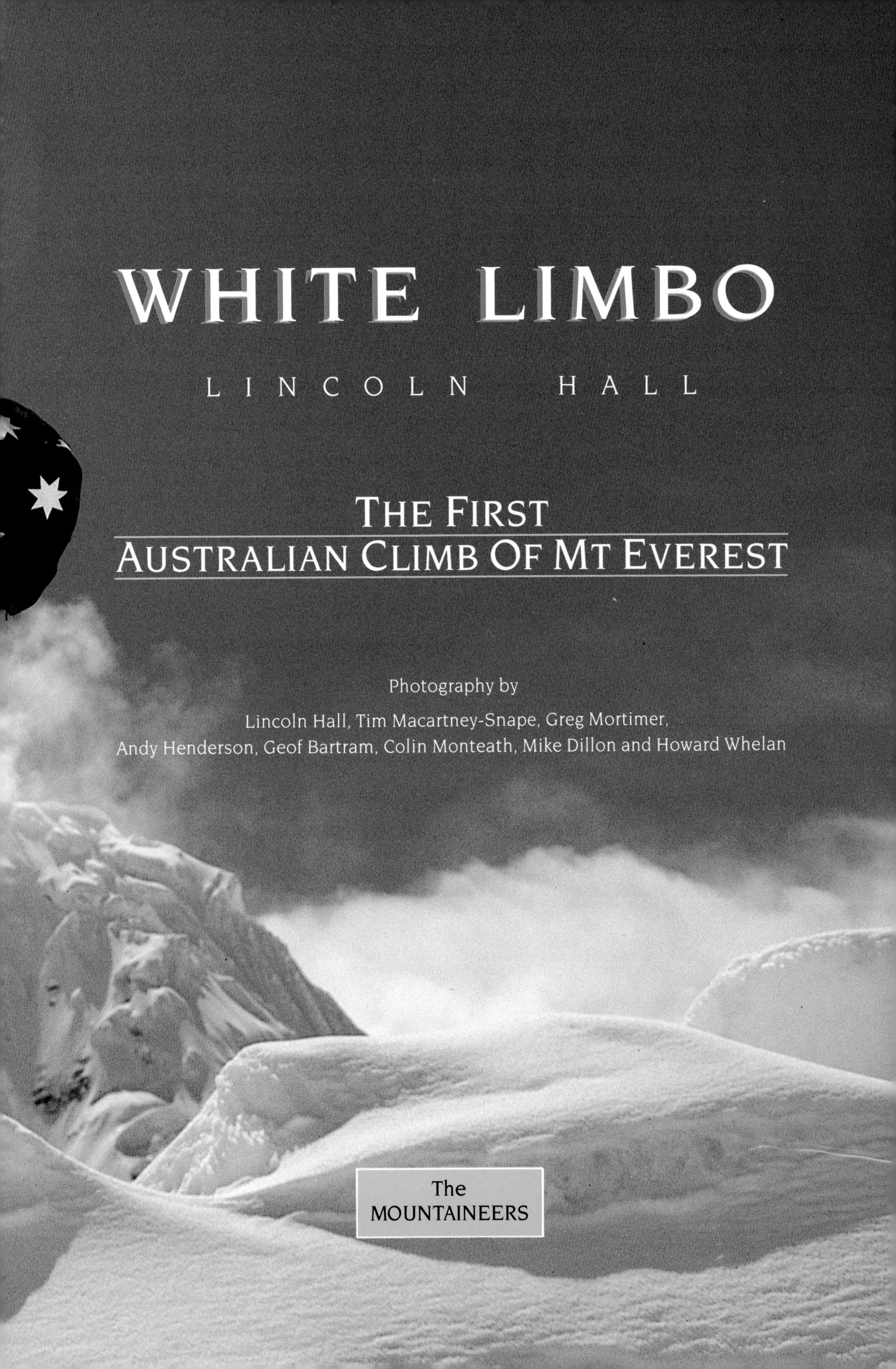

WHITE LIMBO

LINCOLN HALL

THE FIRST
AUSTRALIAN CLIMB OF MT EVEREST

Photography by

Lincoln Hall, Tim Macartney-Snape, Greg Mortimer,
Andy Henderson, Geof Bartram, Colin Monteath, Mike Dillon and Howard Whelan

The
MOUNTAINEERS

The Mountaineers: Organized 1906 "…to explore, study, preserve and enjoy the natural beauty…"

Copyright © 1985 by Lincoln Hall

Published by The Mountaineers
306 Second Avenue West, Seattle WA 98119

Published simultaneously in Canada
by Douglas & McIntyre Ltd.
1615 Venables St., Vancouver BC V5L 2H1

Published in Australia by Weldons Pty. Ltd.
43 Victoria St., McMahons Point
NSW 2060 Australia

Printed in Japan by Dai Nippon
Library of Congress Catalog Card Number 86-062806
ISBN 0-89886-135-7

A KEVIN WELDON PRODUCTION

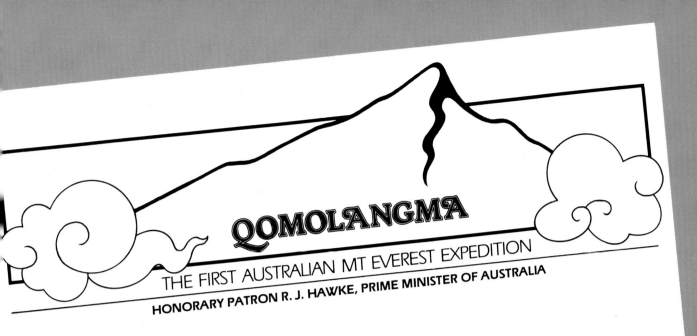

QOMOLANGMA

THE FIRST AUSTRALIAN MT EVEREST EXPEDITION

HONORARY PATRON R. J. HAWKE, PRIME MINISTER OF AUSTRALIA

31 March 1985

Exciting stories, whether real or imagined, tend to depict a world apart from the rest of us. The heroes and heroines of bestselling thrillers never have repayment problems with their Lamborghinis and never suffer jet-lag. The storyteller omits details in order to keep unlikely characters plausible, or to avoid disturbing the reader with too many reminders of reality. After all, the important thing is to track down, somewhere in South America, the fascist spy ring which terrorises Switzerland and Bondi. This, or some other equally gripping goal, leaves no room for human weakness, apart from love, of course.

The world of climbing Mt Everest is apart from us for different reasons. When the book of the climb is written by a mountaineer, much is left out, partly because it seems unexplainable to the uninitiated and partly because to other climbers those omissions are unwritten truths. The only question asked in the story is "Which mountain?" never "Why climb at all?" The consequence is a tale of overcoming the bone-chilling dangers and impossible obstacles which lie between the climbers and the summit. The climbers seem to be almost inhuman in their disregard for danger and discomfort.

When you are part of a climbing story, as I have been often, you know that the only cardboard characters are the people modelling gear in the pages of the climbing magazine that someone brought along to Base Camp. You know that on the mountain emotions do run high and close to the surface; nobody is superhuman; no one is never frightened.

My wish to show people the human side of climbing Mt Everest led to this book being written. The facts are here as well, but I have expanded the record with my impressions and my feelings, so it is very much my story. How much of the essence of our adventure I have managed to capture is impossible for me to judge. Perhaps we will seem more convincing as people if I add that on our return to Aust- ralia we all suffered from jet-lag.

Lincoln Hall

PROLOGUE

9 October 1981

Once our path topped the ridge it dropped straight down to the river as if it, too, needed to escape the icy wind. The wind seemed to have felt no sunshine since leaving the frozen wastes of Mongolia, one thousand kilometres to the north.

At the crest I threw my heavy pack from my shoulders and sat back against it to wait for my five friends. This spot provided our last panoramic view of the mountains amongst which we had been climbing for the past month. I sat with my thoughts while I watched my three climbing companions approach and pass me, each alone and silent. Following a hundred metres behind, Mr Ran and Mr Zhung were talkative. No doubt our interpreter and liaison officer were eager to see their wives again, and to return to the basic luxuries of their homes in Xining, the capital of the Chinese province of Qinghai.

The end of an expedition allows time for reflection. One's mind is no longer concerned with uncertainties: whether the snow will be firm enough to climb upon, whether the glacier is passable, what that type of cloud means in this part of the world. There had been so many unknowns here on the northern limits of the Tibetan Plateau. Until this season no foreign expeditions had climbed this range. When we had arrived in Beijing six weeks before we knew nothing about the Anyemaqen massif apart from the names of its principal peaks. Now, with the main peak climbed by a new and difficult route, our minds were free to cope with the questions that mountaineering always asks.

I looked to the mountains. All were visible except for the snowy tip of Anyemaqen. Only that peak broached the sea of dark cloud which floated above the tumble of ridges and glaciers. Neither I nor my three companions needed to see the hidden summit. We knew what was there. The clouds were heavy with snow and misery for anyone who was up there now. An imaginary suffering, for with our departure the range was empty again.

LEFT: Geof Bartram contemplates a steep step in the glacier, an obstacle between him and the East Face of Anyemaqen, behind.

ABOVE: Geof Bartram, Andy Henderson and Lincoln Hall at a makeshift camp on Anyemaqen.

There had been times when the suffering in the mountains had been real. A sudden storm can turn a peaceful day into a nightmare. The horror of the cold and danger is forgotten when every thought and energy are needed for survival. We had been lucky on Anyemaqen. The only storm we had experienced hit us late in the day when we were above the avalanche-prone slopes of the mountain, and it had abated entirely during the night we spent huddled on ledges hacked out of the snow face.

On this our last day of walking from Base Camp it was appropriate that the weather should be so foreboding. On days like this, I thought, the best thing to be doing in the mountains is to be leaving them. That raised the question that so often plays in my mind: why be there at all?

Part of my mind dismissed the question as irrelevant. My existence was irrevocably bound with the challenge, the friendships and the lack of confusion which makes mountaineering separate from the illusions and pretensions of everyday living. It did not matter that there was no pot of gold at the top. It was enough to climb the rainbow. I suppose it was the danger and fear of dying that made me ask myself why I climbed mountains. Without that moderating fear caution would be thrown to the winds. And that caution is the only thing that keeps mountaineers alive. In the mountains all decisions have to be weighed very carefully but one is never certain that everything has been considered; there is always the worry that a vital factor has been overlooked with consequences that could be fatal.

We were pleased with our climb here in China. The route had not been easy, nor the conditions favourable. We felt content that our experience and judgment had taken us to the top and back safely. But more than that the climb reminded us of the value of everything on earth, from the feeling of companionship one experiences struggling against the cold and the danger together, to sunsets so beautiful that our eyes and ears ached from the colours and the silence. Now, back on comparatively level ground, our minds were relaxed but alert, eager to appreciate all that was happening around us.

At times our thoughts would drift to the future. Already we had expeditions planned for years in advance. An unclimbed spur of Annapurna II was the next big objective for Tim, Andy and myself, and Mt Pumori for Geof. These were the challenges nearest to hand. However, what preoccupied us was Qomolangma. In Tibetan the name means Mother Goddess of the Earth, but to people around the world the peak was known as Mt Everest.

Though the crest of the Himalayan range forms the border between Tibet and Nepal, the bulk of the mountain lies in Tibet. When in Beijing six weeks earlier we had asked about the possibility of attempting Qomolangma. We wished to attempt the only-once-climbed North Face. The Chinese Mountaineering Association considered our application and agreed, granting permission for 1984. We greeted the news with excitement and apprehension, then put it to the backs of our minds. Anyemaqen was our immediate concern.

Now, with Anyemaqen climbed, we had time and room in our heads to think about Everest. Were we ready for the biggest mountain of them all? Were our plans overambitious? Though far from the steepest mountain in the world, Everest's size made it the ultimate mountaineering challenge. Even here, with our most recent success still in sight, the question took a permanent place in each of our minds. Could we climb Everest? We all knew there was only one way to find out.

BELOW: From left, Andy Henderson, Lincoln Hall, Geof Bartram and Tim Macartney-Snape after descending from Anyemaqen, behind.

PHOTO CAPTIONS FOR PRECEDING PAGES:

2–3   Sunset on Makalu, the world's fifth highest peak, over thirty kilometres east of Everest, viewed from foothills in southern Nepal.

4–5   Yaks at Advance Base Camp by the Rongbuk Glacier after a fresh snowfall.

6–7   By the end of the expedition our flag at Camp I was torn to shreds by the wind which regularly blew up the Rongbuk Valley in the morning and down in the evening.

8–9   Sunshine breaks through the afternoon storm clouds to light peaks south of Everest.

10–11   Howard Whelan skis towards the Lho La. Across the Rongbuk Glacier, the West Face of Changtse rises through the mist.

12   Climbers ascend the fixed rope up the lower part of Everest's North Face. The bottom climber is about to cross the bergschrund.

FOLLOWING PAGES: Storm clouds roll in, obscuring Tim Macartney-Snape's view from the top of this subpeak of Anyemaqen. Several days of bad weather kept the climbers in their tents on the glacier before they were able to climb the East Face of Anyemaqen.

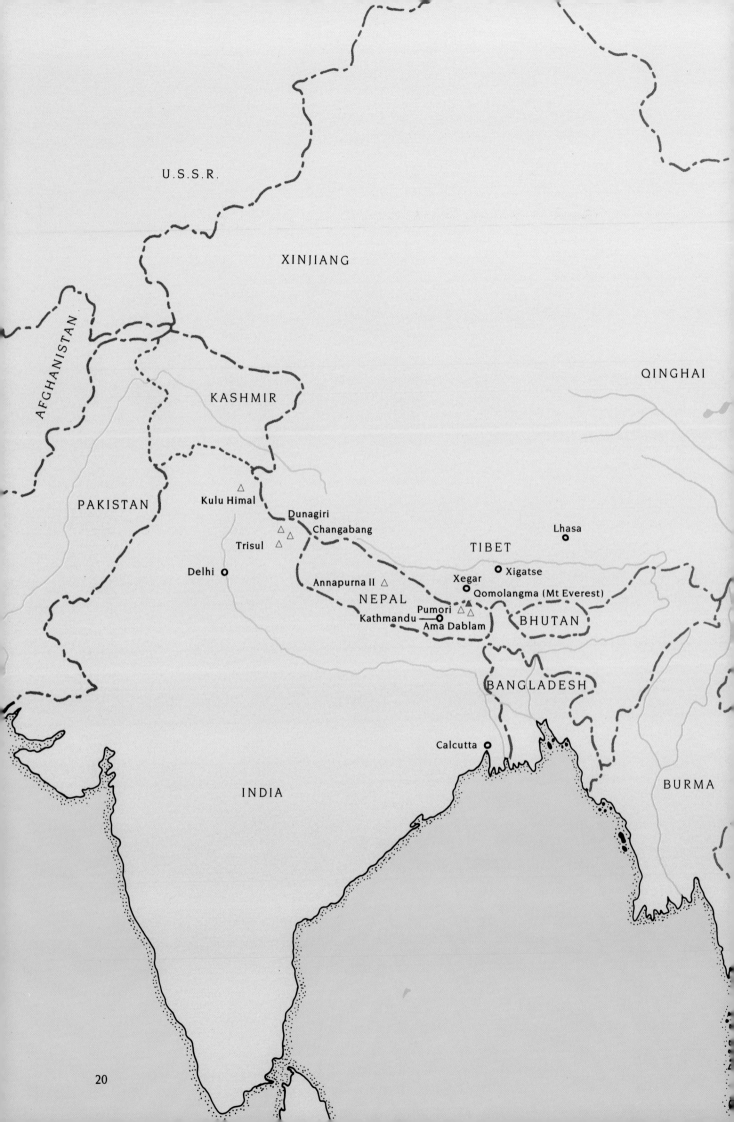

U.S.S.R.

XINJIANG

AFGHANISTAN

QINGHAI

KASHMIR

PAKISTAN

△ Kulu Himal

Dunagiri
△ Changabang
Trisul △ △

Lhasa ○

TIBET

Delhi ○

Annapurna II △

Xegar ○ Xigatse

Qomolangma (Mt Everest)

NEPAL

Pumori △ △
Kathmandu ○
Ama Dablam

BHUTAN

BANGLADESH

Calcutta ○

INDIA

BURMA

MONGOLIA

Beijing ○

Anyemaqen

CHINA

NORTH
KOREA

SOUTH
KOREA

VIETNAM

LAOS

Hong Kong ○

AILAND

KAMPUCHEA

AREA MAP

From the Tibet/Nepal border, Tim Macartney-Snape looks into the Western Cwm of Everest

Avenue of broken dreams
No-one calls the angel falls
Alice is in wonderland

from the song 'White Limbo' by Australian Crawl

Limbo/limbou/, n., pl. **–bos** **1.** (oft.cap.) a supposed region on the border of hell or heaven, the abode after death of unbaptised infants, ... **4. in limbo** → **no-man's-land** (defs 4, 5 6). [ME from ML **in limbo** on the border (of hell).]

The Macquarie Dictionary.

CHAPTER ONE

MOUNT EVEREST IN PERSPECTIVE

TODAY'S modern world is epitomised by technological excess. Entertainment comes from electric toys; dental hygiene from toothbrushes whose bristle length and flexibility are determined by computers; telephones answer themselves with pre-recorded messages then lapse into muzak; petrol bowsers turn themselves off at pre-selected quantities; fast food is made by machines to chemical formulae, packed by machines, dispensed by machines and eaten by people whose tastes have become mechanical. Behind the cities loom suburban hills, their summit lookouts serviced by cable-cars. Most people in our society will never experience the adventure that still exists in places other than King's Cross and, for a privileged few, in space rides to the moon. This is our world. Its benefits are enormous but so are its dangers. The dangers are those of existing for personal security and comfort, of remaining unaware of other sides to life. We worry whether our clothes and cars and emotions and opinions match the current fashion. We allow these things to assume more importance in our minds than the magic of being alive. Meanwhile most people on earth manage to live full lives with only the simplest of trappings. Living the city life it is easy to forget that man is not the centre of the universe.

Beyond the suburbs the bush begins. Our lifestyle does no more than acknowledge the existence of wild places. For most, the bush is seen as the distance between two towns, or as a place for a picnic, or to drive through for a change of air. Yet the stillness of green forest smells of life so much more than the noise and haste of concrete jungles. Mountains radiate confidence in their own worth. They are harsher than the forests, less malleable to the whims of industry. In the high mountains there is no question of values. Humans are simply insignificant. In the wilderness we can feel that something larger than us exists, and it is independent of our petty ambitions and frustrations, irrelevant to our complex society. Reality "is", although we cannot describe it with words or photographs or mathematics. It is the need to seek out this essence that has driven man from the comforts of civilised life to the remotest mountains and widest oceans. The struggle for the right to live is the ultimate challenge of life. People in our society are fortunate to be able to choose that challenge, when so much of the world faces the fight to live every day.

LEFT: Andy Henderson climbs down to Tim Macartney-Snape high on Ama Dablam in Nepal. In the background, Mt Everest rises behind Nuptse.
ABOVE: Morning sun on Mt Everest's summit.

Nature's forces are beyond human control. To visit the mountains people must go on nature's terms. Climbers must use their judgment to survive the threats of weather, avalanches and hidden crevasses. The skill of climbing is to work between these dangers and one's own limitations. The satisfaction comes not only from achievement but also from the intensity of the activity. One becomes totally involved, totally committed, totally alive.

There have long been people in Western society who have felt the need to live life at this level. Some have become soldiers, sailors or bandits, and others mountaineers. Mountaineering is the most recent addition to this list as it is essentially a pastime of the wealthy, or at least, of wealthy cultures. Mountain climbing became an organised and socially acceptable activity in the middle of the last century when British and European scientists claimed research and exploration as reasons for their climbs amongst the Alps of Europe. International rivalry began to exert an influence. Mountains were climbed by difficult routes even though easier ways to the summit could be found. Achievement rather than pursuit of knowledge was acknowledged as the reason for such climbs. This style of climbing became respectable when the climbs were seen to enhance national prestige.

The earliest expeditions to the Himalaya and Karakoram took place at the beginning of this century. Increasing human knowledge of the earth was the professed aim. Many found satisfaction in filling in blanks on the map, but I am sure few would deny that the joys of the experience were personally just as worthwhile. It was only when Mt Everest became the objective of the expeditions that the emphasis changed from geographical and anthropological exploration to a search for the limits of human endurance. No one knew whether people could survive the incredibly harsh environment of the highest mountain on earth. Such a challenge had to be met.

Interest in an expedition to Mt Everest began to gather in the early years of this century amongst British explorers and mountaineers. At that time India provided the only feasible access to the mountain so the British, because of their control of India, regarded Mt Everest as their province. Political difficulties did exist – Everest was not actually in India. Though only one hundred kilometres north through Nepal, the mountain was closed from that direction. The Nepalese kingdom was forbidden territory to foreigners, so access had to be gained through Tibet. The Indian government (then British) had political reasons for not wanting expeditions to visit Tibet, which meant that for many years all plans were stillborn. The First World War changed the political situation, as did the withdrawal of the Chinese garrison from Tibet. Negotiations began afresh and in 1921 an expedition left Darjeeling in India to make a reconnaissance of the mountain. George Mallory, a member of the party, wrote these first impressions: "**There is no complication for the eye. The highest of the world's mountains, it seems, had to make but a single gesture of magnificence to be Lord of all, vast in unchallenged and isolated supremacy.**"

Encouraged by the success of the reconnaissance in finding a suitable approach route and in assessing the climbing conditions, the Alpine Club and the Royal Geographical Society organised another expedition in 1922. It was the first full-scale attempt to climb the mountain. The route taken was the North-East ridge, the way pioneered by the 1921 party. The team consisted of thirteen British climbers, sixteen Sherpas from Nepal to act as high altitude porters, and Tibetan porters and yaks to transport the supplies to the base camp on Tibet's Rongbuk Glacier. Months were devoted to establishing and stocking camps, gradually pushing the route higher up the mountain. Mallory, Somervell and Norton were able to climb to 26 800 feet (8160 metres) above sea-level before admitting defeat. No man had climbed above 7300 metres before this expedition so the climbers were unprepared for the debilitating effects of high altitude. There was no understanding of the mechanisms of acclimatisation whereby one's body gradually adjusts to the absence of oxygen. They attempted to cope with anoxia by using cylinders of compressed oxygen, but there was debate amongst the members as to whether the weight of the cumbersome apparatus offset its usefulness.

During the next expedition in 1924, Norton and Somervell were able to climb to 8300 metres without the aid of artificial oxygen. Norton pushed on to 8440 metres where he turned back with the summit only four hundred metres above him. Three days later

ROUTES OF ASCENT

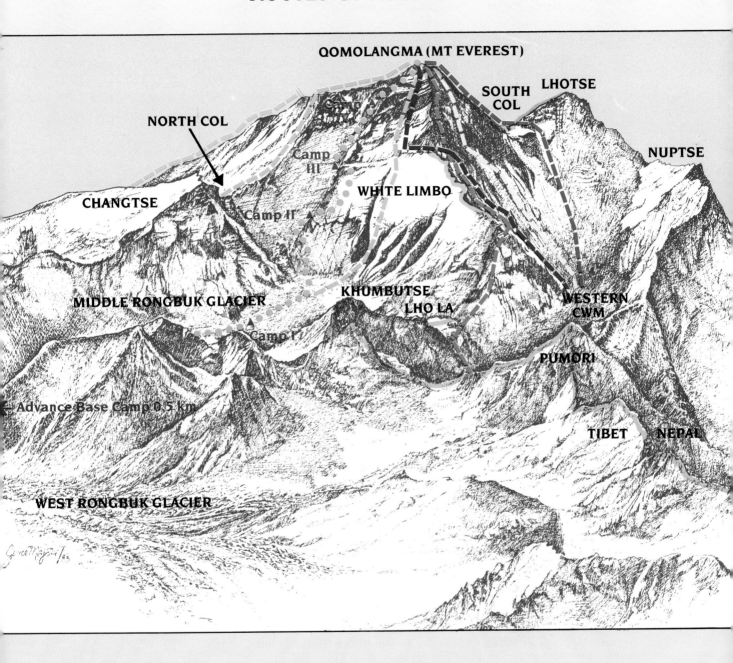

KEY TO ROUTES

■ SOUTH-EAST RIDGE	First Ascent, British Expedition, 1953
◻ NORTH RIDGE	(Pre-War British Attempts) Chinese, 1960
■ WEST SHOULDER AND HORNBEIN COULOIR	Americans, 1963
◻ SOUTH-WEST FACE	British, 1975
■ WEST RIDGE DIRECT	Yugoslavs, 1979
◻ JAPANESE NORTH FACE 'SUPER COULOIR'	Japanese, 1980
◻ NORTH-EAST RIDGE	(uncompleted) British, 1982
◻ AUSTRALIAN NORTH FACE 'GREAT COULOIR'	3 October 1984
◻ NEPAL/TIBET BORDER	

Mallory, veteran of the two previous Everest expeditions, and Irvine, took oxygen sets with them when they left for the summit. They climbed away from their sole companion at the top camp into thickening mist and were never seen again. The story of the courage of that attempt and the loneliness of their unknown grave has become a legend. Public imagination was captured by the thought that their deaths were for no other reason than, as Mallory had explained, **"Because it is there"**.

It was not until 1933 that the British mounted the next expedition. Wyn Harris and Wager, then Smythe a few days later, were able to climb to the same height as Norton had reached in 1924. The mountaineers remained convinced that Everest could be climbed with the right combination of preparation, fitness and weather. Back in Britain opinion was not as optimistic. The public questioned the appropriateness of large and expensive expeditions to Tibet during the Great Depression, a period of extreme hardship at home.

At the time public attention was focussed on Everest – natural enough as the expeditions were sponsored by newspapers – even though the climbs were unsuccessful. Neglected by the press were the climbs undertaken by two of Britain's most respected and competent mountaineers. The trips organised by Bill Tilman and Eric Shipton and their companions may have seemed small fry compared to the Everest expeditions but their objectives were anything but small. Most importantly, several of their climbs were successful. Shipton, who had been a member of the 1933 expedition, was chosen to lead an Everest reconnaissance in 1935 to re-examine strategy and to assess conditions during the monsoon season. All previous attempts had taken place during the pre-monsoon season. Shipton was given the chance to prove the potential of small, light-weight and therefore inexpensive expeditions. His team consisted of Tilman and five others. Rather than take a huge supply train of yaks for the approach, they lived from the land, saving their few luxuries for high in the mountains. Shipton thought the best way to test the condition of the monsoon snow was to climb upon it, and the best way to choose the most suitable route up Mt Everest was to view the mountain from the summits of smaller satellite peaks. It was the perfect excuse for a climbing spree. Consequently the expedition climbed twenty-six peaks from 6000 to 7000 metres. These ascents were made despite the poor climbing conditions of the monsoon. The snow was deep and unstable above 7000 metres, and snow fell virtually every afternoon

The 1935 trip was a prelude to another summit attempt in 1936. Shipton and Tilman had hoped that their reconnaissance would convince the organising committee that small expeditions spelt the way to success. The committee interpreted the success differently, and reasoned that if a small expedition could achieve so much then a large expedition could bulldoze its way to the top. That attitude set the style for the 1936 expedition, even though Shipton and Smythe (another small team advocate) were members. As it turned out the weather in Tibet in 1936 was exceptionally bad, preventing progress above the North Col.

A lightweight team led by Tilman attempted the mountain in 1938 only to fall prey to equally bad weather. The climbers were able to establish Camp VII at 8200 metres and had the weather been good it is likely that they would have demonstrated conclusively that Everest was climbable by a small expedition. As it was, the conquest of Everest had to wait another fifteen years.

During the years that the mountain remained untouched, momentous changes took place back in the human world. Some of those changes had direct bearing on the history of Mt Everest. The first was the independence and partitioning of India, which meant that Britain lost its commanding geographical advantage. This was further weakened in 1950 by the opening of Nepal's borders to foreigners and the invasion of Tibet by Chinese forces, leading to those frontiers being firmly closed.

The British were granted permission by the Nepalese authorities to make a reconnaissance of Everest's southern approaches in 1951. Shipton led a team of six which included the New Zealander, Edmund Hillary. Hopes of a feasible route were confirmed when a way was found through the dangerous icefall on the Khumbu Glacier. From there it seemed possible to climb to the South Col and thence (hopefully) to the summit. Shipton's assessment that the icefall would be the most dangerous part of any climb made from the south has proved to be accurate. To date over a dozen people have been killed there, more than half of them Sherpas carrying supplies for higher camps.

An ice-sculpture on the Rongbuk Glacier frames Mt Everest's West Ridge.

An ice-sculpture on the Rongbuk Glacier frames Mt Everest's West Ridge.

It was a shock to the British Himalayan Committee when, in 1952, permission to climb Everest was given to a Swiss group. Discussions were held with the Swiss in the hope of organising a joint expedition, but instead it was agreed that the British would attempt the mountain in 1953.

The Swiss Foundation of Alpine Research planned a pre-monsoon expedition and, if that failed, another attempt during the post-monsoon season. The Swiss had to cope with the psychological factor of breaking completely new ground where the dangers ahead were totally unknown. Of the British route in Tibet only the last three hundred metres to the summit remained unclimbed. The Swiss faced 2000 metres of untouched mountain. Given this, and the infrequent but severe storms that plagued the expedition, Lambert and Tenzing Norgay did well to break the altitude record and climb within 250 vertical metres of the summit before retreating exhausted. They returned in autumn (post-monsoon) but bad weather prevented them from climbing above the South Col (7986 metres).

Meanwhile the British had expended the energy of their impatience on an attempted ascent of Cho Oyu, an 8000-metre peak west of Everest on the Tibetan border. The expedition, led by Shipton, failed to reach the summit, although its members climbed high on the mountain.

Shipton was in favour of taking a small experienced team to Everest in 1953. The Himalayan Committee was more concerned with success than with the style of the climb. It believed a large expedition had more chance of success, so it was a large venture which it began to organise. It was assumed by all mountaineers in Britain that Shipton with his proven experience and obvious talent would be the leader. He had been selected for that position when it was presumed by the British that they would be given permission for 1953. As they no longer held a monopoly on the mountain the British Himalayan Committee decided that the 1953 expedition must be the successful one. It would be several years before the Nepalese allowed Britain another chance if it failed this time. While the Committee did not question Shipton's ability, it did doubt his capacity to lead successfully a large expedition of the style that was being planned. The result of a great deal of behind-the-scenes intrigue, while the expedition was being organised, was that Shipton was ousted from leadership and replaced by John Hunt. More accurately, Shipton was asked to accept such absurd conditions and qualifications to his leadership that he was forced to challenge them with his resignation from the position. This was exactly what the Committee had been playing for; his resignation was graciously but firmly accepted.

Through no fault of his own, the furtive politicking that led to John Hunt's appointment as leader put him under enormous pressure to live up to Shipton's reputation. It was an unenviable position and a very difficult one for a man who had never visited Everest. However, he was a competent and determined organiser, and by 1953 he had made sure that the British Expedition was in the strongest possible position. The team was proven in ability and determined to succeed. Wartime research had led to improved equipment and a better understanding of physiological needs in extremely harsh conditions. The Swiss had come very close to success in 1952. Everyone knew that the mountain was climbable. It remained for the British to use the momentum of this conviction to carry them to the summit.

That was exactly what they did, though of course a great deal of hard work and co-operation was called for as well. On 29 May 1953, Edmund Hillary and Tenzing Norgay Sherpa stood on the earth's highest point. It was a great personal triumph for Tenzing Norgay, having come so close to success the preceding year. A few days before, Bourdillion and Evans, who made the first attempt to reach the summit from the top camp on the South Col, had turned back exhausted from the South Summit. When Hillary and Tenzing made their successful bid it took two and a half hours to climb from the South Summit to the main peak. The size of the expedition and the logistical build-up which Hunt had planned allowed for a third summit team to be in position at the South Col if Hillary and Tenzing failed. As it was they escorted the victorious pair down the mountain.

LEFT: Andy Henderson high on Ama Dablam. Strong winds blow clouds from Everest's summit, behind.

The ramifications of the first ascent of Everest were numerous. British nationalism was given a firm boost, even though neither of the two summiteers were British nationals. The successful formula for Himalayan climbing had been shown to be a large elaborate expedition which used oxygen apparatus, organised and administered along the lines of a military operation. Had Shipton led a successful expedition the consequences for Himalayan mountaineering would have been different. It is only in recent years that small lightweight expeditions have become popular. The world's major peaks have been climbed and most of them by several different routes. The barrier of the unknown has been broken. Today the challenge of mountaineering is maintained by attempting difficult or unclimbed faces or ridges, or by attempting large or difficult peaks with a small team. With a small group of climbers the backup resources are not there, so the commitment to each other and to the climb is necessarily greater. The problems encountered are much more those of the mountain than ones of the logistics of establishing a hierarchy amongst the many group members. Shipton and Tilman preferred small expeditions because, though the chances of success were fewer, they felt the rewards to be immeasurably greater.

As the highest mountain in the world Everest has always been in the forefront of mountaineering developments. The South Col route was climbed again in 1954 by a strong Swiss team which also made the first ascent of the adjacent peak of Lhotse (literally South Peak). In 1960 the Chinese managed to climb the North-East Ridge by the route the British had attempted so many times. Their expedition was thoroughly planned and determined to succeed. During their summit bid night fell with the climbers still a considerable distance from their goal. They climbed the rest of the way in darkness, crawling the last section because their oxygen sets had run out. They arrived at the summit at four o'clock in the morning. Caution did not play a big role in the final ascent.

The next dramatic development was in 1963 when members of an American expedition climbed Everest's West Ridge and descended the South Col route. Ten years later a Japanese team became the first to climb the mountain in the post-monsoon season by repeating the original route. By this stage the mountain had been climbed by several Sherpas. The first non-Sherpa Nepali to climb Everest was Sambhu Tamang who was a member of the 1972 Italian expedition. He still holds the record of being the youngest person to have climbed Everest. When he stood on the summit he was only eighteen years old.

In the twenty years after the first ascent, Everest had been climbed several times and by three different routes. In every case the expeditions were large in the traditional style. The culmination of this era came in 1975 with the first ascent of the South-West Face by a very strong British team led by Chris Bonington. Bonington had led an attempt in 1972, one of several expeditions from different countries to fail on this intimidating face. The successful climb in 1975 was a showpiece of large-scale expedition strategy, relying as much on precise planning of supply and equipment movements (meaning tactful delegation of load-carrying and climbing roles) as on the climbing abilities of the members.

Other difficult climbs have been made on the mountain's southern flanks. The West Ridge was climbed direct by Yugoslavs in 1979 and the South Pillar in 1980 by a Polish expedition. Although hard climbs, these were consolidations of technique rather than developments in style. The most spectacular breakthrough came in 1978 when Rheinhold Messner and Peter Haebler (members of an Austrian expedition) climbed Everest without the use of artificial oxygen – a feat that many had thought impossible despite the oxygenless climbs of Norton, Wager, Wyn Harris and Smythe to within four hundred metres of the summit.

Oxygenless ascents opened new dimensions in terms of lightweight expeditions. Messner took this to the ultimate in 1980 when he climbed Everest alone in a remarkable display of confidence and daring. His route of ascent was a variation on the North-East Ridge. Earlier that year the Chinese authorities opened their borders to foreign mountaineering expeditions. The first foreign expedition to climb Everest from Tibet was a huge Japanese team. They repeated the British/Chinese route on the North-East Ridge

LEFT: A huge avalanche plunges down the 2500-metre South Face of Nuptse (Everest's West Peak).

33

and climbed the North Face for the first time, but not without loss of life. The vast expanse of rock and ice that forms the North Face is a forbidding prospect. The most obvious line of weakness – a huge couloir (gully) – was the route chosen by the Japanese. At 8000 metres their line joined the route taken by the American West Ridge team in 1963. Couloirs are natural channels for avalanches and it was an avalanche that killed Akira Ube high on the mountain.

The tactic of alpine-style expeditions (as lightweight teams are called) is to climb up and down the mountain in one committed push. For the short time the climbers are making their ascent the dangers are great. There is no row of secure camps down the climb, and there are no others to help if luck turns against them. For all that, the duration of the climb is much shorter so the chances of being involved in a big avalanche or trapped by a severe storm are much smaller.

Since the first ascent in 1953 it has been large expeditions which have opened the frontiers. The most recent avenue of exploration is winter climbing. In 1980 a large Polish team made the first winter ascent of Everest via the South Col route. The weather in winter can be stable for long periods but above 7500 metres the fierce winter winds seldom cease blowing. The long fine spells are balanced by long storms, even more severe at this time of year.

In terms of objectives, alpine-style climbs have tried to emulate what larger teams have shown to be possible. A small British team had recently failed in an attempt to climb the West Ridge during winter, and then in 1982 four of Britain's most talented high-altitude climbers mounted an expedition to the long unclimbed North-East Ridge. Their attempt to climb a new route without oxygen ended in disaster. The disappearance of Pete Boardman and Joe Tasker high on the mountain was a tragic echo of Mallory and Irvine's death almost sixty years before.

The trend in the future will be the repeat of existing routes by small teams, at first during the normal seasons then perhaps in winter. With five routes and several variations climbed, Everest's problems are known quantities, but there are still some new routes to be found. Hopefully the new ground will be trodden by small expeditions as it is for them that the challenge of mountaineering still exists. Small teams of superbly fit climbers can use all the knowledge gained by their predecessors to test themselves at the limits of the possible. Only at that level does mountaineering become more than a sport. For a while at least, competition between egos is swallowed by circumstances which redefine all of one's values. It is sad that in lectures, books and interviews, this truth cannot be adequately expressed. One begins to believe that perhaps, after all, the climbs have been made for reasons which other people seem to expect and understand. It is not a thirst for fame, nor the fires of competition which drive me to climb. In the dangerous world of mountaineering such petty desires are tempered by the need to survive.

LEFT: Water from snow melted by the intense sun of Tibet forms deep pools in ice-hollows on the Rongbuk Glacier.

RIGHT: Ice towers complicate the approach along the Rongbuk Glacier to the North Face. Mt Everest rises in the background, with the West Ridge running down to the right from the summit.

ABOVE: The mass of Nuptse and Lhotse obscures the southern side of Mt Everest at sunset.

RIGHT: As the ice of a glacier melts, boulders are left perched on stalks of ice. Below the North Face, a rock on the Rongbuk Glacier near Camp I posed a problem of balance and agility to Greg Mortimer.

BELOW: Sunset on Lhotse from high on Ama Dablam in Nepal.

Strong winds distort clouds over the top of Everest's North Face at sunset.

CHAPTER TWO

THE AUSTRALIAN EXPEDITION

A FANATICAL ambition to climb Mt Everest was not the common need which brought our team together. None of us viewed mountaineering with quite that single-mindedness. We climbed mountains which rewarded us with their uncomplicated demands and their beauty. Such climbs sustained our faith in the supremacy of nature over the intrigue and obsession-ridden world of humans. Yet sometimes we needed to reinforce our faith in ourselves by attempting a mountain that drew out the last of our reserves. To climb Mt Everest with a small, lightly equipped team, unencumbered and unassisted by oxygen apparatus, had always seemed a project beyond our league. Until, riding high on two successful climbs in 1981, Tim Macartney-Snape and I, encouraged by Geof Bartram, felt that Everest was within our grasp – perhaps. Without the "perhaps" the attraction of the summit lost its gleam. It was the challenge that mattered; the uncertainty which is the essence of adventure. For us Everest would offer both, as well as the journey to our limits which we craved. When the Chinese Mountaineering Association casually agreed to our idea of an Australian expedition to the mountain through Tibet, we were jolted from hesitancy and conjecture into accepting Everest's perpetual, uncompromising invitation.

Only in the late seventies did Australian climbers venture beyond the friendly cliffs of home and the accessible alps of New Zealand and Europe to the ultimate mountains of the Himalaya. Those mountains treat novices rudely. Nothing but experience can give an understanding of the debilitating effects of high altitude. Mt Everest in particular requires an apprenticeship on lesser Himalayan peaks. In 1981 few Australians had served that apprenticeship. Tim Macartney-Snape and I headed the list with three successful Himalayan climbing trips behind us. We did not consider it presumptuous that we should organise Australia's first attempt to climb Mt Everest. Geof Bartram's toughness and mountain sense was demonstrated to us in China in 1981 and confirmed in India in 1982. His position as the third inaugural member was logical. At that time Geof's only Himalayan climbing venture had ended in tragedy when Stafford Morse, Nick Reeves and Richard Schmidt were killed on Annapurna III in 1980. His high-altitude

LEFT: Difficult climbs on "lower" Himalayan mountains provided the depth of experience needed to tackle Everest. After reaching the summit of Ama Dablam (6854 metres), Andy Henderson, Tim Macartney-Snape and Lincoln Hall descend with other members of the expedition.

ABOVE: As this sign suggests, Everest Base Camp is a common destination for walkers in Nepal.

experience came from the many 6000-metre peaks he had climbed in South America, where he worked as a mountain guide.

Good teamwork is essential for a successful Himalayan climb, especially when only a few climbers are involved. Unlike football or other sports where the teamwork must operate for an hour or two, a mountaineering expedition demands that everyone work together happily for two or three months without respite. Every day is spent living in each other's footsteps. There is no room for the brilliant technician whose personality happens to be intolerable. Since we wished to climb Everest with a small team we needed only two or three others to complete our group. The sensible approach was to ask people we had climbed with before and found reliable and compatible. Andy Henderson met these credentials. He had climbed to the summit of Ama Dablam in Nepal with Tim and me in 1981, and joined with Tim, Geof and me in making the first ascent of the East Face of Anyemaqen in China the same year.

A characteristic of successful alpine climbers is their drive to achieve. Often that is a destructive energy on expeditions where much time is spent on the approach, in the technically boring task of ferrying loads between camps, and in sitting in tents waiting for bad weather to clear. The achievements of Greg Mortimer in mountain ranges around the world were impossible to ignore in the selection of an Australian team. Luckily, Greg's determination to succeed on the mountain blended with an exceptionally easygoing nature. Greg completed our team of five.

The bond between us was the compulsion to climb mountains. Our compatibility did not necessarily mean any likeness in character. Our differences in attitude and opinion had given us much to talk about during the long mountain nights and lazy days at base camps.

Geof in particular was open about his views. He had packed a great deal into his thirty-three years but his focus had always been on life in the outdoors. He had an unsuppressable urge to explore the world, and probably more than any of us his interest was to see what was at the top or over the other side, rather than to discover where his personal limits lay. He had a quiet but unassailable confidence in himself. That did not prevent him from continually questioning what he should be doing with his life and how best to respect the privilege of being born into a wealthy culture. While he asked those questions he travelled, mostly in the poor countries of South America, India and Nepal. The poverty and injustice he encountered only fuelled the guilt he felt at being free to choose how to spend his life. The paradox came when he found examples of people living full, rewarding lives within inescapable social confines and with little more than the necessities of existence.

LEFT: Early mornings are cold at 6900 metres. Geof Bartram, wearing a down-filled suit, gears up for a day's climbing.
RIGHT: Geof, weather-beaten by the climb of Everest.

Though it was not a conscious decision, Geof escaped the insoluble problems of the world by climbing. Survival in a mountain environment is such a full-time occupation that other concerns are forgotten or overwhelmed by nature. He removed any hint of self-indulgence from mountaineering by making it his profession. His responsibility was to the people he was leading to the top of mountains. At the same time he created employment for local guides, cooks and porters. Working as a mountain guide did not obscure the rewards of being amongst the mountains but simply made those pleasures a lesser priority.

In the five years that I had known Geof he had not spent more than two weeks a year in his homeland. Before that he had lived in many different places in Australia doing all sorts of work. He was undeniably fond of his country but he could not accept its insularity and self-absorption. Geof's appearance, while in no way outlandish, said much about his separation from our culture. Free from the indoctrination of advertising his dress depended on comfort and practicality. He could not identify with those whose pleasure came from the image or impact they created. Geof's blond hair was worn long in the style of the early seventies, not in defiance of fashion but because of total unconcern with it.

Andy was a radically different character. Earrings, dyed hair and a hot pink bicycle with matching socks were his acknowledgments of current fashion. He lived the inner city life rather than simply tolerating it as I did. His tastes and interests were cosmopolitan, restoring a reasonable balance to the wilderness- and nature-oriented view of the rest of us. Somehow he was able to absorb and assign worth to everything that happened around him. His mind continually needed to feed on ideas, opinions and fantasies, both his own and other people's. As a consequence he was a compulsive reader, devouring everything from newspapers to Clausewitz on war to science-fiction westerns.

Andy often joked disparagingly about himself, a habit which invited us to make him the butt of our jokes as well. His sharp, well-disciplined mind coped easily with our jibes. When in Sydney he relaxed by the traditional methods of drinking and smoking. Hardly suitable training for climbing I would tell him, yet in the mountains he was never more than a few minutes behind. He could be stimulated by a classical concert as well as by a smoke- and punk-filled dance hall. On weekends he would often leave the pace of the city behind and delight in the peace of the bush below the steep sandstone cliffs upon which he climbed. Andy was able to enjoy almost any situation if he shared it with a companion. Close friendships were important to him. The dangers and worries of climbing a big mountain bind the participants together with a cement of shared experience incommunicable to others. It was that which made Andy addicted to climbing. His determination to push on in the face of exhaustion demonstrated the strength of his will to survive. Some of that strength came from knowing that his companions were struggling equally.

LEFT: Andy Henderson back at Camp I after the Everest climb.

RIGHT: Andy tackles "Mindbender", a climb on the steep granite cliff at Blue Lake in the Snowy Mountains, New South Wales.

RIGHT: Greg Mortimer at Camp I on Tibet's Rongbuk Glacier.

LEFT: The heat of the sun, intensified by reflection from the snow, is the reason for Greg's attire, and allows water to be melted from pots full of snow outside the snow cave at 5800 metres on Annapurna II.

My sister, a good friend of Andy's, summed up accurately: "It's not that he likes going on these expeditions with you. It's more that he doesn't like being left out." His sense of humour and good nature had become an indispensable part of our recent Himalayan climbs. There was no question of climbing Mt Everest without him.

During my first visit to New Zealand in 1974 I had spent time climbing with Greg. Following him up mountains had left me impressed and scared, and determined to restrict myself to the safe warm granite of my home cliffs. That resolve was made too late, for mountaineering had already claimed my soul. The challenges were fiercer and more sustained in the mountains than on small cliffs and the rewards were correspondingly greater. Seven years later I felt more at home in the mountains than anywhere else. Now, perhaps, I would be able to keep up with Greg.

One's first impressions of Greg were of a man who was content with his lot. His attitude seemed to say that everything would work out well in the end. It was a misleading impression since Greg's life had been full and rewarding, not by chance, but because he had made it so. He applied himself wholeheartedly to every scheme he considered worthy, whether it was his climbing, his marriage or building a house on the land he and his wife had bought near Christchurch in New Zealand. Greg was a geologist by profession. He was apologetic about his delight in the patterns and formations of rocks as if he realised we thought his enthusiasm childish. After all, cliffs are for climbing not for looking at. When it came to climbing rock he was efficient. The gentleness of his everyday manner was balanced by the aggressive determination of his climbing. This aggression was directed at himself, allowing no space for fear or hesitation to interfere with his judgment. That approach made him a very strong mountaineer indeed.

Greg had climbed throughout the world and had made difficult ascents in many countries. At the time we invited him to join the Everest team his experience of high altitude was limited to several difficult peaks in the Peruvian Andes. In every other sphere of mountaineering he was more experienced than any of us. Despite that, in discussions of tactics away from the mountain, he offered his opinions only when invited, as if he were storing his ability to make instant decisions during the climb. His anger flared infrequently. Instead he would resolve problems by himself in the hope of avoiding confrontation — not that he was afraid of facing it, just that anger left a dark smear on his day.

When a joke was played on him he reacted with almost mock annoyance because he could always see the joker's side of the prank. That attitude of unselfish appreciation flowed into everything in his life as he determinedly did what he thought should be done.

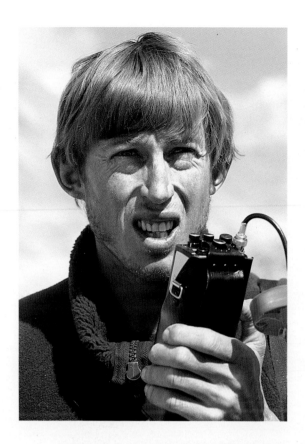

ABOVE LEFT: Tim Macartney-Snape discusses tactics with climbers at another camp on Everest.
ABOVE RIGHT: In mountainless Australia, Tim rock climbs at Victoria's Mt Arapiles.
RIGHT: Tim and Lincoln (the photographer) needed rockclimbing techniques to reach the summit of Mt Geru in the Kulu region of India, 1979.

It was Tim whom I knew best. We had met at university where, rather than studying, our time was spent ski-touring and rockclimbing. Tim's determination and his ability to survive comfortably in the mountains combined well with my fairly narrow field of expertise in technical climbing. During our first season together in New Zealand we managed to climb some difficult mountains.

Our youthful zeal almost caused our doom during our first Himalayan climb. After a night in the open without sleeping bags at almost 7000 metres a blizzard made our return from the summit into a fight for our lives. Utter exhaustion was compounded in my case by severe frostbite. Having come so close to death together Tim and I shared a fresh appreciation of life, and that appreciation has evolved through our subsequent climbs with their incidental ordeals. Between us developed a real but unspoken intimacy, unencumbered by the analyses, jealousies and obligations common to relationships with a sexual basis.

Tim's lanky build and quiet manner belied his physical and mental stamina. Projects of his were never half-hearted affairs, though sometimes rushed as he tried to achieve more than time allowed. Things were done today instead of tomorrow to leave room for whatever tomorrow would present. If a stove needed maintenance or a candle-holder improvised it would be Tim who fiddled away by torchlight. He had definite ideas on everything and a stubbornness for what he felt to be right. Decision making on our expeditions was always a process of talking until we agreed upon the best alternative. Often it was Tim's plans we carried out because his practical mind was quick to solve the problems we faced.

For Tim part of the attraction of high mountains was their continual ability to demand more energy than one's body and mind could supply. No other sphere of activity offered that to him. Accordingly, it was when the mountains drew the utmost from us that he felt satisfied. The pleasure was not one of masochism or displaying bravery but of feeling his body and mind working efficiently when his life depended upon it. Tim always seemed to know where he was in terms of both self-confidence and geography.

His skill in finding the best route in a storm or at night was little less than magical.

Away from the mountains the fierceness of his determination remained hidden behind his politeness and modesty. Self-control and self-reliance were the foundations of his self-respect. As a consequence he kept his ambitions, needs and emotions to himself. Though he had many friends it was difficult for anyone to know him well because the different facets of his life existed independently of each other. Only within himself did they come together.

Rockclimbing had been part of my life since I was fifteen. Its major impact at that impressionable age was that it gave my life a purpose beyond school. Climbing asked much more of me than anything I had done before. Tackling and overcoming situations where fear was a big component boosted my self-confidence. Climbing became a prop for my ego, an escape from everyday worries, and gave me glimpses of a world where the adventure lasted more than an afternoon or a weekend. The exploration of that world grew to be my aim in life.

Gradually, climbing became essential to my existence. Everything else seemed facile or shallow by comparison. Other satisfactions were short-lived and hollow. I had become a fanatic. I realise now that there is nothing in climbing that is inherent to it alone. What is important is the arena of constant challenge. Others find that challenge in their work or in becoming rich. The returns are the same but in climbing the triumphs are more obviously spectacular, and there is the added spice of danger.

It was not until I visited India in 1978 for my first Himalayan climb that the self-indulgence of my activity occurred to me. The challenge for so many people in the world is simply to survive. There is no need for Indians to invent frightening games in order to prove themselves to themselves. India made me realise the narrowness of my outlook. I began to share my life with other interests. Climbing has remained my avenue of experience, but these days I spend more time looking around me. No longer is my head down in a beeline for the summit.

In 1979 I began work as a trekking guide in the Nepalese Himalaya. Fifteen adventure-hungry Australians were entrusted to my care for up to a month at a time, and I had to ensure that their adventures stayed at the gentler end of the scale. I began to value other people's views of the world and to appreciate that many had their own private Everests to climb. It was humbling to work with the Nepalese. For them, performing a job well was reward in itself. Life was lived for what it offered, not in constant hope of a better but never attainable future. I have learnt as much from the people of the Himalaya as from the mountains, and have felt some of the satisfactions of helping others to the same appreciation.

The dangers of mountaineering are very real to me. Several times I have come near enough to death for it to feel as close as the darkness beyond a candle flame. Those occasions prompt a lot of thinking. On every big climb I keep a diary to try to capture not only the events but my feelings. Some things remain inexpressible so I turn my hand to poetry

BELOW: Tim at the first of five camps on the steep North Ridge of Ama Dablam in 1981.
Across the valley, the bulk of Nuptse and Lhotse obscure all but the summit pyramid of Everest.
RIGHT: Cornices form the unstable crest of Ama Dablam's North Ridge. The patches of snow on the steep rock beyond Tim make for difficult climbing.

in the search for their essence. My approach to climbing and, I suppose, to life is more introverted than that of my companions. Usually suggestions of soft options and words of caution come from me because of my healthy awareness of my own mortality.

Each of us had our own strengths and weaknesses. Individual shortcomings were offset by the strength of the group so that together we made a harmonious and formidable team.

By the end of 1982 our planning was complete. Ahead of us was the task of raising the finance, then assembling and shipping our food and equipment. Just as important was preparing ourselves for the climb. The only satisfactory training for mountaineering is climbing mountains. To that end Geof organised an expedition to Pumori, an outlier of Everest. For Andy, Tim, Greg and myself our objective was Annapurna II. Certainly those mountains provided problems we would encounter on Everest. At the same time they were mighty climbs in their own right. And for a while, as we faced their particular challenges, Everest was almost forgotten.

CHAPTER THREE

ANNAPURNA II

NORTH OF the lowland town of Pokhara in central Nepal the Himalaya soar up in an uninterrupted sweep to the crest of the Annapurna range. It is as if in this one place the geographical formality of foothills has been forgotten. The obstacles presented by the gorges that cut through the vertical flanks of the mountains more than compensate for the lack of intermediate ranges. With nothing to obscure the view the mountains catch the eyes of all who travel by road from India or Kathmandu. Though the whole Annapurna range is visible from Pokhara one peak in particular attracts the interest of mountaineers.

Behind and to the east of the spire of Machapuchare rises the huge mass of Annapurna II. The summit pyramid of stark black rock dominates the skyline. The spur which falls directly from the summit and divides the pyramid's south face into its east and west facets suggests to climbers an obvious though difficult line of ascent. All four previous attempts to climb that route had failed.

Over several years our work as trekking guides had taken Tim and myself to the Annapurna region many times. Always that south spur of Annapurna II tempted us, and finally we yielded to it. Our style of climbing lent itself to the difficulties of the mountain. A small team minimised the logistical problems of the exceptionally rugged approach. As for the peak itself, its situation was magnificent. Just to be on its slopes amongst the clouds would be reward enough. To leave the summit untrodden would not spell absolute failure. At least, acceptance of the likelihood of defeat was how we justified to ourselves our decision to attempt such an awesome objective. The South Face of Annapurna II remained the major unclimbed route in the Nepal Himalaya so we half expected to fail as all previous expeditions had done.

Tim, Andy, Greg, Queenslander Mike Groom and I met in Kathmandu at the beginning of August 1983. I had been working in Kashmir and arrived in Nepal a few days early. The casual style of the expedition was set when I was an hour late in meeting the other climbers at Kathmandu airport. The only way to cope with the lazy chaos which is the modus operandi of Kathmandu life is to operate at that same level of disorganisation. Consequently not only was I an hour late but I arrived on the back of my friend Ang

LEFT: Outside the snow cave at 7100 metres, Tim looks west across the huge crevassed glacier between Annapurnas II and IV to the twin peaks of Machapuchare.

ABOVE: Leaving Advance Base to try for the summit, the rock buttress above was made more difficult by fresh snow. Lincoln climbs the fixed rope.

Karma's motorbike, hardly the vehicle to transport my companions and their mountains of equipment. Various plans of action were discussed above the insistent attempts at bargaining from half a dozen unwanted taxi drivers and hotel touts. Eventually it was with the help of Ang Karma's brother, Kunga Sherpa, and a well-travelled jeep which Kunga had borrowed that we transferred ourselves and all our gear to Kunga's place.

Kunga's big new house at Bodnath on the outskirts of Kathmandu was our base for the next few days. We had worked with Kunga for several years and during that time we had become firm friends. An intelligent, well-educated man, Kunga had no illusions about the corruption and incompetence of sectors of the Nepalese government. He had learned efficient ways to deal with the Mountaineering Section of the Ministry of Tourism. Often that meant ignoring the rules completely, which suited our somewhat anarchistic style of organisation. To our minds, more essential than the compulsory bureaucracy imposed on mountaineering expeditions was the buying of supplies and equipment. For these tasks we were helped by five Nepalis who were to work with us during our adventure. Narayan Shresta was to be our sirdar ("boss"); Maila Tamang, expedition cook; Lobsang Tenzing Sherpa, sometime cook and all-time pillar of strength and dependability; general dogsbody Tomai Magar (Tomboy-sahib); and our mailrunner and practical joker Onchu Sherpa. As well, Ang Karma accompanied us for the first three weeks of the climb.

Each year Nepal's mountains attract not only dozens of mountaineering teams but thousands of trekkers who come to walk in the foothills and high valleys. Tibetan traders and the wives of Sherpa men who work in the trekking and climbing business make good money dealing in secondhand equipment. The bulk of our gear was bought from their shops. With Maila and Tenzing we calculated the food quantities for two months in the mountains. After six days of fossicking in crowded bazaars, prolonged sessions of bargaining, and overloading battered taxis with our purchases, everything was packed into porter loads at Kunga's house. It was Friday evening, and we were ready to leave. When Kunga told us it was bad luck to leave on a journey on Saturday we postponed our departure, despite wanting to send Onchu and Maila ahead to arrange porters to carry our loads. Kunga suggested a way that they could avoid leaving on Saturday. On Friday night, they left their rooms down the road from Kunga's place and came to stay with Kunga. First thing in the morning they left, having technically begun their journey the

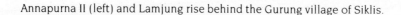

Annapurna II (left) and Lamjung rise behind the Gurung village of Siklis.

night before. For a Himalayan climb every portent of good luck must be courted.

One good omen (at least that was our interpretation) was our first glimpse of Annapurna II. As we roared along the narrow winding road on the roof of our bus a parting in the monsoon clouds revealed our route. No other mountains could be seen.

In order to climb in the settled weather at the end of the monsoon it is necessary to arrive in Kathmandu and travel to the base camp while the rains are still in progress. The day we made the eight-hour bus journey from Kathmandu to Pokhara the rains held off. Yet on steep hillsides beside the road the rice paddies were running with water. The local farmers kept the long irrigation canals clear and repaired the washed-out walls of terraces. At some places rice was being planted; at others the fields were already a vivid emerald green. The monsoon was a very busy period. For us it was a good time to relax and begin to concentrate our mental energies on climbing the mountain.

Usually the walk-in is the time to prepare one's mind for the rigours ahead. My already fit body tuned its muscles as I walked through the lowlands, but my mind needed to be flexed. I contemplated my reactions to danger, wondered whether I'd have the strength to push myself to the limits that the lack of oxygen would demand of me. I imagined the fear, the discomfort of the extreme cold, and the breathlessness which comes with an adrenalin rush at high altitude. I had coped with these things in the past, but this time the mountain was tougher and bigger than anything we had climbed before, on top of which the short walk-in gave less time to prepare ourselves.

Onchu and Maila flagged down our bus as we drove into Pokhara, and took us to meet the forty-odd local men and women who were to carry our food and equipment. After half an hour of chaos while the porters argued amongst themselves about the size of their loads we walked away from Pokhara, north towards the clouds. The first afternoon was an easy stroll along the banks of a river. The next day's walk was straightforward but made oppressive by the muggy heat. Interest and refreshment came from wading side-streams, sometimes dangerously swollen by the monsoon rains. We cut over a minor ridge into the valley of the Mahdi Khola, the river which drains the southern slopes of Annapurna IV, Annapurna II and Lamjung. Occasionally the sun broke through the clouds making the heat almost unbearable. The parting of the clouds did give us another view of our mountain, a reminder of why we were sweating up and down the muddy lowland trails.

The southern slopes of the Annapurna massif is the wettest part of Nepal. The monsoonal clouds drift north high above India and empty the last of their rains upon the immense barrier of the Annapurnas.

There are no foothills to intercept the storms. The exceptional wetness is reflected by the flooded streams and the lush, impenetrable jungle that clothes the lowest slopes of the mountains. To us, a reminder of the ruggedness ahead was the fact that virtually all our porters deserted shortly before Siklis. It had taken two days to cover the thirty-five kilometres to this last village at the base of the mountain. We waited a day there while Narayan employed more porters, this time locals who claimed they knew the terrain and the rigours it would demand. A day of slashing and hacking to clear the path through the jungle took us only a few kilometres nearer. Mirjan, our chief track-cutter, assured us we would reach Base Camp the next day. As we struggled through the giant stinging nettles and plucked dozens of leeches from our bodies the crisp air and simplicity of life in the high mountains seemed a long way ahead.

The next morning we came upon the settlement of Hoga – a couple of hectares of fertile river flat. The people who farmed the area reached Siklis by a high route through their alpine pastures. It was a very long way around but it saved them the continual work of keeping a path cut in the quick-growing jungle we had travelled through. We bought and devoured some fresh buffalo milk yoghurt and arranged for supplies of beans and potatoes to be carried up to our Base Camp another three hours' walk further on.

Base Camp was still in the jungle at an altitude of 2600 metres. We cleared sufficient vegetation to set up our camp and considered the enormity of our project. The summit was more than five kilometres above us. During the next six weeks we would work our way up the slopes till we established a high camp at 7000 metres. From there, if our careful planning had been accurate, we would have strength enough left to climb the most difficult part of all, the steep rock pyramid to the oxygenless summit.

The route of the climb on the South Face of Annapurna II. From the Base Camp in the gorge to the summit is over 5000 vertical metres. These photos, taken in winter 1984, show less snow on the peak than at the time of the climb.

The immediate problem before us was the gorge. The sight of the steep rock walls was enough to send most of our porters hurrying back to Siklis. It was fortunate that amongst the three men willing to stay was Mirjan, our track cutter. Though Narayan had employed him in Siklis he lived with his parents at Hoga. He had acted as guide for several of the previous expeditions. With his aid little time was wasted finding a path around and over the thickly vegetated cliffs. After a thousand metres of struggling with vertical bamboo thickets and dense rhododendrons the forest gave way to lower but equally dense under-growth. There we were lucky to find enough level ground to pitch our tents for our first depot.

The labour of carrying loads of food and equipment up to the depot was done in perpetual mist. It was almost a protective cloud, preventing us from seeing the extent that the cliffs rose above us and the doom that awaited us should we slip during the muddy climb. It rained heavily the morning we left Base Camp to spend our first night at the depot. That afternoon the clouds parted enough for us to appreciate our spec-tacular situation. Across the gorge, cliffs rose from Base Camp for three thousand metres. From the glacier at the top of the huge precipice avalanches fell through a thousand metres of air before sliding down steep ramps and gullies to the bottom of the valley. The noise of the avalanches reverberated across the gorge with our camp seeming to be the focus. For that reason we named it the Auditorium.

From the Auditorium our route wound its way up steep tussock slopes and smooth bluffs. In some spots we left ropes in place to make our load carrying a safer operation. We repeated the procedure of moving supplies up the mountain, this time to a camp we called Easter Island because the silhouettes of the rock buttresses above our camp were

Thick leech-infested jungle, nurtured by the monsoon rains, makes the approach to Annapurna II's Base Camp a slow and frustrating struggle. The trail which we cut grew over completely within a fortnight.

reminiscent of the ancient Polynesian statues. Easter Island gave us our first relatively close view of the summit pyramid, though the top was four thousand metres above our lush, rainy camp.

Above Easter Island the terrain began to open up into the huge cirque of mountains whose ice and snow melt had cut the gorge out of the rock. At that point the gorge itself was choked with the landscape-forming ice of the glacier. Our route crossed the jumbled glacier to the slopes of our mountain. Again days were spent ferrying loads, this time up grassy slopes bestrewn with myriads of alpine flowers. The site of our Advance Base Camp at 4700 metres was an idyllic spot with magnificent views out over the ramparts of the gorge to the lowlands.

Advance Base Camp was a place for us to rest while we prepared ourselves for the "real" climbing on ice slopes and snow-covered cliffs above. The tough approach had already conditioned our minds to working in the dangerous vertical environment. Now we had to contend with the extra discomforts of cold and lack of oxygen. We had been mentally preparing ourselves for this stage of the climb for months. It was a relief for us to face these familiar challenges and to leave the rain and mud and leeches behind.

The first obstacle above us was a broken glacier. Andy and I negotiated a way through the maze of ice-blocks and crevasses, and began work on the 200-metre cliff beyond. The next day Greg, Mike and Tim climbed to the top of the cliff. They had followed the route used by previous expeditions and marked by old pitons and tattered ropes. Beyond that we were faced with several options. Greg and Andy returned disappointed from a hard day reconnoitring the route. The direct line we had hoped to take to the Col (high pass) at the foot of the summit pyramid was threatened by avalanches. Mike and I investigated the other option. It proved to be much longer but fairly straightforward and definitely safer. We dumped our gear at the site for Camp I and returned exhausted to Advance Base. The lack of oxygen at these altitudes made physical activity such hard work that after one day of climbing we needed a day of rest. While half the team recuperated the other half climbed. Tenzing and Narayan helped us with the thankless task of carrying supplies up to Camp I.

As we acclimatised, the debilitating effects of oxygen debt lessened. After a week at Advance Base we moved up to Camp I where we were faced again with the painful process of adjusting to the height. Camp I was in a hollow just off the crest of the ridge which came down from the south spur of the mountain. It was that spur, dividing Annapurna II's South Face into its east and west facets, which we hoped to climb.

During our 1982 climb of Trisul Tim, Mike, Narayan and I had experienced gale force winds, strong enough to flatten our sturdy mountain tents. Since then, whenever the snow was suitable for their construction we camped in snow caves. At Camp I we dug two caves – one as a kitchen and one as sleeping quarters. It became such a comfortable camp given the limits of comfort imposed by the cold and the altitude of 5800 metres that it soon earned the nickname of Hotel Annapurna.

Above, we were again faced with two choices. One way meant obviously more difficult climbing and hence was less suitable for the carrying of heavy loads to our next camp site. We decided to explore the easier option, which meant travelling along a glacier below the ridge rather than on top of the ridge itself. Our main worry was that avalanches would fall onto our route from the flanks of the ridge.

That proved to be a real danger. As we made our way along the glacier we crossed piles of avalanche debris. There was reassurance in that – each avalanche that had fallen was no longer a threat. A few hundred metres below the Col the weather, which had been deteriorating all morning, became so bad that we were forced to dump our loads and head back to Hotel Annapurna. A short way before camp we were faced with climbing a fifty-metre cliff we had descended that morning to reach the glacier. We had left a rope in place, so it was a simple matter of climbing the rock with the rope for safety and as an aid. Only one person could climb the rope at a time. A blizzard was blowing when I, the last of us, began to scramble up the cliff. Because of the bad weather the others decided not to wait for me but to continue to the nearby camp.

A short way up the rock I put my weight on the rope. To my horror it immediately went slack. Before I had time to think I heard the rumble of rocks falling down the cliff. The rope had pulled loose some boulders. I flattened myself against the wall with my arms crossed over my head. Rocks showered around me, large pieces striking my right foot, my arm and my helmet with sickening force. When the dust subsided I checked that all parts of my body appeared as they should be. The pain from my arm and foot was already intense. I realised that I had to get back to camp before the shock wore off and the pain incapacitated me. Only determination got me to the top of the cliff. On the glacier again

Mike Groom (top), Greg and Andy at Easter Island. Over a thousand metres below is Base Camp, and almost a thousand metres remain to Advance Base, where the snow- and ice-climbing begin.

LEFT: Glimpses of cliffs through the monsoon clouds at the Auditorium hint at the scale of our undertaking.

BELOW: Tenzing (right) and Maila cook dinner in the improvised mess tent at Advance Base.

the wind and snow blew unobstructedly – with darkness approaching it was dangerous weather for an injured person to be away from camp alone. I hobbled back to Hotel Annapurna, already mentally accepting that the climb was over for me. At the snow cave the others were shocked by the sight of me – clothes and rucksack torn, my glasses broken and my face covered with blood. Luckily my injuries were not as serious as my appearance suggested. My helmet had been split, and it was that combined with my quick reactions which had saved my life. On my return to Australia an X-ray confirmed that a bone in my foot had been broken. For the rest of the climb my stiff mountaineering boot acted as a perfect splint.

I spent the next week recuperating at Hotel Annapurna. The first few days were bad weather. Since heavy snowfall threatened our route up the glacier with avalanches, Tim, Greg, Andy and Mike decided to climb the ridge direct to the Col. The climbing to the top of the sub-peak we had named the Pyramid proved to be enjoyable but not easy. Beyond that snow conditions worsened dangerously. It was nine o'clock that night before everyone was back in the snow cave, with tales of deep soft snow and of Greg triggering two avalanches.

Narayan and Tenzing came up to stay from Advance Base shortly before the weather worsened again. By the time it was safe to climb, a few days later when the avalanches had cleared, I decided that though my injuries were still painful I would be able to follow the footsteps of the others. Mike returned to Advance Base because his cracked sunburnt lips had become badly infected, while Andy and Greg set off via the glacier route to set up Camp II on the Col. Narayan, Tenzing, Tim and I followed the next day. The Col was a windswept spot and the snow was too icy to dig a snow cave. Instead we built an igloo. At a height of 6600 metres we were at last getting close to the main difficulties.

We rested for a day to give our bodies a chance to adjust to the altitude. Our plan to climb a few hundred metres higher and dig a snow cave at the base of the rock pyramid was frustrated by bad weather. We woke after our second night to half a metre of fresh snow. Rather than eating the supplies which had taken so much effort to carry up here we returned to Advance Base Camp.

As quickly as we could we climbed down to Hotel Annapurna. We rested in the snow cave for an hour making hot drinks and eating, during which time another metre of snow fell. On the descent from Hotel Annapurna a slope avalanched while Tim was on it. By reacting instantly and with a little luck he scrambled free just before the avalanche plunged over the 300-metre cliff above Advance Base. We continued down to the place we had climbed up and down earlier. To our horror we saw that the whole nature of the route had changed because the tremendous weight of the ice pushing the glacier down had pushed it sideways to the edge of the cliff. Huge blocks of ice teetered above our route ready to fall at the slightest nudge from the glacier behind. An ice avalanche had swept away the ropes we had left in place. Fortunately, by abseiling down the one rope we had with us, Tim was able to reach the tangle of ropes caught in the gully lower down. From there he made his way to the bottom of the cliff.

While we were waiting for Narayan to follow, a lump of ice the size of a television set bounced down the slope towards us. I was standing on the edge of the cliff and had nowhere to go. The block bounced straight towards me. I was able to jump over it, but caught a glancing blow to the thigh before it disappeared over the edge. We stared nervously at the blocks the size of trucks that were poised over us.

By the time I abseiled down to the others my thigh was so swollen and painful that I could not walk. My companions pushed, pulled and carried me down the glacier to Advance Base Camp where I spent a second week as an invalid.

Our decision to retreat from the Col was the right one as the weather stayed bad for many days. Everyone except Tenzing and I made the journey down to Hoga to fetch more food. Three thousand metres down and back in two days was hard going and it was the only time I was at all thankful for my injuries.

After nine days of waiting we set off from Advance Base, this time to reach the summit. I was still unsure of my leg but was determined to try. The others had reconnoitred a line up the cliff which avoided the worst of the falling ice. We climbed that line to the top of the cliff and plodded through knee-deep snow up the ridge to Hotel Annapurna. The camp had disappeared under two metres of snow so the next two hours

were spent digging out the snow cave entrances and the one tent we had previously pitched. The tent, of course, had collapsed. The amount of snow led us to worry about the safety of the route up to the Col. The next day proved to be hard work through deep snow and fresh avalanche debris, but reasonably safe because most of the big avalanches had already fallen. Col Camp was partially buried and the poles of one tent were broken. Exhaustion dictated that the next day be spent resting to allow us to build up our strength for our climb to the summit.

The following morning we shouldered our loads and climbed slowly upwards. Though the high altitude made the going hard the magnificent scenery and the perfect weather made the day enjoyable. The snow was firm and the climbing safe and straightforward. Early in the afternoon we reached a place at an altitude of 7100 metres where we could dig a snow cave. Mike, Tenzing and Narayan dumped their loads, wished us luck, and headed back to the Col. Now it was up to the four of us to climb to the summit. Our first task was to dig the snow cave, exhausting work at that height. From where our heads lay at night, Tim and I could see the lights of Pokhara through the door, over 6000 metres below. The warmth and humanity of the town were brought nearer by the glow of its lights.

We expected to spend at least one night out on our climb to the top so in the morning we took food, stoves and sleeping bags with us. The rock of the 800-metre summit pyramid was friable and devoid of ledges, a difficult combination for climbing. Where it was possible we climbed patches of snow on top of the rock in preference to the rock itself. By mid-afternoon it was obvious that we would get nowhere near the summit that day. What's more, there were no ledges at all, let alone places to dig snow caves. We decided to stash the food and extra climbing gear and return the next day. With lighter packs, familiarity with the terrain, and an extra night to adjust to the altitude, we hoped to make much better time.

Once again our decision to retreat proved wise. That night a snow storm began which lasted two days. When the snow stopped falling a strong and intolerably cold wind kept us in the snow cave for another three days. During the long wait we became weaker day by day because our muscles were not getting enough oxygen to sustain them. The sixth morning was fine and windless. In our eagerness to push on with the climb we left before dawn. It was bitterly cold until the sun rose. As our senses thawed we were able to appreciate the beginning of a perfect day. By mid-morning we reached our previous high point. Again we had to worry about selecting the best route up the rest of the Face. Slowly we worked our way diagonally to the left. The difficulties were exaggerated by the altitude of 7500 metres. Every step which was in any way awkward required a few extra breaths for concentration. Every pull up was a real exertion. The way to cope with the enormity of the climb and the effort it demanded was to take each small problem as we reached it, and deal with that without worrying about all that lay above.

One thing we did have to worry about was where we were going to spend the night. There were no ledges more than a few centimetres wide. As the sun was setting in the lowlands Tim reached a steep snow-filled gully. There the snow was deep enough for us to dig ledges large enough to sit on. The sunset was magnificent. Annapurna II cast a shadow which stretched above and beyond Manaslu into the sky and gave to the heavens an eerie impression of solidity.

The ropes from our waists we tied to anchors hammered into the walls of the gully. We huddled on our tiny ledges nursing our small gas stoves until two in the morning, melting enough snow to quench our thirst because a vital part of surviving at high altitude is preventing dehydration. For the remainder of the night we dozed intermittently and waited for the sun. Our drowsiness and the cold spoiled our appreciation of the beauty of the dawn.

PRECEDING PAGES: A hollow in the ridge provides a sheltered spot for "Hotel Annapurna"
Beyond the ridge of Annapurna IV (across the valley) monsoon clouds cover Nepal.

LEFT: After five days in the snow cave at 7100 metres, the climbers leave for the summit. Pyramid on the left, the subpeaks of Annapurna IV on the right, and beyond, the lowlands of Nepal and India.

BELOW: Tenzing and Greg en route to Col Camp early in the morning. They are about to descend the rock cliff onto the glacier which runs up to below the Col.

Since we planned to make the summit that day we left our stoves and sleeping bags on the ledges. Immediately above our bivouac was a hundred-metre-high vertical gully of extremely rotten rock. The climbing was so difficult that we needed the whole day to climb those hundred metres. Again our plan to reach the summit was frustrated. We left our ropes hanging down the gully for a quick ascent the next morning and descended to another long and miserable night on the ledges.

By the morning the lack of oxygen and proper food, combined with the cold, had left us drained of energy. Only determination to succeed pushed us back up the ropes to our high point. The short rock wall above presented no problems. Beyond that a steep but firm snow slope led to the summit. The peak itself was corniced with an overhanging lip of ice so we stopped on the steep slope a couple of metres below.

There was no place to sit and an extremely cold wind blew across from Tibet. Clouds obscured the familiar view to the south but we could still see the mountains and valleys to the north. As we stood there, catching our breath and feasting our eyes, the clouds thickened beneath us, slowly filling the valleys. Soon the lesser mountains were buried in the clouds. We were left alone in a circle of Himalayan giants – Manaslu, Himalchuli, Annapurna I and Dhaulagiri. There were hand shakes and slaps on the back, gently given so as not to unbalance our precarious footing. The real elation was to come later. Foremost in all our minds was not celebration but the task of descending the mountain. It was only seven hours later as we sat in the snow cave with a violent electrical storm raging outside that we were able to relax and appreciate our success.

Despite a solid sleep we were still exhausted the following morning. We packed and staggered down against a strong wind. At Col Camp we stopped to melt snow for a drink and could not muster the momentum to move again. We spent the remainder of the day sleeping, drinking and eating. Our rest had been painfully earnt and was much needed.

That night over a metre of snow fell. In the morning we were faced with descending the avalanche-prone slopes between Col Camp and Hotel Annapurna in the worst possible conditions. Every step through the thigh-deep snow was a struggle. The bad conditions increased the time we spent exposed to the dangers. At nine p.m. we reached Hotel Annapurna, having survived avalanches which fell in front, behind and between us. It was the worst day any of us had spent on any mountain.

The next day proved to be even more dangerous and exhausting. The storm continued through the night. Tim, Greg and I, who had slept in a tent, had to dig through three metres of snow to free Andy from the snow cave. Because the snow was chest-deep it took two and a half hours to travel the first two hundred metres from camp. Beyond that the slopes had avalanched and we were able to descend much more quickly though still threatened by avalanches from far above. The next problem was the glacier above the cliff leading down to Advance Base. Huge crevasses obstructed our path and blocks of ice overhung the cliff. We could not find a route through the maze before nightfall so we were forced to camp again, this time on the glacier with no food, no drink, and with one tent for the four of us. We were so worn out that we slept despite the discomfort. In the morning another shock greeted us. Advance Base Camp seemed to have disappeared. The area was covered in snow and there was no sign of the tents. The whole day was needed to negotiate the terrifyingly dangerous glacier and the cliff beneath it. Again our ropes had been swept away by icefall; we felt very much in the firing line as we set up new abseils. Everything was made more difficult by the metre of new snow.

Shortly before dark we floundered exhausted into Advance Base. It was deserted but to our delight the collapsed kitchen tent was still there. From somewhere we found the energy to dig away the snow and to whoop with joy when we discovered the food the Sherpas had left. Though we were a week late they had not given us up for dead as we had feared, but had simply moved below the snow line to wait for us.

That night we feasted. The fare was not elaborate but there was plenty of it and plenty of drink for our insatiable thirsts. It was with minds at ease that we crawled into our sleeping bags. The sun woke us in the morning and for the first time in days we knew that we would be alive at nightfall. The danger was behind us. We had time to enjoy the warmth of the sun, to taste the elation of success and to appreciate the privilege of life.

ABOVE: Greg climbs the steep rotten rock of Annapurna II's summit pyramid aided by rope fixed by Lincoln (right) and Tim (obscured, on the skyline).

PRECEDING PAGES: On the crest of the snowy ridge Tim, Andy, Greg and Mike Groom slowly make their way to the top of the Pyramid. The main summit of Annapurna II rises imposingly behind.

CHAPTER FOUR

THE MAD MONTHS

"CLIMBING Mt Everest is unquestionably dangerous."
The heat from the spot lights in the television studio made me sweat through my make-up. "Do you have a suicidal urge? Are you crazy?"
I stared back at the carefully painted face of my interviewer. I could not believe the mindlessness of her question. Her concern was with confrontation, not with any rational discussion of mountaineering. But I was here to publicise our expedition, to convince people that the challenge we faced was worthy of their support. My reply was tempered accordingly.

"I'd go crazy if I spent my life safe and secure in boredom behind a desk". Or in front of a television camera, I added to myself. "Craziness has nothing to do with proving yourself to yourself, which is what I do in the mountains. And suicide is giving up the game rather than playing it for all it's worth."

"So life is a game to you?"

"It's more of a game than death is, so when you're alive you're obliged to get the most out of it. That means putting all you've got into it."

The night was warm and peaceful outside the lecture theatre. A low wall near the entrance made a comfortable seat for the four of us as we waited.

"There must be something good on Brisbane television tonight," said Kate.

"When we were in Adelaide our slide show coincided with the final episode of 'A Town Like Alice'." I laughed at the memory. "We had an audience of twenty-three."

"We might break that record tonight," said Tim, but without any gloom in his voice. Gloom did not have much of a place in his world.

The next minute four people walked up. I hurried inside behind the table piled high with Expedition T-shirts to accept their admission money. They were the catalyst. Two cars pulled up. A cyclist locked his bike to a tree. A few more pedestrians arrived. A quarter of an hour after our scheduled start several dozen people made the hall look only half empty. It was time to begin. Tim and I left the doors and took the stage. Silence fell as Tim nervously tapped the microphone.

LEFT: Tim and Tenzing during a climb of the Three Sisters, Katoomba, broadcast live by Channel Nine's Wide World of Sports.
ABOVE: Tim (left) and Lincoln conquer a truckload of gear about to leave Manly for Tibet.

"Good evening, everyone. Thank you for supporting our expedition to Mt Everest by coming along to our lecture. If you'd like to support us further there'll be T-shirts and posters for sale afterwards. I'm Tim Macartney-Snape and this is Lincoln Hall. We're here tonight to show slides of our recent climb of Annapurna II, which was part of our training programme for Everest as well as being a worthwhile climb in its own right. I'll begin by talking about the planning and approaches and the first part of the climb, then I'll hand over to Lincoln who'll take you to the summit ..."

That was my cue to leave the stage and switch on the projectors. A dozen shows had made us familiar with our equipment and with telling our story. Always we were nervous until we became lost in the memories the projected images never failed to arouse.

Dappled shapes of sunshine played upon our bodies. The patterns changed as the warm wind swayed the casuarina branches above. The sun reflected brightly from the river and the sand. The heat of the Australian summer lived through everything around us, presenting no option but to relax and forget the tension between us.

"How have you been?" I asked.

"Really, life could not be better." She smiled gently at me, as if to say she understood how that reply would hurt. "I love it here."

"I can see that you might," I said. "It's a beautiful place." I paused. "It's only now, afterwards, that I can see what you tolerated from me. With me being away from you so much, and expecting you to wait, and the worry, and the hope that every climb would be the last. Yet as soon as I was back I'd be planning the next."

"You were impossible. You were worse than that."

"I know," I interrupted. "I'm not suggesting we start again."

A gust of wind rustled the leaves of the trees shading the river and sent ripples across the surface. A currawong's call rang out pointing to a reality beyond our own, reminding us both that life was so much simpler when unclouded by emotion.

"I've been here three months now. There are some really good people. There's so much to do, so much to learn about myself."

"Rather than about me?"

"It didn't take long to learn about you."

I laughed.

She did not allow the conversation to dwell on our past. "What have you been doing since you got back from Nepal?"

"Relaxing back into Australian life. I've been rockclimbing a couple of times. Beginning to worry about how we are going to get the money together for Everest. The organisation is horrifying."

And now she interrupted, "I'm so glad I'm not involved in any of that anymore."

How much climbing rules my life, I thought, while she talked on about her new friends. The important thing in life is to have something to live for. Here she had found it.

Soon it was time for me to leave.

"You must visit more often," she said as we stood up.

"I will." The implication was that the initiative must be mine.

I kissed her quickly and turned away.

One day, perhaps.

But meanwhile, priorities.

In the past, mountaineering had always been an intensely personal experience. The satisfactions were private and of little interest to anyone else. We soon learnt that Mt Everest was something different. By planning to climb the world's highest peak we had become the vehicle for satisfying some kind of public need. People looked for symbols which could be identified with displays of courage and patriotic determination. Many found such a symbol in our attempt to climb Everest.

Our wish was to climb the mountain. At the most courage and patriotism were incidental to our aim, yet at every organisational level the people we dealt with and were encouraged by understood our drive only in those terms. Like explaining the beauty of a sunset, the rewards of mountaineering are deep and fully appreciable only by the initiated. Consequently, when support was given to our expedition we were especially grateful for the faith shown in a project which no one quite understood.

Interest in Everest was bountiful, but converting that interest to concrete assistance was difficult. Most of those who had the means to sponsor our expedition were the least likely to wish to do so. So often the power of distribution of large amounts of money belonged to those who saw financial prosperity rather than adventure as the worthwhile pursuit in life.

Sponsorship certainly was necessary. Organising an expedition through Tibet proved to be several times more expensive than through India or Nepal. We had been able to finance expeditions to those countries ourselves but a climb in Tibet was beyond our means.

Sponsorship was a moral question for all of us. No one felt happy about accepting money for vague promises of publicity, especially when such promises were often difficult to fulfil. The media were understandably reticent to provide free advertising which was how they saw acknowledgment of sponsors. We preferred the situation whereby our sponsors made use of the expedition in their advertising and publicity campaigns.

The task of raising the finance was left to Tim and me. Geof decided his skills did not lie in a job that required his presence in Australia for the best part of a year. Greg was committed through his marriage and his work to living in New Zealand. Though Andy lived and worked in Sydney he lacked the necessary organisational experience. The world of high finance was foreign to Tim and me as well, but slowly we began to discover it. A mosaic of meetings, formal and surreal, where we made reluctant protestations of our ability, introduced us to lifestyles whose tenets were completely different to our own. Through those meetings and by carefully worded letters and nervous phone calls we sent out one message – Help Us Climb Mt Everest. We left it to the advertising managers and public relations people to sort out exactly why they should.

The first encouraging response came from the Brisbane-based company Mountain Designs which agreed to provide the expedition with sleeping bags and specialised clothing that the company would make to our specifications.

The potential for our expedition to benefit relations between Australia and China was recognised by the Australia–China Council which gave a generous grant to our cause. Part of the Department of Foreign Affairs, the Council's brief is to work to develop and deepen the understanding between the two countries through cultural and sporting exchanges.

Further help came from the Hong Kong and Shanghai Banking Corporation. Its sphere of influence extended through Asia in a fashion which tried not to regard political borders as barriers.

When we left Australia in August 1983 to climb Annapurna II we had raised less than a third of the necessary funds. Our success on Annapurna II provided the impetus we needed. That climb received a great deal of publicity in Australia, largely because we were reported missing by the press and our return had some of the appeal of a resurrection. We capitalised on the publicity in an attempt to make people aware of our planned Everest climb. Public knowledge, we hoped, would lead to public support.

The support we needed came from a major television network. The promise of a dramatic documentary was enough to prompt Sydney's Channel Nine to cover the remainder of our costs and outlay the enormous expense of filming in Chinese-administered Tibet.

The deal with Channel Nine was a clear-cut business arrangement. The Channel financed the project, and in return we would co-operate in the making of the film. Our only concern was that the filming did not interfere with the climb, either by demanding too much of our energy or through personality conflicts with the climbers. The compatibility of the film crew was vital. Its members needed to be able to relate comfortably to both the climbers and to the harsh environment of Tibet. Being able to meet the second requirement almost assured compliance with the first. People who could appreciate life in the dusty wastes of Tibet had by definition the same broad outlook on existence, whether they sought to grapple closely with the challenges presented there or simply observe them. None of those who came to Tibet would need to complain about the cold and the barrenness, nor of the altitude, nor ask why climbers needed to go to such inhos-

Mike Dillon, cameraman and on-site producer.

Jim Duff, sound-recordist and doctor.

Colin Monteath, climber–cameraman.

Howard Whelan, sound-recordist and cameraman.

Simon Balderstone, reporter from the "Age".

pitable places. The lure of the unknown, the indefinable romance of adventure would be our common bond. The climbers sought to experience that mystique by living through a struggle with a mountain. The film crew's object was to understand that struggle by faithfully recording it.

The selection of the film crew was made easier by the limited size of Australia's population of professional adventurers. The one person about whom no decision had to be made was Michael Dillon. Mike had worked as a cameraman and producer all over the world, including making several films in Nepal with Sir Edmund Hillary. In terms of camera expertise and the ability to shoot with the final product in mind he had few equals. For our small expedition it was necessary that the film crew be kept as small as possible to prevent the project becoming more of a film-making event than the climb of a mountain. Mike was ideal for the job as he could perform the work of both on-site producer and cameraman.

With David Hill, the executive producer, Mike Dillon reviewed our list of suggested additions to the film crew, and from it chose Mike's three assistants.

Most experienced in the realm of mountaineering cinematography was Jim Duff, a British doctor who lived in Hobart. Jim had climbed up to 7500 metres on Bonington's Everest South-West Face expedition in 1975. Apart from his role as doctor he worked as sound recordist with the BBC-TV team which made a documentary of the climb. He had also done the sound work for the 1978 British K2 Expedition film, and helped make a climbing documentary of Mt Cook in New Zealand. At the age of thirty-nine he had twenty-five years of climbing experience behind him, including several expeditions to the Himalaya and the Karakoram. He was also one of the world's most experienced high-altitude doctors. Jim's travels had left him with a large stock of stories which he had learnt to tell well.

The assistants to Mike and Jim were Colin Monteath and Howard Whelan.

Born in Scotland and raised in Australia, Colin had for many years been living in New Zealand where until recently he had directed operational aspects of the New Zealand Antarctic programme. He had climbed widely in those three countries and also in South America and the Himalaya. He was well practised in catering for the whims of scientists in harsh Antarctic conditions. Little effort was needed for him to adapt to the needs of film-makers in inhospitable Tibet.

Howard's background was as much in mountaineering as in cinematography. Most of his life had been spent in the mountains of Utah where he was born. He trained as a journalist and cinematographer but his work in those fields was eclipsed by his need to be in action out in the mountains. He worked in ski patrols, ski-raced and helped make skiing films, before he married an Australian and eventually moved to Australia. Though life had not been easy for Howard it was always fun, or as close to it as he could manage. His dynamism and eagerness to learn blended well with Mike's quiet but busy professionalism.

Largely through the encouragement of staff journalist Simon Balderstone, the "Age" newspaper came to appreciate the news potential of our climb. Simon's enthusiasm came from his wish to join the expedition. He and I were friends from guiding work we had done together in Kashmir, and it pleased me (and eventually all of the expedition) that when the "Age" bought the newspaper rights to the climb, the deal included Simon as the reporter to accompany us. Though he had little technical experience, he had visited the Kashmir Himalaya many times and was certainly familiar with the rigours which his work as journalist would demand.

Channel Nine's sponsorship through its Wide World of Sports programme came at just the right time. With only six months before we were due to leave for China we needed to be able to forget about financial worries and switch our concentration to the logistical aspects of the expedition. Channel Nine's involvement and the inclusion of four extra people added to our organisational burden. Time was short, but with money to pay the bills, our food and equipment orders could be quickly filled. This did not mean that our deadlines were always met. Much of our gear did not arrive in Australia from specialist factories overseas in time to be shipped to Beijing. The Chinese Mountaineering Association required our equipment two months in advance of our arrival, which meant shipping everything at the end of March 1984. It wasn't until the end of May that our goods left Australia. Tim, Andy and I packed everything into sacks and barrels and delivered the lot to Scotpac, the packing agent which had donated its services to the expedition. In turn Scotpac delivered it to the dock. Unfortunately the arrival of the intended carrier to Hong Kong coincided with a wharfies' "go-slow". As our timing was tight even without the delay at the wharves, we gave up and airfreighted the entire thirteen hundred kilos. It arrived in China six weeks before we did, two weeks late but in enough time to be transported overland to Lhasa in Tibet.

After our climb of Annapurna II we realised the benefit of two or three climbers working in a support role. The task was a difficult one as it held no promise of the summit yet shared most of the risks. Narayan and Tenzing, who had contributed so much to our Annapurna II success, eagerly accepted our suggestion that they come with us. Both were thoroughly dependable in the mountains and Tenzing had the extra virtue of speaking fluent Tibetan.

In April I left the organisational problems of shipping the gear to Tim and went to Nepal. There I guided the ascent of an easy Himalayan mountain, arriving back in Kathmandu at the same time as Geof and Narayan. Both of them were jubilant, in a modest way, about reaching the summit of Pumori. Geof in particular had a good reason to be proud. He had organised the expedition, and all seven members made it to the summit of the 7000-metre-high outlier of Everest. Narayan, Tenzing, Geof and I flew from Kathmandu together after our friend Kunga wished us good luck at the airport. Geof continued through to Australia while Narayan, Tenzing and I stopped in Bangkok to arrange their visas for Australia.

After living in the crowded rural country of Nepal the affluent city-oriented lifestyle of Australia was a shock to the two Nepalis. Through their work as trekking guides they had made many Australian friends. There was no shortage of people to visit nor of things to do and see. Tenzing was very shy and openly questioned little, forming his opinions by constant observation. Narayan was always alert and never worried about appearing naive by asking too many questions. Because of his interest and directness he was a refreshing person to be with. In Nepal our different cultures imposed a gap between us and our Nepali friends which our different roles exaggerated. It was satisfying to be with Narayan and Tenzing in a situation where they were not our employees.

Tenzing Sherpa, ready for anything, during an extended period of bad weather at Annapurna II's Advance Base Camp.

Narayan Shresta rockclimbing at
Sublime Point in the Blue Mountains
during the pre-climb visit he and
Tenzing made to Australia.

The seven weeks between our return from Nepal and our departure for China was a hectic time. The previous year Tim had become a director of the adventure travel company "Wilderness Expeditions". As well as worrying about Everest, he had to train someone to replace him for the three months we planned to be away. The others, too, had to perform similar shufflings of their lives, except for Geof and me who led less timetabled, more itinerant existences. Andy and Howard resigned from their jobs. Greg and Colin flew over from New Zealand. Jim was busy until the last moment moving out of his professional premises and into new ones.

We spent a couple of late nights packing and labelling the perishable foods and odds and ends we had accumulated since dispatching the bulk of our gear to China. Our plastic boots were widened and insulative gaitors permanently attached to them. An extensive repair kit was assembled. We bought spares of everything, as little would be available in Tibet. We made sure we found the time to keep fit and go rockclimbing, and even devoted the best part of a week to a cross-country skiing trip.

It was an exacting time for us, not only because of the many last-minute things that needed to be done. The emotional pressures of leaving for a major expedition are immense. For all of us adventure was a basic need. The people we cared for and who cared for us knew that, even if they could not understand it. Their promise of loneliness contrasted with the excitement we felt at our imminent departure. The problem was not one that could be resolved, only accepted.

The base of our operations in Sydney was a large ramshackle house in Manly which Tim and I shared with several other people. For months the underneath of the house had been jammed full with kitbags and barrels labelled "Australian Mt Everest Expedition", and the hallways and corners cluttered with obscure pieces of equipment. The night before we flew out of Sydney was the occasion of a party to celebrate not only our departure but also the cessation of the endless phone calls for the Mt Everest Expedition.

At last we told ourselves that what we had not done by now would have to remain undone. The long months of preparation were behind us. A good feeling came from knowing that the mountain awaited us, that within a couple of weeks we would be beneath its flanks. Our excitement kept us fired with energy. For the last time we put Mt Everest to the back of our minds, then kicked up our heels to the music.

CHAPTER FIVE

TO CHINA

T HE ONLY traffic noise was the quiet swish of bicycles carving paths through the warm air. The few cars on the road were slowed to a crawl as they doggedly drove through fleets of two-wheeled, man-powered machines. The green trees which grew in lines between the footpaths and the roads almost obscured the low buildings. The modest advertising and unpretentious window displays revealed only at second glance that most of the buildings were shops. The paths were crowded by many people walking with definite and different purposes but without the eager rush we had seen in Hong Kong two days before.

A few blocks away it seemed like another city. The streets were as broad as airport runways. Along the flanks were streams of bicycles, cars, trucks and concertinaed buses all driving in clearly marked lanes. Wherever the huge avenues met, giant Ts supported horizontal traffic lights. On the wooden platform beneath the signals there sometimes stood a policeman, illustrating the essentially Chinese precept that however sophisticated the mechanisation only human presence could ensure perfect operation. In the West, technology had become a drug, immortalising and addictive. In China it was a fallible, impersonal, yet vital tool.

It was good to be in Beijing again. After one day the overwhelming impression was the same as that which had flooded our senses three years before – the uniqueness of the Chinese way of life. If they existed, and no doubt they did, ripples of discontent passed unnoticed before us, since our eyes were glazed and our ears deafened by the novelty and appeal of China. Nowhere else in the world had we encountered so pervasive an atmosphere of peace and tolerance in such an inescapably crowded place.

During our previous visit I had realised the futility of judging a country about which I understood neither the ethic of government nor the sophisticated and complex civilisation. Yet it was impossible not to contemplate facts that were driven home at every street corner, in every shop, and at every tourist attraction we visited. China was bursting with humanity.

To me, as a casual observer, it seemed that the unaggressive atmosphere I sensed in the Chinese had evolved as the social conditions tightened and eliminated personal space. That was many centuries ago now. History has shown that when the dam of accepted provocation breaks, the flood of violence is merciless. There was no hint of that emotion amongst the people who laughed at our frisbee games or patiently gesticulated the price of fruit in the markets. However, the vast plazas and intimidating architecture of Mao's Tomb and the other huge buildings around Tiananmen Square, spoke of a fervour and dedication hidden from an outsider's scrutiny.

LEFT: In Beijing, a city of eight million people, air pollution is a major problem, largely because of the wide use of coal as fuel for heating and cooking. However, the murky skies do make for beautiful sunsets at Tiananmen Square.

RIGHT: The whole of China and its Autonomous Regions operate to one time zone, as shown by the clock at Beijing airport. The minute hand points to Mt Everest (on the border) at twenty-two minutes to the hour.

All mountaineering expeditions to China are organised through the Chinese Mountaineering Association, a body whose main function is to act as travel agent for foreign climbing teams. All our transport, accommodation and sightseeing were arranged by the C.M.A. Although this approach made operations very smooth and comfortable, it further insulated us from reaching any real understanding of the Chinese people. In a land where very little English is spoken there was some relief in passing on the important responsibilities of moving all our equipment and ourselves from Guangzhou, our arrival point in China, to the mountains. But there was also regret at losing the satisfaction, insight and sense of freedom that would have come from coping by ourselves.

From the time of our arrival in China we were in the C.M.A.'s hands. Its representative in Guangzhou met our train from Hong Kong and made sure we and our luggage caught our connection to Beijing. We travelled by luxurious "Soft Class". There were four-berth compartments with bed linen, curtains, a pot plant and a thermos for topping up our tea.

The thirty-six-hour journey allowed us time to relax and forget the rush of the last few weeks in Australia. As the kilometres rolled by we began to appreciate what it meant to be in China, the most populous nation in the world. Every view from every window showed intense cultivation or dense and crowded towns and cities. The huge rivers of the Yangste and the Hwang Ho hinted at the hugeness of the country which they drained. Our mission to climb a mountain somewhere far beyond all this seemed foreign, which indeed it was. China was our pathway to Tibet, a country which until twenty-five years ago had been an isolated mountain theocracy. Now Tibet was administered by the Chinese. Our ten-day approach through China allowed only a superficial look at the enigmatic nation.

There was, however, enough time to assemble a series of images in each place we stayed. In Beijing the traffic scenes were contrasted by the quiet of the Temple of Heaven. The huge park surrounding the Temple was only five minutes' run from the Bei Wei Hotel where we stayed. Each morning we would jog down and through the grounds to the Temple.

The fifteenth-century architecture captured with lasting effect the peace and mightiness of the Chinese conception of heaven. Every year on the day before winter solstice, the Son of Heaven – the Emperor – had travelled ceremoniously to the Temple where he prayed for good harvests.

These days thousands of Chinese took their daily exercise there. People of all ages performed the graceful martial art form of Tai Chi amongst the trees, sometimes in classes of a hundred or more, but often alone or in small groups. Old men met at the same places every morning to chat and admire each other's caged birds. They sat and smoked while the birds sang to each other. Younger people played badminton, hackysack or handball. After our run the others would play frisbee while I practised yoga. By the time we had jogged back to the hotel we were invariably late for breakfast. It was worth hurrying the meal to make such a refreshing start to the day.

ABOVE LEFT: Trains are an important way of transporting people and goods across China. Steam trains are still in common use.

LEFT: As travellers in "Soft Class", we were given huge meals three times a day during the train journey to Beijing.

RIGHT: Chinese trains are well maintained. At one of our many stops our carriage and Andy were hosed clean. Transliteration of Chinese words into roman characters is becoming increasingly common in an attempt to lessen the communication gap between China and the rest of the world.

北京 特快 广州
BEIJING — GUANGZHOU

ABOVE: With most of the first two weeks of our trip spent travelling, we made the fullest use of every opportunity to keep fit by exercising. Jogging through the streets of Beijing in the early morning avoids the heat of the day.

RIGHT: Mike Dillon getting down to work in the streets of Beijing while Tenzing pretends to be a spectator.

FOLLOWING PAGES: Chinese tourists, both expatriots and those from China itself, considerably outnumber Western tourists at the Great Wall.

The C.M.A. encouraged us to keep busy. Its officials, too, appreciated how much there was to see in China. We made a day trip to the Great Wall. At one time the wall had stretched in a continuous length for 5000 kilometres. The first sections were built in the third century BC, though the part we visited had been restored to the extent of being totally rebuilt during the Ming Dynasty (1368-1644).

The wall itself was as it had been at our visit three years ago – and for centuries before that. Below, where the buses parked, the tourist facilities had multiplied tenfold. The wall snaked over the rugged and empty hills like a hollow Chinese dragon. For the couple of kilometres open and accessible to tourists, the dragon came to life as thousands crowded the ramparts. Most of the sightseers on the wall, choking the souvenir shops and filling the restaurants, were Chinese. The road as we drove back to Beijing was busy with buses. The tourist market had become big in China.

Other things had changed since 1981, even to our blinkered eyes. Three years before, equality amongst the Chinese was shown by the universally worn blue uniforms of the Revolution. Now other clothes could be seen, some with more than a hint of fashion. Women in particular, or perhaps it was the women whom we noticed, wore clothes that actually flattered them. See-through blouses and skirts, though modestly cut, were a big step from shapeless blue trousers and square jackets and skirts. Such changes were evasively justified as logical developments of policy rather than being acknowledged as about-faces in attitude. The people had such faith in the Communist government that dramatic changes and improvements in lifestyle could be made quickly and without question. The government was not shackled by fear of the electorate's reaction, nor by petty politicking against it.

The highlight of our stay in Beijing was an acrobatic show. In an old hall opening onto a narrow street a team of fifteen gymnasts, jugglers and magicians kept us amazed with their flexibility, poise and showmanship. Though many Westerners were in the audience, the show was essentially entertainment for the Chinese. The applause of the old men in singlets and the young Chinese couples was as vigorous as ours. The dedication and discipline of the performers made us feel like amateurs. Yet, for the duration of our expedition, the climbing of Everest would rule our lives as completely as the nightly performances governed the acrobats. Though our fields of expertise were vastly different I found the show inspirational. Far from being relaxing, it fuelled my impatiently contained eagerness to reach the mountain.

At other times we organised our own entertainment. Simply walking the streets watching the daily routine filled out our view of the giant city. Bicycles played such a large role in the lives of the people of Beijing that Mike decided he needed to film a cycling scene. With Mr Xia, the young English student who was our interpreter, we combed the backstreets near Tiananmen Square in search of a shop which hired bicycles. Eventually we found the place, only to be told that the bicycle owner had moved his

premises. Since it was our last morning in Beijing we did not have time to hunt around other parts of the city. We encouraged Mr Xia to ask two young men eating ice-creams by their bicycles whether we could borrow their machines for ten minutes. When they agreed, we persuaded the ice-cream vendor to let us hire the tricycle-trolley he used to transport his stall. Howard pedalled the tricycle with Mike kneeling on the platform at the back while Tim and I rode behind. It must have been a curious sight, for some European tourists stepped out of their bus to take photos of us as we rode by. The Chinese were interested in our performance but not enough to be distracted from whatever they were doing for more than a few moments. Foreign tourists had become an accepted presence and their behaviour was expected to be peculiar. Travelling the flat streets by bicycle was an enjoyable way to see Beijing. Unlike other big Asian cities the roads were not ruled by the dual evils of anarchy and speed.

From a subject's point of view it was interesting to see the amount of work that Mike put into the film. He needed a great deal of co-operation from us in order to shoot the same scene from different angles. When filming, he became oblivious to the reactions of the people around him apart from those who featured in the footage. His concentration on the job made it easier for us to forget our embarrassment as we ran up and down the ramparts of the Great Wall in front of huge crowds, or made seemingly natural comments about the food at the C.M.A.'s banquet in Beijing, despite the bright lights, the camera, and Jim hovering in the background recording the conversation.

The film added another dimension to our expedition. A group of twelve is naturally less cohesive than one of half that size. During our approach to the mountain our common aim was the film. Once we reached Base Camp the idea of the film would drop from the climbers' minds as we concentrated on the enormous task of climbing the mountain. The intimacy of a small group working together would return. Above Advance Base Camp we would operate as two separate groups to allow each person to concentrate on his own special problems. There would be co-ordination of filming and climbing by radio and other areas of co-operation, but essentially we would be two independent teams. Meanwhile we made no distinction, only that those behind the cameras were busier than those in front of them. As we travelled through China there was a real sense of biding our time, of twiddling our thumbs until the action started. The twelve of us joked and carried on like a football team on end-of-season holiday. Once the climbing started there would be little energy to spare for frivolity.

Our next stop was Chengdu. Instead of simply overnighting en route to Lhasa we spent a day there absorbing the atmosphere of another part of China. Though a large city, Chengdu had a definite provincial atmosphere. Built on the banks of the Min Kiang, the climate was tropical. The thickly treed avenues and parkland running by the river, together with the vegetables in the markets, gave the city a lushness which stopped the heat and humidity from seeming out of place as they had in Beijing. There were many things to do and see – more than time allowed. Howard and I visited a massage clinic where all the masseurs were blind. In a country with a thousand million people to support no resources are ignored. The only people who would feel left out would be those who did not wish to conform. No such people were obvious to us.

Away from the main roads the streets were narrow alleys. It was as if the broad avenues serviced by buses and trams were the city's concession to the modern age. In the backstreets the houses seemed to tower above the cobblestones, only because the passageways were so tight. Here was the China of my imagination. An old man under a big straw hat waddled along the street, his legs bowed under the weight of two huge baskets of vegetables. Each basket dangled on four strings from the ends of the worn bamboo pole which lay across his shoulders. Leaning against a doorway was a grey-haired grandmother. The small black shoes upon her once-bound feet, together with the black legs of her trousers, suggested two exclamation marks; a contrast in emotion to her wrinkled yet expressionless face as she stared back at me.

What changes those eyes have seen, I thought. How foreign China is to me. And how long it would take for me to begin to understand what these people thought. Their appreciation of the world would remain entirely theirs. The next day we would fly to Tibet, where the only Chinese were transient bureaucrats and soldiers tolerating hardship postings.

ABOVE: The amount of food for sale in the markets seems stupendous until one remembers the number of people in China.

BELOW: Advertising reflects China's drive to become a major industrial power.

CHAPTER SIX

TIBET

UNDERNEATH us an ocean of clouds stretched from horizon to horizon. During the two-hour flight from Chengdu the few breaks in the cloud revealed hilly landscapes dramatic in their lack of habitation. And once, a tantalising glimpse of an ice-capped peak lying directly below, the dirty plastic windows distorting its shape. Then, again, endless clouds censoring our view of the unknown country.

Suddenly the plane dipped its nose and we were plunging through whiteness to emerge, it seemed, in another world. Beneath was a huge riverbed flooded muddy brown from one bank to the other. The walls of the valley soared dramatically skyward from the water's edge.

Purple, red and yellow scree slopes rose steeply above the river, sometimes jumping vertically for hundreds of metres over darker cliffs. Bluffs formed the summits of the barren mountains which flanked the valley in merciless monotony. Gentleness was found in neither the landforms nor our approach. The plane continued to drop rapidly so that soon the mountains towered above us, and the expanse of water below seemed uninvitingly close. Then, relief to the eye, greenness filling the floor of a major side valley. I spotted a village at its head, but even there the houses were cluttered together as if crowding helped combat the bleakness and immensity of Tibet.

Just as it seemed inevitable that our touchdown would be in water the concrete runway appeared below. We hit the ground once ... twice ... three ... four times. At 3500 metres, the thin air rushing the upturned flaps was slow in bringing us to a halt. Stairs were wheeled up and we stepped out into the cool sunshine of one of the world's remotest airports.

Over the mountain range to the north of the runway lay Lhasa, the city supposedly serviced by the airport. Six hours' drive away, the capital of Tibet was built many centuries before accessibility by air was a consideration.

Our luggage filled most of the aeroplane's hold. We waited a couple of hours for it to be unloaded, firstly onto trucks, then into the small enclosure surrounded by mud and puddles which was the luggage claim area. There we transferred what we could into the comfortable bus which was to take us to Lhasa. The padded seats did little to compensate for the appalling state of the road.

In comparison with tropical Chengdu, Tibet was desolate, yet in the bus we were close enough to notice what vegetation did exist. We passed through irrigated areas where fields were the green and brilliant yellow of ripe barley and mustard. Most of the countryside was of rock – pieces of all sizes from huge cliffs to scree and gravel. A hospit-

LEFT: The floodplain of the Yarlung Tsangpo River is our first view of Tibet when our aircraft breaks through the thick layer of cloud.

RIGHT: Detail from a fresco in a small Buddhist monastery outside Lhasa. Tibetan religious paintings depict incidents in the life of Buddha or his reincarnations or manifestations. The process of painting is a religious act, as is meditating upon the art.

91

able environment for lichens and a few small flowering bushes but very little else. The road followed the river the Tibetans called the Tsangpo; further downstream it is known as the Brahmaputra. In places the road was less than a metre above the muddy, swirling torrent. At other spots, side-streams had washed the road away so that our bus had to take the even rougher detour around the washout. At a small cluster of Chinese-style houses which could hardly be called a village, a long bridge crossed the river. From there we continued to follow the river until the road branched up the valley which held Lhasa.

It was late afternoon by the time we approached the legendary city. Visible from the outskirts was the Potala Palace, perched on the summit of a rocky peak high above the city. Once the residence of the fourteenth Dalai Lama and his previous incarnations, the Potala stood in stark contrast to the solid but rough concrete factories, warehouses and barracks, built by the Chinese on the city limits. The broad modern streets were flanked by similar buildings. Functionality was the prime criterion for design. As we neared the centre of the old city the atmosphere changed. Long three-storey apartment blocks, obviously new, were built in Tibetan style. Large windows filled with a dozen smaller panes were surrounded by carved and brightly painted frames. The doorways were similarly decorated. It was refreshing to note, even as we arrived, that in the old part of the city the Chinese administration was complying with the broad, squat style of Tibetan architecture and its distinctive manner of decoration.

One of the privileges of a mountaineering expedition was that we were able to stay in the Centre for Physical Culture and Sports. Though the facilities were basic it had the enormous advantage of being close to the middle of town. Most tourist groups were accommodated in a big hotel seven or eight kilometres from the city.

The kitchen staff at the Centre had been expecting our arrival and as soon as we had unloaded the bus we were whisked off to the dining hall. The good food fuelled our appetite to see something of the city. As dusk approached we left the compound in groups of

At Lhasa airport, our baggage is unloaded, then sorted into piles of what is needed immediately and what can follow later by truck.

92

In contrast to Tibet's barren hills, some of the river valleys are very fertile. Three Tibetans return from their work in the fields through crops of yellow rape and barley.

two and three. It was natural that we all ended up in the same place as the flow of people led in one direction. That was to the Jokhang Temple, the spiritual centre of Lhasa, and hence of Tibet. The main street was broad and guttered and uncrowded. Each side street we took became narrower and busier until we came to an intersection which made us stop and stare. Chinese had vanished from the crowds. Tibetan men and women in their heavy clothes of wool or sheepskin walked clockwise as if part of a procession. From the time I had spent in Nepal, I was familiar with the tradition of walking clockwise around Buddhist monuments. We were to discover that the object of veneration was the Jokhang Temple complex that dominated the block around which the people walked. We joined the crowd which thickened as we approached the Temple. Many of the Tibetans were from places a long distance from Lhasa and had never seen Westerners before. They stared and laughed and chattered to each other and to us. Their rough and weather-beaten toughness, as we were jostled in the crowd, made us glad that their reaction was one of amusement.

Many of the men had long plaited hair wrapped around their heads with red cotton. Neatness was not a mark of fashion, except perhaps in a negative sense. Rough jewellery featured prominently. The men decorated themselves with ear-studs of turquoise. Sometimes a turquoise pebble was suspended from an ear by a short length of cotton. A red coral bead prevented the cotton from slipping through the pierced ear-lobe. Around their necks they wore two beads of coral and one of turquoise and, sometimes, a translucent agate bead appeared as well. The jewellery of the women was finer and more elaborate with many of the pieces set in silver. The turquoise stones were larger and less blemished, with amber and silver beads included amongst the coral and turquoise on their necklaces. Often smaller pieces were set in silver to form a pendant. Many of the Tibetan people are semi-nomadic herdsmen and, for them, jewellery is a logical way to carry their wealth. Other possessions are cumbersome, but jewellery can be sold or traded easily when money or goods are needed.

The women seemed equal to the men. They joked and teased just as much, although less noticeably because they were fewer. Their long black hair was always worn in plaits, sometimes hanging down their backs, sometimes wrapped around their heads, but always neater than the men. At their waists, on top of their black ankle-length skirts, they wore finely woven, multicoloured aprons. The words ''dress'' and ''skirt'' suggest a fineness of cut that did not exist. Clothes for the harsh Tibetan climate were above all else practical – heavy yak or sheep woollens designed for warmth and protection from the weather.

The crowd came to a virtual standstill outside the Jokhang. The evening light was diminished further by the clouds of juniper smoke from sacred fires. The courtyard of the temple was covered with people prostrated towards the entrance. It was not a matter of dropping to their knees, then walking away considering their religious service done. They lay full length on the ground, forehead touching stone and hands extended. Each person repeated the procedure dozens, sometimes hundreds, of times. The paving stones were worn smooth from centuries of this practice. Many people came with mats on which to lie and small hand-pads to slide forward. Others sat on the step by the road watching or repeating mantras with their malla beads. It was an extraordinary sight. We had come to Lhasa knowing of the Chinese suppression of Tibetan Buddhism during the Cultural Revolution twenty years before, and had expected the temples and the Potala to be stale museums of past glory. Our surprise was great, and we found the display of religious fervour uplifting.

The next day we were allowed to see the interior of the Jokhang. The front gate opened into a courtyard surrounded by a covered walkway. Red wooden pillars supported the second storey. Where the pillars met the ceiling were elaborate carvings painted bright blues, yellows and greens. Similarly decorated pillars separated the second storey from the third. From the ground we could catch glimpses of sculpted, gilded roofs above. An old lama (priest) dressed in traditional scarlet robes hurried us inside. His face was expressionless and remained so for the two or three hours we spent exploring the temple.

The splendour of the main hall outshone all other religious monuments I had seen anywhere in the world. A huge statue of Shakyamuni Buddha took pride of place. From the floor to the tip of his gold- and jewel-encrusted headdress was a full three storeys. The whole bronze figure was plated with gold. The walls of the hall were painted with elaborate murals; each painting told a different story about the life of Buddha or his different reincarnations and manifestations.

Opening directly from the main hall were a dozen rooms, each barely large enough to house a life-size image of one of the holy people associated with spreading Buddha's teachings in Tibet. Each figure was bedecked in gold and jewels. Butter lamps and offerings of rice, scarves and money lay at their feet. Upstairs more statue-filled rooms opened onto the walkway surrounding the main hall. The skill of the artistry was consistently fine. The worth of the religious art was stupendous in monetary terms and its spiritual value impossible to assess.

From the roof of the Jokhang we looked out over the buildings of Lhasa. Rather than isolated houses, the buildings were in big blocks, each with a central courtyard. The roofs were flat with low walls around the perimeter and were used as part of the living space – a place to dry grain, to store yak-dung for fuel, or to sit outside away from the dust and bustle of ground level.

A few kilometres away was the Potala Palace, rising proud and aloof above the city as if to capture in its location and architecture the other-worldliness of the spiritual rulers who had lived there.

The following day we were permitted to tour the inside of the palace. The same feeling of extravagant holiness pervaded the hallways and chambers of the ancient building. Our appreciation of the artistry of the famous tomb of the fifth Dalai Lama and of the exquisite murals colouring the walls of the rooms was limited by the lack of light given out by our candles. Electric lights hung from the ceiling in the most incongruous places, but an electrical fault had started a fire a few months before so the lights were no longer used.

The roof of the Potala looked up at nothing but the rocky mountains which ringed the valley. The human world with its endless suffering and ephemeral joys was in the dusty and primitive city below. Above soared the heavens in all their purity. In the Potala we could feel that what lingered from the days of the Dalai Lama's rule was the sense of separation between the monks, whose thoughts were with the heavens, and the lay people, who were very much of the earth. For us, Lhasa was part of a different pilgrimage. Our Higher Path involved keeping our hands and feet firmly on the ground.

After flying from sea-level up to 3500 metres, it was essential that we spend several days at Lhasa adjusting to the reduced amount of oxygen in the atmosphere before proceeding any higher. Our time was divided between visiting the most famous of the city's monuments, sorting our equipment and wandering, fascinated, around the town. Days could have been spent sitting and watching Tibetan life go by but we were driven on by our carefully planned itinerary and our impatience to reach our mountain.

The roads in Tibet are amongst the worst in the world – an endless succession of potholes, fords, washouts, rockfalls and sand-dunes. The bus we caught from Lhasa liked the road even less than we did. The route to Xigatse (that night's destination) involved several high passes where the road zig-zagged its way up from the valley floor. Our bus refused to cross even the first of these. The driver scurried down the hillside with a bucket to fetch water for the radiator. We stepped outside to realign our heads and shoulders after the hours of continuous shaking. Walking gave more time to appreciate the immensity of the landscape. From Lhasa we had driven through huge grass-covered hills buttressed with gigantic cliffs. There were neither buildings nor trees to give perspective. The only scale we had was the long time it took for the bus to approach and leave behind each roadside hill. The pass itself was surrounded by rocky peaks. On the crest was a sizable collection of Buddhist prayer flags which had been placed there in appreciation of the power of nature and to acknowledge the humility of humanity before such forces. Beyond, the road descended more gently. The plateau had taken a step up and opened out and for the first time the emptiness of our surroundings came to me with force. It was little wonder that one of the world's most complex religions had evolved here as the inhabitants, driven by hardship and awe, sought to explain reasons for existence.

Our vehicle caught up so we hopped aboard for the few hours it took to reach the next climb. This time the bus almost made it to the top before we had to walk. The pass gave

The Potala, residence for many centuries of the Dalai Lama, spiritual head of Tibetan Buddhism.

LEFT and ABOVE: Inside Lhasa's Jokhang Temple, offerings of butter burn in front of a gilded, jewel-encrusted statue of a Buddhist deity, and ceremonial scarves are draped over an image of Princess Weng Chu.

BELOW: Beyond the decorated roof of the Jokhang Temple rises the Potala Palace.

ABOVE RIGHT: On the roof of the Jokhang Temple a monk blows a ceremonial horn while two others study scriptures.

BELOW RIGHT: Afternoon tea at the Tashihlunpo Monastery in Xigatse.

ABOVE: Mike and Colin record our crossing of the flooded Tsangpo (Bhramaputra) by yak-skin coracle while Greg jokes about swimming.

BELOW: The ferry village by the Tsangpo. The unused ferry lies by the near bank, and a queue of trucks wait on the far side.

magnificent views to the south and west of hills and mountains disappearing into the distance. Two more days' travel through the vast land lay between us and the Himalaya.

At about five that afternoon we stopped for a different reason. We pulled up behind a queue of trucks waiting to be ferried across the Tsangpo. When we walked past a dozen trucks to the bank of the swollen muddy river we learnt, to our horror, that the first few trucks had been waiting for six days. The flooded river was too powerful to allow the ferry to operate. Rather than incur the expenses of fuel and damage to their vehicles from retracing their paths on the rough roads, the truck drivers chose to wait, however long it took, for the waters to subside. We did not wish to waste time driving back to Lhasa and taking an alternative route, but at first we seemed to have no choice. The officials from the C.M.A., who were to stay with us for the duration of the expedition, rushed off to the nearest telephone. It was to solve exactly these sorts of problems that the C.M.A. insisted the expedition employ at least one liaison officer. After an hour or so the officials returned looking pleased. Through our interpreter, Mr Xia, we were informed that a truck from Xigatse would meet us on the other side. That was good news, but it did not solve the problem of how to cross the fast-flowing river which was about three hundred metres wide where we stood.

An extended shouting-match with people on the other side seemed to achieve nothing until we noticed a man launching a boat about half a kilometre upstream. Though he rowed furiously, the force of the river carried him down almost to where we stood by the time he reached our bank. The man's boat was a very curious craft. The idea for its construction may well have inspired the rhyme "Three Men in a Tub". The framework was of willow, each pole little thicker than a broom handle. Over that, to form the hull, was a covering of yak skin. The result was a light and surprisingly watertight rectangular coracle. Though its river-worthiness had been proven before our eyes we were still a little fearful about entrusting to it both ourselves and the gear we had in the bus. However, as there was no alternative we agreed to be ferried across the river.

While we unloaded our baggage from the bus the boatman dragged the coracle from the water, turned it upside down, crawled underneath, then stood up with it on his back. As he staggered upstream along the shore he looked from behind like an enormous two-legged tortoise. By the time we had carried all our luggage half a kilometre upstream, another coracle had rowed across to us. The boatmen tied the two craft together and motioned for us to pass our luggage aboard. Half the baggage and almost half our team filled the first boatload. There was little daylight left so we quickly pushed off. Immediately we were swept downstream. By rowing hard the boatmen were able to keep our cross-stream progress slightly ahead of our down-river speed. They grinned at our obvious delight in this unusual form of transport. Mike kept his movie camera pressed to his eye, panning and zooming left and right. We beached on the far shore without shipping any water at all.

The boatmen carried their craft back upstream to make the second trip. Immediately the local villagers began to descend upon us. They were obviously astonished to see a group of Westerners calmly sitting by the river with a huge pile of baggage. There was a sizable audience to witness the arrival of the second boatload of climbers and gear at dusk. We thanked the boatmen as they strode off, tortoise-like, with an air that implied they rescued stranded mountaineering expeditions every day of the week.

The impending darkness drew with it heavy storm clouds. We were led by a mob of enthusiastic children to the shelter of the schoolhouse as the first few raindrops began to fall. With all our gear inside, there was little room to move. The children jammed the doorway and window in their eagerness to watch the behaviour of strange foreigners. Our dinner that night was a packet of biscuits and a few cups each of Tibetan tea. The tea was made with milk, salt and yak butter, and was definitely an acquired taste. We soon gave up hope of the truck from Xigatse arriving that night, so we bedded down on the tables, benches and floor in our sleeping bags.

The next morning we had time to explore the village. Both the houses and the high walls that sheltered them from wind were made of mud brick. The courtyards, and some-times the roofs of the buildings, were piled high with yak-dung and firewood. Few trees grew anywhere within sight and firewood was mostly the twisted and stunted trunks of the low bushes which grew in the sand-dunes behind the settlement. From the sand-

A photo stop below the Pang La, en route to Base Camp from Xegar.

dunes I could see a fertile and heavily cultivated side valley which presumably provided the village with its grain and other crops. I guessed that the village itself had been built on the banks of the Tsangpo to serve as a ferry town, at a time when yak-skin coracles provided the only way of crossing the river.

Our truck arrived at the village shortly after midday. We threw our gear in the back, climbed on top of it, then bounced off along the road towards Xigatse. Though I had not believed it possible, the road was even worse than the one we had endured the previous day. In a few spots it had washed away leaving deep gullies. Since an unladen truck had a better chance of crossing the gullies left by the flood, we hopped out at those places. It was obvious that even if our bus had been able to cross the river, there was no way it could have negotiated this road.

The dusty and bumpy journey lasted two hours. Xigatse, the second city of Tibet, was in a large valley. A ruined fort of enormous proportions overlooked our barrack-style hotel. We stayed in Xigatse for two nights, both to aid our acclimatisation and to allow time to explore the city. Xigatse was most famous for the huge Tashihlunpo Monastery, the centre of the Panchen sect of Tibetan Buddhism. We spent an afternoon wandering around its many passages and hallways. The most impressive sight was a giant statue of Buddha. It stood twenty-six metres high and had been completed in 1914 after four years of labour. Like all other important statues we had seen in Tibet the figure was gilded and inlaid with gems and semi-precious stones. By now we were no longer impressed by the ostentatious wealth. It was easy to understand the popularity of the famous sage Milarepa who, after years of study, scorned his monastery and wandered Tibet preaching the word of Buddha in ballads and poems.

Despite the wealth of the monasteries, most of the monks live austere lives. One luxury they are allowed is afternoon tea. It was an anachronistic sight to see the red-robed monks, who live by rules laid down centuries ago, lining up to receive their ration of tea in thermoses. The tea-kitchen was an amazing place. A furnace heated a tub with a built-on roof ("lid" seems inappropriate for a pot three metres in diameter), and the tea was drawn from different points around the tub. The size made us appreciate the population of the monastery which in itself indicated the force of Buddhism in modern Tibet.

Xigatse itself was a much slower city than Lhasa. There was a great deal of building going on but little of the bustle and air of business that had pervaded Lhasa. The essential difference was that in Xigatse the Tibetan people greatly outnumbered the Chinese.

The monsoon in Tibet takes a strange form. There are constant storm clouds but only occasional rainfall. We arrived in time for one of the biggest downpours of the season. The streets and alleyways immediately turned to deep mud, but the smoke and haze which had been hanging over the town was cleaned from the air. We were concerned that the road to Xegar, our next stop, would have become impassable. Luckily the rain did little damage and in fact helped settle the dust. We left Xigatse early so that we had time to visit the hot springs of Lhaze. The springs were in the middle of an open plain so, to protect the bathers, walls and even buildings had been constructed around the springs. We savoured the hot bath, knowing it would be our last proper wash until we returned in two months' time.

From Lhaze we crossed a minor pass then drove along fertile river valleys. The valleys were narrow and the green fields of barley with the occasional vivid yellow patch of mustard seemed especially bright against the brown rocky hillside which soared up steeply from the valley floor.

As we approached Xegar the mountains receded, leaving an open plain. The town was nestled at the far side of the valley on the lower flanks of a peak almost steep enough to be called a spire. The ancient fort of Xegardzong topped the peak and its ruined walls flowed down the slopes to the town. It was a magnificent situation for a fortress. As Xigatse had been smaller and quieter than Lhasa, so Xegar was smaller and more primitive again. Each day we drove further and further away from civilisation. Nature, always the undisputed master of Tibet, was soon to take over completely.

RIGHT: The hill with the ruins of Xegar fort shelters the town of Xegar from the Tibetan wind. The days when the fort provided military protection are long since past.

Sun-dried clay tablets depicting the form of Buddha or other holy images are made by lamas as a religious duty. This pile of thousands is one of many such collections found in rock caves near the ruined nunnery a few kilometres north of the Rongbuk Monastery.

Our Chinese staff were worried that the heavy rains might make it impossible to cross the Dzakar Chu River, the final obstacle before Base Camp. Rather than joining the Tsangpo, the river flowed around the eastern side of the Everest massif to join the Arun River which flowed south through Nepal into India. Jim, who had travelled to Base Camp before, and Tim and I, spent the evening discussing alternatives, only to decide there was no option but to find a way across.

The next morning we set off early. It was a beautiful day. After a few kilometres we branched off the "highway" to Nepal on to an even rougher road, sometimes barely a track, which led over a 5000-metre pass named the Pang La. Our truck slowed almost to a crawl as it wound its way slowly up the mountainside. Near the top all vegetation had disappeared, leaving a sea of scree. When we crested the pass we were amazed to see, forty kilometres away, the Himalaya stretched out before us. Cho Oyu, Gyachung Kang, Makalu and, in the middle of them all, Qomolangma – Mt Everest. We stopped the truck and jumped out. The monsoon clouds soon closed in, but not before we were given enough time to appreciate the scale of our objective. The giant mountains of Makalu and Cho Oyu seemed dwarfed. Of all of us, only Greg had not seen Mt Everest before, and he was now adjusting his expectations to the unimaginable reality.

Back in the truck we coasted down the southern side of the pass. At the river, the sight of our two truckloads of gear and food waiting for us on the far side gave us confidence. It was an exciting ford across the fast-flowing rocky river. Five metres from the far shore, and luckily not before, our driver stalled his vehicle and had to be towed out by one of the other trucks. We celebrated with lunch in the sun, a quick affair since we were all eager to reach Base Camp as soon as possible. After an hour we passed the small village of Chobuk, built in the middle of a boulder field several kilometres long and as wide as the open valley. It was the most imperfect spot for a village that I could imagine. From there the road branched off from the river and led up the Rongbuk Valley.

The valley which drained the northern slopes of Everest was appropriately magnificent, gradually narrowing until it was almost a gorge. A thousand metres above us on both sides rose gigantic cliffs. The skyline was a jagged ridge of pinnacles and turrets balanced against the call of gravity – perhaps an example of the power of Mt Everest, looming huge somewhere hidden in the clouds at the head of the valley. In the midst of this setting were the ruins of Rongbuk Monastery. The few monks who lived there, and the many who had lived there in the past, could have held no doubts about the insignificance of humanity compared to the forces of nature.

The road crept around the rocky hillside a hundred metres or so above the noisy Rongbuk River while the clouds sank low over us. What an inhospitable place to spend the next two months! We tried to keep from our minds the thought that on the mountain itself, conditions would be much harsher. Comfort would be a peripheral issue from now on, one we would worry about but which could not receive priority if we were to climb the mountain.

The valley opened out of the gorge into a river flat. On one side only was a small grassy area. Everywhere were scree and the smaller rocks of the river basin. This was it, our Base Camp. We had arrived.

ABOVE: "A thousand metres above us on both sides rose gigantic cliffs.
The skyline was a jagged ridge of pinnacles and turrets balanced against the call of gravity."
BELOW: Our truck stalls while fording the Dzakar Chu River.

105

ABOVE: "A thousand metres above us on both sides rose gigantic cliffs.
The skyline was a jagged ridge of pinnacles and turrets balanced against the call of gravity."
BELOW: Our truck stalls while fording the Dzakar Chu River.

106

ABOVE: The North Face of Mt Everest from Rongbuk Monastery.
ABOVE LEFT: After light rain from heavy monsoon clouds, a rainbow is cast over fertile fields along the banks of the Tsangpo River.
BELOW LEFT: Tibetan roadworkers admire the huge rock sculpture of Buddha which looks out over the Tsangpo.

CHAPTER SEVEN

BASE CAMP BLUES

I WOKE in the morning to a familiar yet unexpected silence. Missing was the subtle background noise as the tent flapped and stretched in the gentlest of breezes. Several centimetres of snow cloaked our tents, freezing all movement and causing darkness to linger as dawn broke outside. I peeked through the door and saw that the whiteness extended into the sky. There was no point in waiting for the sun, since the clouds would continue to keep it distant. I crawled from my cozy sleeping bag, dressed quickly and stepped out to face the first day of a different world.

Now that we were at Base Camp a new stage had begun. Our journey from Australia through China and Tibet had been a necessary preamble to our climb. Travelling was a disorienting process which freed us from the comforts of routine, encouraged our minds to become alert and aware, and so made us live in the present. Our climb of Mt Everest would involve incredible hardship because of the cold, the lack of oxygen and the dangers of avalanche and rockfall. Once on the mountain we could afford to ignore none of those things because our survival would depend on constant concentration. But meanwhile, at our secure and comparatively comfortable Base Camp, the sensible approach was to let our immediate problems absorb our attention.

Automatically I looked to the south where the mass of Mt Everest lay. Clouds blocked all view as if to remind me that as there was plenty of time, there was no immediate necessity to see the mountain. The weeks ahead would breed a familiarity with the peak whose beauty and challenge would attract us while its dangers repelled. Here at 5100 metres we had first to allow our bodies to adjust to the reduced amount of oxygen in the upper limits of the atmosphere. The higher we went, the less oxygen there would be. For the moment we had to take things easily and limit our ambitions to more gentle heights.

The lack of oxygen was self-limiting. The boundless energy we had been bottling up inside for months evaporated in the thin air. We felt no desire to do more than the menial tasks that were necessary and possible at Base Camp.

That first morning we sorted and repacked our food and equipment. With the food that the C.M.A. had bought in advance, the total weight of equipment and supplies for three months was about three tonnes. Though we had cast our eyes over the intimidating pile in Lhasa the prospect of checking the contents had been too daunting to tackle there.

LEFT: As the clouds clear, the overnight fall of snow melts at Base Camp and the North Face of Mt Everest is revealed.

RIGHT: For Lincoln, yoga relieves the stiffness caused by days of travel in the back of a truck, and helps dissipate the tension that results from the excitement and nervousness felt during a dangerous climb such as Everest.

In such a rocky landscape, we were lucky to find an area near a stream on which to pitch our Base Camp.

Despite the lack of sunshine the air warmed sufficiently to melt the snow. Late in the morning Greg looked up from what he was doing and immediately shouted "Hey, look at that!"

We turned to the south. Beyond the hillock of moraine in the foreground the cloud had opened to reveal a face of snow buttressed with indistinct rock ridges. As we watched, the clouds lifted further to reveal the shape which was familiar to us all from photographs – the summit of Qomolangma, Mt Everest, the highest point on earth. It was a sobering view. Even from twenty kilometres away the peak loomed high above us. There was no hint of the way the mountain lay back from the vertical, a truth told by our maps and distant oblique views from Nepal. No one found much to say. Quietly we each absorbed the fact that there before us was our objective. After years of planning we were finally here. At last, there were no distractions, only the thought of climbing the mountain. The piles of rope and ice-axes at our feet assumed a new importance now the peak was in sight. The expedition had begun.

Our Chinese staff faced a different prospect. Base Camp would be home to them for the next two months at least. Within a week we would move up to our Advance Base and the Chinese would be left to themselves.

The C.M.A. had provided us with an abundance of personnel. There was a liaison officer – an official troubleshooter – for the climbing team and one for the film crew. Three technicians manned the radio which sent Simon's reports out to Beijing and hence to the Age in Melbourne. Mr Xia acted as interpreter for everybody. We employed Namagel, a Tibetan from Xigatse, as cook for the Chinese. As our jeep driver had little to do most of the time, he helped with the cooking. After the initial settling-in period all but the radio operators would have nothing to do but pass the time. Theirs were jobs we did not envy. Mr Qu, the liaison officer for the climbing team, and Mr Yang, who performed the same job for the film crew, were old expedition hands so Base Camp was no hardship for them.

Mr Qu reached the summit of Qomolangma Feng, as he called Everest, during the epic climb the Chinese made in 1960. They followed the North Ridge, the line attempted by the British before World War II. Everest posed its usual obstacles. Lack of oxygen was combatted with breathing apparatus. The task of stocking the camps on the mountain was performed by a support team of over a hundred people. As for bad weather, no amount of planning or Communist inspiration could help with that. The climbing itself was relatively straightforward, with the exception of a couple of short steep sections towards the top, where they least needed to encounter difficulties. The second of these involved a vertical section of rock a few metres high. Unable to scale it by any other means Mr Qu removed his gloves, shoes and socks, in order to be able to use the small holds. Thanks to his efforts and with the help of his rope, other climbers were able to climb up to him and on to the summit. It was an expensive solution to the problem as he lost his toes and parts of his fingers to frostbite. His stay with our expedition was much more relaxed, for he limited his excursions to within a few hundred metres of Base Camp.

Mr Xia, though, was at a loss in the mountains. He had never ventured far beyond the walls of the various educational institutions where he had studied. The intellectual struggles and pleasures which provided the satisfaction in his life were missing. It was not that they did not exist in the mountains, for life there posed questions as bluntly and directly as anywhere else on earth. The Himalaya were a foreign world to him, one whose language he could not hear, let alone begin to understand.

At Base Camp we were returning to a style of living that had become familiar to us through many expeditions. The goings-on in the world at large would be forgotten. On these occasions, when we possessed a radio, the news it gave always seemed unreal and distant, belonging to a place which existed independently of our mountain arena. In the world outside, the major events were the clashes of people or nations who were breaking or redefining rules, be they accepted conventions of behaviour or international borders. Here the mountain set the problems. We coped by defining our own rules and living by them. That was much of the satisfaction of a long climb such as this since, in the end, we had only ourselves to answer to.

Base Camp was simply the place where the road stopped. It was too far away from the mountain to be of any practical use as a climbing camp. Nevertheless, it was good to spend a few nights at the roadhead at an altitude of 5100 metres, before moving higher into thinner air.

The second day at Base dawned fine. We needed to explore the upper reaches of the Rongbuk Valley to find a site for our next camp. A walk of about a kilometre over river flats led to the Rongbuk Glacier. As with any glacier, the ice of the Rongbuk carved away the walls of the mountains on both sides as it flowed down the valley, leaving unstable slopes similar in appearance to huge road-cuttings. Rocks and landslides continually fell onto the ice so that the lower parts were concealed by a blanket of stones and boulders. The rock-cover slowed the melting of the glacier so that it extended to where the climate seemed too warm for permanent ice. Finally the glacier ended and a series of streams poured from the snout of the gigantic frozen river. As it melted, the rocks which had been on its surface were dumped in huge piles.

Those piles, called terminal moraine, interrupted our gentle walk along the river flats. We were lucky to find that here, where the valley had widened, a trough had formed on the true right bank between the valley wall and the piles of moraine pushed to the side by the ice. The moraine trough made travel up the first part of the valley unexpectedly simple.

An hour and a half from Base Camp we reached the major side valley of the East Rongbuk. We were faced with crossing a mighty torrent, the river which had sprung from the East Rongbuk Glacier several kilometres upstream. The volume of water was not great but the watercourse was steep and cluttered with boulders splashed wet and slip-

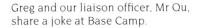

Greg and our liaison officer, Mr Qu, share a joke at Base Camp.

pery by the churning stream. The faint trail we had been following disappeared into the river. Even if we managed to cross near the lower trail we still needed to find an easier path for the yaks that would be carrying most of our food and equipment up to our next camp.

About a kilometre upstream the gorge of the East Rongbuk opened out into an area which was almost flat. As I approached, the low rock walls and rusty tins and other rubbish told me that this was the site of Camp I for the earlier expeditions that had attempted Everest's North Ridge. The sunshine disguised little of the spot's bleakness. The landscape consisted of scree slopes, crags and snow-capped peaks. Nowhere did there seem to be any earth, only boulders, pebbles and powdered rock.

The river had divided into smaller streams separated by tiny islands. It seemed a sensible place to cross. When I had removed my shoes, socks and trousers, I noticed that water splashed on the rocky banks and protruding boulders had frozen despite the warm sunshine. Expeditions always involve a certain amount of discomfort, I told myself, and these icy boulders and the murky, fast-flowing, freezing water are about to provide the first of it. I floundered across, dancing on each of the rock islands to restore some feeling to my feet.

The way ahead was pathless scrambling over the scree which ran down from the peaks towering above. After a couple of hours we came to a fork in the wide glacier. The West Rongbuk branched to the right and the main Rongbuk turned left around a spur to travel its final ten kilometres up to the North Face.

At the junction of the spur with the lateral moraine a tiny valley had formed. Half the hollow was filled by a pond which was fed and drained by a small stream. The combination of sheltered flat ground and running water was rare in the surrounding rubble of broken-down mountains. Just to make sure there was no better alternative nearby we walked around the corner formed by the spur. A superb view of the North Face confronted us. We forgot the search for camp sites and feasted our eyes on its huge sweeping snow slopes. Much of our planned route up the Face was obscured by a ridge running down from Changtse – the bulk of Everest loomed above and behind the 7500-metre north peak of the massif. Ahead of us lay ten kilometres of broken glacier travel to the bottom of the Face. There seemed to be no practicable place for a camp and with ten kilometres to return to Base Camp we felt we had come far enough for one day. We lay back and admired the view for half an hour. The Rongbuk Glacier at that point was not yet covered with loose moraine rocks. Instead, huge ice towers rose in the shapes of shark fins, as if a school of giant fish were preserved in white ice. Crossing the glacier would be difficult here, and thankfully unnecessary. Half a dozen steep ice peaks, which our maps neglected to name, flanked the West Rongbuk Glacier. We were surrounded by mountains that rose from a glacier which was itself higher than almost every other mountain range in the world.

The breathlessness we all felt came neither from the magnificence of our surrounds nor from the feeling that finally we had arrived. The cause was the lack of oxygen at an altitude of 5500 metres. For the next two months the thin atmosphere would be a constant limit to what we could achieve. The effect would be worst on the upper reaches of the mountain where every step would be a tremendous effort. That time was many weeks away. Until then our bodies would gradually adjust to the oxygen lack. Attempting to climb high without allowing time for acclimatisation would induce severe sickness that would almost certainly result in death. Survival in these mountains depended on caution and a thorough knowledge of both the physical and physiological dangers.

For the moment we were content to put our energies into setting up our Advance Base Camp in the small valley at the fork of the Rongbuk Glacier.

The next day was a rest day. I relaxed my body and mind with a long session of yoga, then scrambled about six hundred metres up the rocky ridge directly above the camp. The rock was friable, giving enough spice to the steep sections to evoke the intense concentration which provides much of the satisfaction of rockclimbing. I returned to Base wearily in the evening and reached the tents at the same time as a couple of Tibetan men.

They were the owners of the yaks that were to carry our equipment up to Advance Base. We had not expected them to arrive until the following day but, as we sat down to

Geof, Narayan, Tenzing, Lincoln and Andy relax by a small pond during the reconnaissance up the Rongbuk Valley in search of a site for Advance Base Camp. By the pond was a good camp site, but it was too far from the mountain.

dinner, twenty-five yaks herded by another three Tibetans walked over the low piles of ancient moraine to the small meadow which was our camp. That night we organised supplies into suitably sized loads for the fifteen yaks we chose to hire, though in the morning the Tibetans insisted on rearranging the loads.

So that they would be able to tolerate the cold of the high mountains, the C.M.A. had provided the yak owners with suitable clothing. Rather than carrying these things until they were needed, they wore them. The sunglasses for snow glare were worn permanently on their heads, with the tinted lenses looking backwards in blatant admission that their main purpose was to keep their long hair in place. Down jackets replaced their heavy sheepskin coats but they were worn in the same style. In all but the most intense cold one sleeve dangled empty like a spare arm, leaving their throwing arms free, as the Tibetans' method of herding and directing their yaks was with carefully aimed pebbles.

Despite carrying heavy packs weighing perhaps forty kilos, the walk up to our Advance Base site was relaxed, since we were limited by the slow pace of the yaks. The water-level in the East Rongbuk River had dropped considerably so we were able to follow the lower trail by leaping from rock to rock. We supposed that it was only during a hot day after a big snowfall that the river was swollen. Certainly the lower route saved a great deal of time and effort.

As we neared the small valley we walked ahead to decide the best place to unload the yaks. A beautiful grassy area had been cut into small islands by the stream that poured out of the moraine above but inspection revealed the ground to be uneven and therefore unsuitable for tents. Eventually we chose a muddy but level spot near the lake. Above and behind lay more uneven turf where we could sit when the weather was kind to us.

ABOVE: A few minutes' walk from our sheltered Advance Base Camp was a spectacular view up the Rongbuk Glacier past Changtse (left) to the North Face of Everest.

LEFT: Because it is much closer to Advance Base Camp, the 7550-metre peak of Changtse looks as tall as Qomolangma, 1300 metres higher.

RIGHT: The North Face of Qomolangma from a 6000-metre peak to the west of the Rongbuk Glacier. Camp I was established on the glacier near the ridge of Changtse which comes down diagonally to the bottom right corner.

ABOVE and RIGHT: The fast-flowing river which drains the East Rongbuk Glacier and the unstable moraine rock provided no real obstacles for the sure-footed yaks that carried our equipment to Advance Base.

LEFT: Tenzing crosses a glacial stream where a fallen ice tower has provided a bridge. The stream undermined the tower until it collapsed. The constant erosion of the ice by sun and water means that dangerous changes in the glacial structure occur quickly.

RIGHT: A natural mosaic, stones and gravel set in deep blue glacial ice.

We watched the Tibetans unload the yaks then set about pitching our mess tent and kitchen tent. The kitchen tent was a huge but simple four-sided pyramid with a single central pole. Apart from its weight it was simple to erect. Tim, Narayan and Tenzing battled with that while Geof and I pitched our wits against the tent we had already nicknamed the Quarter Acre Dream. It was a large and luxurious tent complete with windows, a verandah, removable curtains and a dozen poles. The Sydney firm of Goodearl and Bailey had donated it to the expedition. It was robust and weatherproof when erected but complicated to assemble. An added problem was that as we unrolled it heavy snow began to fall, driven by a bitterly cold wind. I read out the instructions while Greg, Geof and Andy struggled with the many poles. Immediately it was up we bundled all the gear inside to keep it dry, so that soon there was no room for us. We sat in the kitchen tent which was roomy and cozy from the heat of the stoves. For the rest of the trip the Quarter Acre Dream, which we had brought to use as our mess tent, remained our store.

When the storm subsided we pitched our two-person sleeping tents. Being away with a smaller group evoked the familiar feeling of camaraderie which had always been an important part of our climbs, so it was with some reluctance that we returned to Base Camp the next morning with the yaks and yak drivers. But there was food and equipment to be packed into loads and we knew we would be back up within a day or two.

Making up the loads was a routine process. Everything had to be carried up to Advance Base eventually; it was simply a matter of determining priorities.

Tim was worried when he could not find his boots.

"When did you last see them?" I asked.

"Sunday night. In Manly."

"Oh ..."

Bags and boxes were turned inside out and the kerosene lamp burnt late into the night as he searched.

"I can't believe they're lost. They'll turn up," were my sleepy words of half-hearted reassurance when he finally came to the tent to sleep.

Advance Base was a flat oasis among endless slopes and ridges of broken rock. Behind lies the cloud-covered 7000-metre peak of Ring-ri.

Yaks arrive at Advance Base Camp.

The next day we headed up to Advance Base, this time to stay. For the whole walk Tim was trying to work out where his boots were. At camp, when we were unpacking the yak loads, Tim questioned Andy. By that time he knew the exact location of everybody's boots except his own. Andy, who as usual had been floating along in his own daydream, admitted to having a pair of boots in his kit bag.

"But your boots are still at Base Camp!" protested Tim.

"Are they?" asked Andy sheepishly. "I'm sorry. I hadn't realised there was a panic on."

It was good to be in residence at Advance Base. Simon, Mike, Howard and Colin remained at Base Camp. They would accompany the yaks and yak-men for the last two ferries of equipment. The sun hit the tents shortly after ten o'clock in the morning, a misleading figure since all clocks in China were set to Beijing time thousands of kilometres to the east. Over the border in Nepal, only a few kilometres to the south, it was half-past seven. Nepalese time was more accurate in that it related to the sun, but we found it simpler to set our watches to the rest of China. The only real advantage was that we were encouraged to get up earlier. Such confirmed sleepers-in as Andy and myself felt guilty about staying in our sleeping bags much past ten-thirty, and even that sounded decadently late.

The next day we set about making our camp as comfortable as possible. One thing there was no shortage of was rocks. We built a lavatory magnificent both in its construction and its view of the mountains. With the summit of Mt Everest directly ahead we had no need to be frightened of constipation. Fear is the great laxative. By hunting around we found enough flat rocks to pave the floor of the kitchen tent which would otherwise soon have become a quagmire.

The good weather continued, allowing us to make our first excursion along the Rongbuk Glacier from Advance Base. We discovered that the obvious comforts of our camp had been ignored by other expeditions for a less hospitable spot on the glacial ice. About an hour closer to the mountain we came to the site where the big Japanese expedition of 1980 had camped. Huge piles of half-burnt rubbish littered the area. Even perfectly good equipment had been destroyed. Empty tins and cooking-gas cartridges were scattered in all directions.

Ice towers, ten to twenty metres high, make the glacier impassable for yaks. From this dump of gear we carried our supplies the last few kilometres to Camp I.

Such abuse of the environment pointed to a type of thinking radically different from our own. Those Japanese climbers had used the mountains as an arena for conquest, a place to prove themselves mightier than the mountain. To them the scars of that battle were irrelevant – it was only the achievement that counted. Our priorities were different. As much as possible we wished to leave the mountains as we found them, aloof and mighty, and unblemished by our petty struggles. On a grand scale our climbs were of no relevance. Only to ourselves was success or failure, life or death, a concern.

The Everest region is one of the most rugged and beautiful mountain regions in the world. The remoteness and recent political inaccessibility of Tibet has ensured that the mountainous country has remained unaffected by the evils of tourism. Despite this, the first foreign expedition to visit in over forty years had left a lasting mark on the purity of the northern approaches to Everest. The sight made us determined to carry all our rubbish back to the roadhead and away on the trucks.

Travelling on a glacier demands full concentration, at least until the route is known. We were able to forget the ugly sight of the rubbish dump as we tried to find the best way up the valley. Just around the corner from Advance Base the hillside was dangerously unstable so we were forced onto the glacier itself. From above it appeared as though the ice was covered with mounds of loose pebbles, the debris of landslides. Once on the glacier we appreciated the illusion. The ice which could not flow around obstacles on the valley floor was pushed up into miniature mountains. Rocks were thinly spread over the surface except where the ice walls were too steep and bare ice barred our way. The covering of rocks permitted us to walk on slopes that would have been impossibly slippery had they remained smooth ice. Nevertheless care was always needed for sometimes the stones slipped away beneath our feet.

At other places we skirted the deep chasms of crevasses, the edges of which had been eaten away by the sun to make very obvious and definitely uninviting funnels leading to the depths of the glacier. Sometimes the crevasses were filled with water, a murky brown from the rock debris. In other places, where the ice was clean, water in the craters appeared a brilliant turquoise blue.

As with most large glaciers the difficulties of travel on the Rongbuk were largely offset by the beauty of the place, especially towards the centre of the glacier where our path wove in and out between the giant ice pinnacles. Between the icy spires, shallow streams flowed, bubbling up out of the ice for no apparent reason and disappearing just as suddenly. In places the streams tunnelled through the towers and the caves they carved were filled with beautiful soft blue light. Sometimes icicles had formed over the entrance like bars; in other places they hung from the overhanging walls of the towers.

When we walked further up the glacier we were able to work out how the remarkable spears and towers of ice had formed. The higher reaches of the glacier (the nevé) was a big snow basin. As the ice slid slowly down the valley the surface began to break up. At one place it was a honeycomb of gaping crevasses; slightly further down the thin walls melted to form jagged ridges. In the next stage the saddles and low walls between the peaks had weathered away, leaving spectacular minarets of ice. These grew smaller and sparser until finally, near Advance Base Camp, the last of the towers melted or collapsed into blocks of ice. It was a continuing process for, while the glacier moved down the valley and as the final ice peaks fell, the ice at the head of the glacier was breaking up into crevasses, creating the beginnings of more towers.

A short way past the site of the old Japanese camp the towers and walls of ice became a maze impossible to walk through. We scrambled back to the edge of the glacier. The problem there was continual rockfall from the hillside above. The danger was not so much from being hit by falling rocks – alert ears and eyes avoided that – but of the unstable rocks underfoot. Rocks had been dumped on the slowly moving glacier by landslides. As the glacier groaned over the irregularities of the valley floor the piles of rocks were continually readjusting. Any rock that was stepped on was likely to roll over, pitching one headlong onto more loose boulders. The result could easily be a twisted ankle or an arm broken in an attempt to break the fall. Towards the end of the expedition Howard stumbled and fell heavily and, though he did not realise it at the time, broke three ribs.

Beyond that dangerous area we cut back out towards the centre of the glacier. A few steep ice hills covered with loose moraine were the only obstacles. Past them lay open ground where it was easier to walk. A gradual slope led to the place where we decided to pitch Camp I, at 5750 metres. Changtse rose above for 2000 metres in a steep, uninterrupted and almost vertical face of ice and rock. We decided that it was too steep to hold

Looking down to the Rongbuk Valley from Advance Base, bad weather approaches from the north.

ABOVE LEFT: This lump of ice remained standing while the rest of the glacier melted around it.
ABOVE RIGHT: Colin with the pika he caught in his tent at Camp I.
BELOW: Beyond the ice towers the West Rongbuk Glacier joins the Middle Rongbuk.

enough snow for dangerous avalanches. Since the North Face of Everest was still a couple of kilometres distant there was little fear of our camp being damaged by the huge avalanches which undoubtedly sometimes fell from there.

On one of the several days we spent carrying loads from Advance Base to Camp I the whole of the western side of the North Face avalanched. We were returning to Advance Base when the snow slope at 7500 metres separated from the mountain in a huge slab avalanche with a fracture-line several kilometres wide. Howard and Greg, who were furthest down the valley, had a particularly good view and watched the cloud of powder snow blown in front of the avalanche dust the whole area of Camp I. The conclusion we all reached was that it would be suicidal to be anywhere near the base of the Face after a big snowfall. It was another case of concentrating upon the task at hand, stocking Camp I, while the monsoonal storms exhausted themselves.

The yak herders were easily persuaded to make their beasts carry some of our supplies up the glacier to the Japanese camp site. Beyond there it was impossible for yaks to travel. Having a depot of supplies on the glacier was a great help as it meant we could stay at Camp I and fetch supplies from the depot as we needed them. The round trip took only a couple of hours.

Before moving up to Camp I we decided to reward ourselves for the hard work of load carrying with the hard work of exploring the country near Advance Base. Geof, Greg, Andy and Colin headed up the East Rongbuk while Tim, Tenzing and I crossed the main Rongbuk and climbed the western side of the valley. Our aim was to look into the valleys to the west and to amuse ourselves with some skiing.

The ridge we climbed from the glacier was, like everywhere around us, piled with loose boulders. Occasional low bluffs provided opportunity to practise my rockclimbing skills. I soon noticed that the granite boulders were studded with garnets, usually tiny but sometimes the size of a fingernail. Tim found a lump of white granite the size of a cricket ball which was studded with the large red crystals.

"A good paperweight," he said as he put it in his pack.

Unfortunately the weather frustrated our skiing plans. The first evening we had good views of the North Face. Since our camp was ten kilometres away at 6000 metres there was less of the foreshortening which had distorted the mountain from the lower and closer vantage points of Advance Base and Camp I. Tim, Tenzing and I sat staring at the huge Face, stunned by the enormity of the task we had set ourselves.

"It's only a thousand metres higher than Annapurna II," I said tentatively, in an attempt to reassure myself.

"You worry too much," said Tim.

Soon the clouds which had been darkening the valley all day rolled in and snow began to fall. It snowed virtually non-stop for the next thirty hours. For that time we lay in our tiny tent reading and sleeping; eating breakfast at three in the afternoon to stretch our one day's food supply into two. The next day it was still snowing so we were obliged to descend. The loose boulders covered with thirty centimetres of fresh snow made the going very hard. As soon as we were back down on the glacier the weather began to clear. The sun shone half-heartedly, but strongly enough to inflict snow-blindness on poor Tenzing. He had been half an hour later than us in donning his sunglasses. The thin atmosphere at 5500 metres was not very effective in filtering the harmful rays of the sun.

When we were sitting around on the grass back at Advance Base I showed Greg the garnet-infested rock that Tim had found, and asked for his professional geologist's opinion. He turned the piece of white granite in his hands as he searched for words to describe it.

"Garnets aren't found in granite when it's first formed," he said, as he rubbed his fingers over the rock. "It shows that the granite's been intensely compressed, probably when the Himalaya was being formed. It's real mother of the earth stuff, this."

I began to share some of his awe. Yet to my mind it was appropriate that the immense forces of nature should be apparent in the smallest details around us. After all, above us as we talked soared the incredible bulk of Mt Everest, testimony of a creation mightier and more lasting than humankind.

Balanced rocks epitomise the unstable nature of the terrain. The finger of rock points to the pond (photo page 113) on the east bank of the Rongbuk. An easier approach to Advance Base was along the glacier itself.

CHAPTER EIGHT

WHOSE IDEA WAS THIS, ANYWAY?

I N A WORLD of ice and snow it was ironic that the heat was intolerable. As we plodded slowly up the glacier towards the North Face we felt like insects attracted to a candle flame – wings burnt, unable to escape the extreme heat. The sun's rays intensified as they reflected down from the brilliant white walls of snow and ice that rose for thousands of metres in every direction. Little of the sun's radiation had been absorbed by the thin atmosphere at 6000 metres, making the heat intense.

Our path was a shallow gully in the glacier. On both sides huge crevasses gaped uninvitingly, though we knew that inside they would be cool. We reached the lip of the gully where the glacier levelled out onto the shelf leading with a scarcely discernible rise to the base of the North Face. Gratefully we drank in the slight breeze which blew across the shelf. As we were on skis Tim and I were ahead of the others. It seemed like a good place to wait so we dropped our packs onto the snow and flopped on top of them.

Geof, Greg and Andy arrived roped together. Without skis they were much more likely to break through the firm crust of snow into hidden crevasses beneath. In this event it was probable that only Geof, who was in the lead, would fall, leaving Greg and Andy to pull him out. The rope was a safeguard for our first journey to the névé of the glacier. Having judged the glacier to be safe, we dispensed with the precaution of ropes for subsequent journeys.

Our purpose that morning was to get closer to the mountain and choose the best line up the Face. Rather than carry empty packs we had each brought some food and climbing gear, and now we needed to cache it in a spot that would not be buried by a heavy snowfall or an avalanche. We had learnt that lesson well. There was some disagreement as to which was the safest place, but finally we decided to leave everything in a kitbag on the edge of a large crevasse. To distinguish it from our dump of gear below Camp I, we called the depot the Stash.

I dumped my load and skied the hundred metres back to where we had first sat. It was there that the breeze was freshest. Meanwhile, Greg had unroped and plodded a few hundred metres further towards the Face. Though his figure grew smaller and smaller he seemed to be getting no closer to the mountain. The illusion helped the rest of us appreciate the incredible scale of our objective. At least from here we could distinguish some detail, and that helped destroy the air of unassailability which more distant views had given.

LEFT: Tim, on the Lingtren Glacier, looks towards Qomolangma, with Changtse on the left. Camp I is situated on the Rongbuk Glacier near the base of the ridge running towards the camera from near the summit of Changtse.

RIGHT: When the snow melted after an exceptionally heavy snowfall, Advance Base was flooded. With everyone else up at Camp I, Tim (in the water) and Lincoln faced the task of shifting the tents to higher ground.

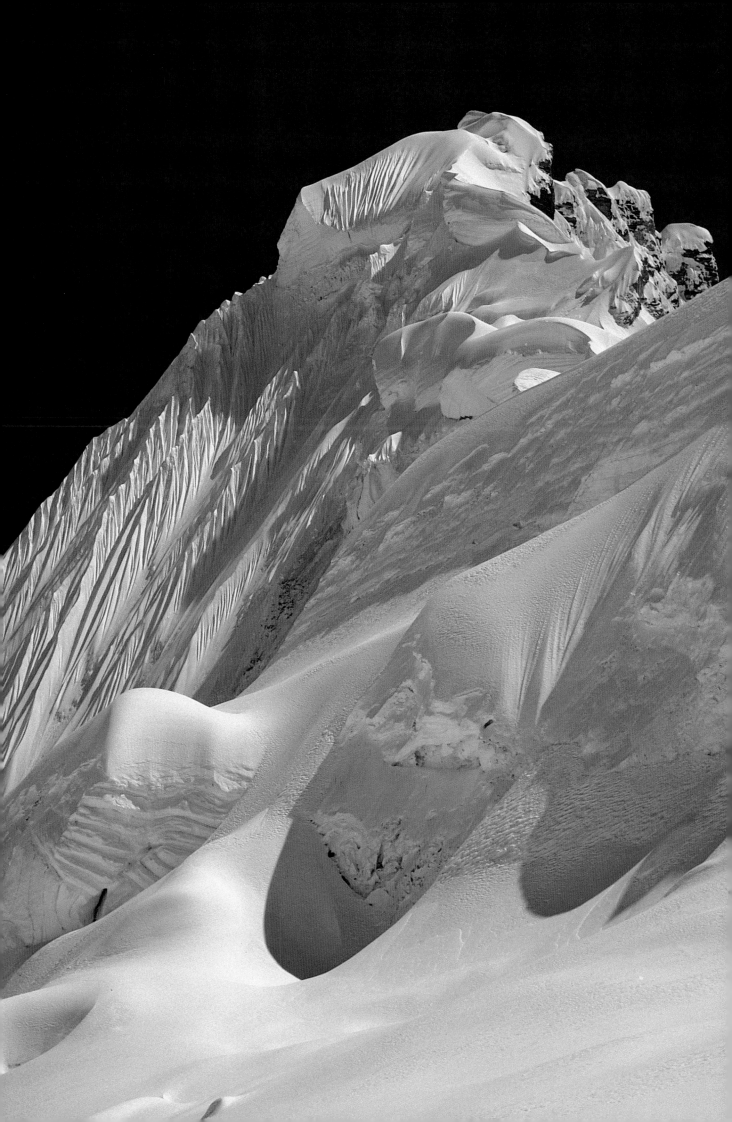

LEFT: Huge cornices form the summit ridge of Khumbutse (6600 metres). Strong winds have carved the flutings in the ice face.
RIGHT: Skiing was a good method of acclimatising to the thinner atmosphere of the Himalaya. Tim on his cross-country skis on the slopes of Khumbutse.

I sat on my empty pack and stared at the mountain. The problem was to select a route which offered the least possible threat of avalanche. Several spurs gave dimension to the lower part of the Face. The obvious choice was to climb one of those. Above, a huge slab of snow almost eight hundred metres high stretched in an unbroken sweep from the North Col across to the West Ridge. It was from there that the huge avalanche had fallen the previous week. It was a danger-zone we would have to treat very cautiously. On the slab itself, we would minimise risks by plotting our route between the shelter of the large rocks (only specks on the snow from where I sat) which dotted the slope at very infrequent intervals.

Andy had already christened the dangerous slab White Limbo. The name was familiar to us from one of our favourite tapes. The song, "White Limbo" by Australian Crawl had nothing to do with mountains. Yet Limbo, as a no-man's land somewhere between heaven and hell, seemed an apt name for the feature which threatened to lower half of the mountain with avalanche. Whether we would know the success of the summit or the hell of an icy death lay in part with the whims of White Limbo's avalanche-prone slopes.

Above White Limbo were two weaknesses through the steep rock. To the right was the Hornbein Couloir, first climbed by an American team who had traversed in from the West Ridge, and repeated in 1980 by the Japanese North Face expedition. Since we wanted to climb a new route we were left with the second option, the Great Couloir. Only the Couloir's top half was safe for climbing. Huge ice cliffs over two hundred metres high threatened the lower slopes with enormous ice avalanches.

Greg returned. "It looks fantastic," he said. "I thought there'd be avalanche debris all the way along the bottom of the Face, but it's as clean as a whistle."

"Good news," I said.

Tim, Geof and Andy had emptied their packs. Andy started back down to Camp I while Tim and Geof joined Greg and me.

"What do you reckon?" asked Tim.

"The Japanese route looks good," said Geof.

"Yes, but it's been climbed," countered Greg. "If we could pull off the line to the right of the ice cliffs it would be a real coup. A new route on Everest would be really something."

"It sure would," I said. "And apart from that it's the safest route on the Face."

Geof looked at the relevant part of the mountain for a few moments.

"It could be difficult getting through the rock below the big snow slab."

"That's some of the attraction," said Tim.

Geof nodded, then said, "I don't mind hard climbing but the advantage of the American route to the left, as far as they got, is that it's easy, and that means you have more strength left for the top."

I disagreed. "The line to the right of the ice cliffs is much shorter than the American route, and with this much snow around, much safer. Besides, harder climbing knocks your

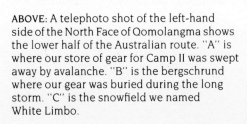

ABOVE: A telephoto shot of the left-hand side of the North Face of Qomolangma shows the lower half of the Australian route. "A" is where our store of gear for Camp II was swept away by avalanche. "B" is the bergschrund where our gear was buried during the long storm. "C" is the snowfield we named White Limbo.

BELOW: The North Face of Qomolangma – Mt Everest.

head into shape. Near the summit, where the lack of oxygen is at its worst, it would be a great help psychologically to tell yourself that the climbing below was harder than what you still have left to do."

Greg returned to the practicalities of the route. "I think that the obvious access to the middle of the Face is no good. Traversing left across the mixed ground could be hard. It looks reasonably safe to climb those avalanche funnels beneath the obvious rib."

"It might be safe," Tim said. "We'll have to have a close look."

"It could be worth climbing up above the icefall here beside us to get a different perspective."

"Time enough for that, Geof. Let's ski down and have some lunch."

My mind was made up. The way to go was the line Greg and I had worked out to the right of the big ice cliffs halfway up the Face. From there we would cut across the top of White Limbo above the ice cliffs, then follow the Great Couloir to within eight hundred metres of the top. The last major obstacle was the steep rock section which ended the Couloir. The barrier of the Yellow Band, as the cliff was known, extended right around the summit pyramid. It would be many weeks before we needed to worry about the problems it presented. Tim seemed to agree that this line was best, and Geof and Andy could be persuaded.

We had done our best to make Camp I as comfortable as possible. The kitchen consisted of the outer shell of a two-person tent pitched on low walls of rocks. Narayan and Tenzing made the kitchen their domain, and had built the walls after we collected the rocks. There was plenty of head-room and flat stones on which to sit stoves. A few metres from the door we pitched our large dome-tent as a dining room. Over the top of both we slung a tarp which kept the weather out of both tents in all but the worst storms. A touch of luxury was our

BELOW: Though we were lucky to find a safe and easy way through the crevasses, the route up the glacier from Camp I (off the picture to the right) was always slow and often unbearably hot because of sunshine reflected from the snow.
RIGHT: Tim is dwarfed by the subpeak of Lingtren which rises above him.

Lincoln skis back towards Camp I after a day trip to explore the Lingtren Glacier; compare with photo on previous page. Mt Everest is 2200 metres higher than the peak shown here.

stereo system, two small speakers connected to a Walkman tape-player.

Living at high altitude is an unavoidably uncomfortable experience. The thinner air of 5800 metres made life at Camp I noticeably harder than it had been at Advance Base. Psychological considerations, such as being relaxed and happy, became increasingly important, since negative emotions would eat away at our determination to succeed. "Psychological consideration" became the justification for the effort of carrying a music system, dozens of books, and a few frisbees and musical instruments.

The best way to assess the conditions on our favoured route was to climb its lower slopes. The prospect of starting the technical climbing at last was exciting. The morning of our first foray up the Face we spent hours adjusting our equipment and making sure we had everything that was necessary. It had been several months since any of us had done any iceclimbing. As well, I think we all stood a little in awe of Everest's reputation. From a practical point of view it was just another mountain, but from somewhere emanated a presence and aloofness none of us had encountered anywhere else.

Again we baked as we trudged up to the Rongbuk nevé. Two kilometres remained up the gradual slope of the Northern Cwm. The mass of Everest loomed above us; the two ridges of the North Face stretched out to either side like the inviting arms of the Mother Goddess of the Earth. The mountain exuded timelessness and power, yet as I walked under that gigantic Face any thought of my fragile mortality was drowned in the sweat that poured from my brow.

Luckily we found shade in the bergschrund, the big crevasse which ran the length of the Face and separated the mountain from the glacier. While we rested there we ate a little and drank as much as we could. The bergschrund created an almost insurmountable barrier, except where the gaping crevasse was filled with the snow of avalanches from above. Just to the left of where we sheltered a choke of snow provided a bridge onto the slope above the 'schrund. The adrenalin-induced alertness as I attached my crampons to my boots and unstrapped my ice-axe from my pack was a familiar and welcome feeling. Three thousand metres of mountain to be climbed and at last we were beginning.

In the interest of speed we did not rope together. After all, if we could not climb this initial steep snow section without the aid or reassurance of a rope, what chance would we have of climbing the difficult ground higher up? After fifty metres or so of snow barely soft enough for good footprints, the snow gave way to ice – much less secure to climb upon – and I began to remember the fear and excessive caution induced by difficult unroped climbing. Here, it was not that the climbing was difficult, rather, my old crampons did not bite firmly into the ice because they were blunt from overuse. Every step felt insecure. I swore that my first job back at Camp I would be to sharpen the points of my crampons. As well, my mind had grown unaccustomed to danger because of the recent safe, sedentary months I had spent in Australia. It was the same at the start of every climb. We all faced the problem of readjusting to the dangers of a vertical environment. There is nothing like the fear of falling to induce precision in one's movements and actions. After a day or two the precision becomes an automatic response, and the joy of climbing begins to resurface.

As Andy reached the top of the ice section he called across, his face bright with relief, "Bit of a savage introduction, eh!"

"Well, this is Everest, after all."

Above us on the steep snow slope Geof, Greg and Tim slowly climbed upwards while I paid out the rope Geof was dragging behind him. At this stage the rope did not provide any security. Our purpose was to fix a continuous line up the Face by tying the rope to anchors hammered into the slope. Here, where there was snow, the anchor was a sixty-centimetre-long aluminium section. Higher up where the underlying rock pushed its way to the surface we placed rock pitons. The purpose of the rope was to provide a safe and rapid way to climb and descend. When we climbed up, unbalanced by heavy loads, the security of the rope would be invaluable.

That first afternoon we climbed about three hundred metres up the Face. Thousands of metres of climbing stretched above us up into the limits of the earth's atmosphere. Our first sortie onto the mountain was little more than knocking on the door, yet that evening, as we skied back down the glacier to Camp I, we felt enormously satisfied. At last we were starting the technical part of the climb. The heat had exhausted us but the effects of altitude were less severe than any of our previous experiences at 6000 metres. We had acclimatised well, and that was cause for great satisfaction. Also, there was the pleasure of the climbing itself, of our bodies and minds coping with the difficulties the mountain presented.

Determined to make the most of the good weather, Tim, Geof, Greg and Andy headed back up the mountain the next day. I felt weak from dehydration so I chose to spend the day at Camp I to recover. In the afternoon, I wandered down to our dump of gear on the glacier to collect some more rope. I made a diversion into the maze of passages between the ice towers, but travel was complicated by wide streams on the surface of the ice and blue, apparently bottomless, pools.

Up on the mountain the others were able to climb a further hundred metres and cache the food and equipment they carried in a small hole dug in the snow slope. It was not a good place for Camp II, but there seemed to be no safe sites anywhere. The weather the next day was bad. Snow fell overnight and continued through the morning. The fine-weather plan had been for me to head up the ropes with Narayan and Tenzing to stock the depot at our high point. Instead we all loafed around Camp I. Those energetic enough spent the afternoon skiing the gentle slope behind camp – a great method of keeping our spirits up in the bad weather. It is during exercise that one's body has to fight hardest to cope with the oxygen lack, and that of course helps the acclimatisation process.

The bad weather continued, so the next day Tim, Andy, Simon and I made the six-kilometre journey down to Advance Base Camp. It was much more comfortable there. Camping on grass is invariably better than on ice, and the 300-metre altitude drop made

"From a practical point of view it was just another mountain, but from somewhere emanated a presence and

aloofness none of us had encountered anywhere else.'' We cross the nevé for our first day's climbing on the North Face.

LEFT: Geof rests while three other climbers ascend the next section of fixed rope.

BELOW: The technical climbing on Everest began at 6100 metres – above most of the world's summits. The steep climbing at the bottom of the Face ensured that our climbing reflexes were tested immediately.

sleeping a little easier and deeper because of the small increase in atmospheric oxygen.

The following afternoon Simon headed down to Base to file a story. Andy chose to have faith in the weather and went back up to Camp I. He could not have misread the signs more completely. That night about thirty centimetres of snow fell. We woke to find the mess tent sagging sadly and the Quarter Acre Dream collapsed with poles bent under the weight of snow. Tim and I shovelled the snow away with pots and the lid of our pressure cooker as our snow-shovels had been carried up to Camp I. We repaired the minor damage then set about making breakfast.

When the sun dissolved the clouds the snow melted quickly. The stream in front of the tent drained through the rocks and the northern end of our little valley. Before long the drain could not keep pace with the snow-melt so the water-level began to rise towards our tent door. As the water was still a couple of metres away there did not seem any reason to panic. A week earlier the water had crept into one corner of the tent but the cold of night froze its advance and by morning it had receded to its usual level. We hoped that would happen again today.

Late in the afternoon, as we sat in the tent drinking tea and eating biscuits with water lapping around our feet, we accepted defeat and agreed we would have to move the tent. For two people it was a major task. Everything had to be carried fifty metres up the hill to the most suitable flat spot: barrels of food, boxes of film gear, pots and pans, books, spices, odd pieces of clothing and equipment, and the tent itself. We dragged it all to the new site. Tim held the centre pole erect while I ran around hammering the pegs into rocky ground. By dusk everything was rearranged inside. Our work wasn't over, for the water had crept the few extra metres to the Quarter Acre Dream. From there we moved everything that might be damaged into the mess tent. Moving the tent itself would have to wait until there were more people to help.

Everyone, apart from Andy, came back down to Advance Base Camp the following day. Because of the amount of snow that had fallen it would be several days before it was safe to climb on the mountain again. The days passed easily in different combinations of reading, eating, talking and sleeping. I spent the sunny mornings doing yoga. There was no urgency to do anything. We could afford no room for impatience; attempting to act before the conditions were right would be foolhardy and dangerous.

On 1 September, after a week at Advance Base Camp, Geof, Greg and Andy went back up to Camp I, and Jim and Colin went with them to film their activities. It was a pleasant change to be at Advance Base with fewer people. Simon had gone down to Base Camp so only Mike, Howard, Narayan, Tenzing, Tim and I remained. Between the twelve of us there had been remarkably few angry words during the six weeks we had been away from Australia. Sometimes there was a little tension between the climbers and the film crew over the film crew not pulling its weight, though the difference was largely imagined. The film-makers not only had to carry loads of food to make sure they were adequately supplied but also had to film everything that was going on in and around the camps.

By making life uncomfortable, high altitude encourages irritation at the same time as uniting everyone in hardship. Certainly for our group friendships grew deeper and stronger as the trip progressed. Flashes of anger were dismissed as signs of tension and impatience with weather, rather than any personal affront. Whenever somebody started taking things too seriously Narayan would seize the opportunity to tease those involved. Personal melodramas were a source of unconcealed delight to him and he enjoyed helping people realise the ridiculousness of their position with a few well-chosen but mispronounced words. As we sat around the kitchen tent while he and Tenzing cooked he would entertain us with stories of the practical jokes he had played on other expeditions and treks. For some of us, many of the tales were familiar for we had been the recipients.

On the first evening that the others spent at Camp I, Greg radioed to say that birds had attacked our food. Andy, who had come down a day after everyone else, had failed to put a few things away and had left a couple of vital tent-door zippers undone. The saddest losses were serious damage to our big block of Jarlsberg cheese and the devouring of nine blocks of chocolate.

Worse news came the following day as Tim and I packed in preparation for our return to Camp I.

Mike walked over to us "Geof wants to talk to you," he said.

Tim took the radio and ran up to the moraine ridge where the reception was best. Ten minutes later he strolled down, looking pensive.

"What's the story?" I asked.

"They left Camp I this morning to head up the mountain. Now they're near the Face and have just spotted bits of Camp II on the glacier. It's been avalanched."

"Hell! That will give them something to think about. It's just as well no one was up there."

"Of course. It's much better to find out now that the place is not safe."

"What did they find?" I asked. "What have we lost?"

"Don't know yet. They only just spotted the tent lying amongst the debris."

"Well, it's good to have that anyway."

It was such a beautiful day and the dangers of the mountain were far enough removed from Advance Base for the news not to affect our mood of excitement at being on the move again. We ate lunch and left camp. Narayan had set off that morning. Mike, Howard and Tenzing were to follow us. The glacier to Camp I was a familiar trail by now and for long sections we could turn our minds off and think.

The most important thing about the avalanche was that it showed we had assessed the conditions on the mountain wrongly. That sort of mistake could be fatal. A place we had thought safe had been removed from the mountain by a gigantic snow slide. The amount of snow dumped on the 3000-metre Face made huge avalanches when it slid from the slope. We had realised that but underestimated the size of the problem. It was a valuable lesson learnt at the cost of some replaceable food and equipment.

At Camp I, more bad news awaited us. Geof, Greg and Andy had just returned from the Face.

"How'd you like to climb Everest in your walking boots?" asked Geof as a greeting, nodding at my Adidas shoes.

"What do you mean?"

Andy answered for him. "The gear we left at the 'schrund has been buried by another avalanche. We couldn't find a thing."

"Bloody hell! That's all the boots and crampons and ice-axes!"

"Well, Geof and I have boots," said Andy, "but Greg's, yours and Tim's are there."

The three of us had left these things on a ledge at the back of the crevasse at the base of the Face to avoid carrying them backwards and forwards as we skied to and from the start of the climb.

"Sounds like a day of digging tomorrow," said Tim. "It can't be buried too deeply where it was."

Later that night Howard found some reassuring words. "These things always happen in threes, so you should be all right from now on."

"How do you mean? What's the third?" My mind was thinking of that day's news only.

"The two avalanches and the birds pillaging our food."

"Oh, right. Thanks, Howard. We can all relax then."

The following day was far from relaxing. We left camp early to avoid the intense heat on the glacier, and climbed up to dig where we thought the gear was buried. The position in the crevasse was readily identifiable from the distinctive icicles which hung from the overhanging back wall. By late afternoon we had shifted a tremendous amount of snow. All we had to show for our efforts was a hole five metres deep over an area of five metres by three. Around our ditch we probed the snow with our extendable ski-poles, but to no avail. Dejected, we returned to camp.

The next day Tim and I searched the slope below our ditch with our ski-pole probes. Geof, Greg and Andy headed up the ropes, hoping to find a safe site for Camp II. They planned to remain there and fix ropes through the steep ground above during the next four days. To make things easier for them Jim and Colin went ahead to free the ropes buried by the recent snowfalls. Narayan and Tenzing followed up the ropes with supplies for the others' planned stay on the mountain.

The day was not a success for any of us. Tim and I did not find our lost equipment, and Colin and Jim found freeing the ropes to be strenuous and tedious work. At about three o'clock a huge bank of dark clouds rounded the Changtse corner of the Rongbuk Glacier

The night after the flood at Base Camp, the Quarter Acre Dream (our storage tent) froze in the pond, and Colin's tent (below) collapsed completely under a fresh fall of snow.

The cache of boots, ice-axes and crampons which we left in the bergschrund at the bottom of the Face were deeply buried by avalanches during a week of bad weather. Mike, Tim and Greg during their shift of digging for the lost gear.

heading for the North Face. By four o'clock it was snowing steadily. Narayan became dangerously cold as he had neglected to take warm clothes with him up the ropes. It had been so warm on the glacier that he thought he would be back long before the weather changed. Within half an hour of the snow beginning to fall, powder-snow avalanches were pouring down the Face. Geof, Greg and Andy decided it was impossible to stay there that night. The big avalanche that had swept away the small snow cave and the gear that was inside it had also removed a hundred metres of fixed rope. It was obvious that nowhere beneath our high point was safe. The small outcrop that we had reached on our first day of climbing offered some shelter so they dumped their food and equipment there in a kitbag. As they began to descend, the avalanches were already becoming serious. Knee-deep powder slid down the slope around them with frightening force.

At the bottom of the Face those avalanches passed by Tim and me on both sides and began to fill in the hole we had dug. The first one dusted us with snow and frightened me considerably. Now we could understand how, during the long storm, snow shed from the Face had buried our gear so deeply. We decided to head back to Camp I before any really big avalanches came down. Visibility was appalling, but luckily Geof had placed flags on the glacier that morning. The bamboo poles with bright orange rags tied to the tips, marked the route down the easily angled nevé. Now the snow cloud was too thick to see one flag from the next though they were only two hundred metres apart. As I peered into the whiteness for a glimpse of the next orange marker, snow driven by the vicious up-valley wind tore at my face. In such bleak conditions the best course was to ignore the discomfort and descend as quickly as possible.

Back at Camp I, Tim and I began to cook dinner. It was several hours before the others arrived. Narayan had begun to suffer hypothermia so everyone stopped at the Stash to warm him up in the tent. By the time they descended the remaining few kilometres to Camp I, everybody was exhausted.

The snowfall during the night made it too dangerous for us to consider going back up the mountain the next morning. At any rate the loss of gear made an immediate return impossible. We sat in the mess tent and considered the options before us. I was the only one with a complete spare set of gear – boots, ice-axe, ice-hammer and crampons. I had everything except a harness. The others were not in such a happy position. Geof and Andy still had their boots since, rather than ski, they walked to and from the Face. All eyes turned to the film crew.

RIGHT: Colin and Jim (behind) arrive at Camp I (5750 metres) during bad weather.

BELOW: Several kilometres beyond Camp I is the Lho La Pass (6006 metres) on the Tibetan border with Nepal. Through the pass and disappearing into the clouds is the West Ridge of Nuptse.

"What size are your feet, Howard?"

It seemed that the route would be too difficult to allow the film crew to climb very high. In that case their boots, ice-axes and other climbing gear would not be used. And anyway, if we didn't borrow what we needed we would have to abandon the climb, which would leave them nothing to film. Tim's huge feet proved to be the only ones which could not be accommodated by loan or improvisation.

"They're the bane of your life, Tim," I said, "along with your surname."

His feet were size twelve and a half. Mike's size twelve boots were the closest approximation. It looked as though Tim would have to climb Everest in his cross-country ski boots. Combined with a pair of Geof's insulated overboots, and rigid crampons with the imaginative name of Foot Fangs, it proved to be a workable solution.

Andy took vicarious satisfaction in writing on a postcard to his housemates: "In one stroke we went from one of the most hideously over-equipped expeditions ever to leave Oz to one of the lightest ever to consider Everest."

We spent the sunny morning airing sleeping bags and improvising harnesses from climbing webbing. Geof sat outside his tent tying flags to bamboo wands so that the whole route to the base of the Face could be marked for bad-weather descents. Andy severely sunburned his face, and particularly his eyelids, by falling asleep in the sun to the sound of his Walkman. Tim and I moved our tent to a flatter site, then, with the help of Narayan and Tenzing, levelled the ground under the mess tent. In the two and a half weeks since we had established Camp I, the ice of the glacier had melted considerably and had left our tents perched on little platforms.

The weather closed in again overnight. Howard, Tim, Narayan, Tenzing and I entertained ourselves by skiing on the slope of the glacier behind camp. I stopped by the mess tent for a drink before heading up the slope.

"If you're going out on the glacier," said Greg, "take Tim's binoculars so that you can see whether that kitbag full of gear is still there."

"Ah no! It's better not to know."

"Nonsense," said Greg. "I've been lying awake at night worrying about it."

"Yeah. It's worth finding out," said Geof.

"Why? Do you want to know whether to write that you'll be coming home soon because you've got no gear?" Geof was taking our mail down to Advance Base Camp that afternoon.

"Yep," replied Geof. " 'Dear Sponsor, from this expedition postcard of the mountain eliminate all dotted lines above Camp II ... No, make that all lines on the Face. Instead I've marked where we lost our gear. X is where we lost most of our boots, ice-axes and crampons. Y is where Camp II used to be. Z is where another avalanche took our kitbag full of food, rope, climbing hardware ...' "

"Okay," I said, "I'll take the binoculars."

The next day was also cloudy and cold but the conditions were not bad enough to prevent Colin, Howard and Jim from carrying the 16 mm film gear up to the Stash. I was not sure why they chose that day of poor visibility to perform a task that could be done at any time, except, as Colin said, "Jim gets restless".

Tim, Andy, Geof, Tenzing and I headed down to Advance Base Camp in the afternoon to meet Simon who was coming up the next morning with our mail. The letters had arrived at Base Camp from Lhasa that day with a German trekking group.

The morning of 8 September was snowy again. Everyone else decided to come down from Camp I, and they arrived early in the afternoon shortly before Simon arrived with the mail. It was almost two months since we had left and so many things had happened that the time seemed even longer. Home was a long way distant, which made mail a real comfort and a reminder of the world we had put out of our minds. The expedition old-hands, Geof, Greg, Tim, Andy and I, had left homesickness behind. It was harder for Jim, Howard and Colin, who had wives and children. The rest of us were warmed by the reassurance of the future which awaited us if we were careful and not unlucky on the mountain. There was some bad news – a good friend of Colin's had been killed in a plane crash in New Zealand. Apart from that, it was a great afternoon as we sat around laughing and swapping news with each other. The miserable weather outside for once seemed irrelevant.

Geof was always the first to get restless. He did not necessarily have to be climbing, he just needed to be doing something. The next day he took the letters we had written down to Base Camp where they would await the departure of the German trekkers. Over the radio that evening he told us of the progress of the large American expedition which had arrived two weeks before. They had left Base Camp almost immediately and walked, with load-carrying yaks, up the East Rongbuk to begin their attempt on the North Ridge. By now they had fixed rope almost to the North Col but had retreated in the face of avalanche danger. In order to rest and to allow time for the slopes to clear they had come down to Base Camp. It sounded as though we were to be camp-bound for a few more days.

Most of us had no problem filling in time. There were many books to read, and endless discussions to be had on topics as varied as nuclear disarmament and who had eaten most of the biscuits. Our letter writing urge had been temporarily purged and pens were put to diaries instead. Greg's diary was a joke for all of us. Most days he wrote the date, where he was, and closed the book.

One day several of us were lounging in the mess tent writing, apart from Andy who was trying to fix his Walkman.

"It's entertaining to watch you all scribbling away," he said. "You concentrate hard, then there's a quick spasm of the neo-cortex and another few words dribble out."

Greg replied, "I've got these fantastic thoughts but I can't get them down."

"About life?" I asked.

"Oh yes," he answered. "Life, the universe, the whole damn lot."

"I'll have to read that later, Greg," I said.

"No, you wouldn't understand it."

"It should sell well in that case," said Andy, "provided you give it a good title."

Andy, Simon and Greg (with his head down) relax in the mess tent at Advance Base.
Hours and sometimes days were passed drinking tea, talking, reading or sleeping while bad weather raged outside.

CHAPTER NINE

ON THE MOUNTAIN

THE FULL MOON is a special time in the mountains. The snow on the peaks glows silvery bright; perspective and distance collapse so that the peaks seem close enough to touch.

The huge moon reminded me that a month had passed since we had moved up from Base Camp to stay at Advance Base. Time was in a different gear. In Australia, one continually ran to keep appointments with people and machines, so that life was regulated by the face of one's watch. Here, the mountain dictated when we acted and when we sat in camp. As far as I was concerned, time from the sun and the weather provided a more preferable style of living to that demanded by a fancily decorated quartz crystal.

The heavy snowfall meant that the mountain was unsafe but, as we were impatient for exercise, we walked up to Camp I anyway. The following day Tim, Narayan and Tenzing skied up to the Stash to sort out five days' food for our first stay on the mountain, which hopefully would be soon. The rest of us skied across to the Lho La, the name of the high pass between the end of Everest's West Ridge and the much smaller peak of Khumbutse. We reached the 6000-metre pass (on the border with Nepal) just as clouds were starting to well up from the valley of the Khumbu Glacier, quickly obscuring our view. Between the West Shoulder and the fluted ice face of the long convoluted Nuptse Ridge, we could still see the infamous Khumbu Icefall where the glacier plunged down several hundred metres from the Western Cwm to the valley floor in a tumbled mess of giant ice blocks and crevasses. The Icefall provided the only access to most of the routes on the Nepalese part of the mountain and any attempts from the southern side were consequently a very serious proposition.

We knew that at that moment four other Australians – Roddy Mackenzie, John Muir, Craig Nottle and Fred From – were climbing with New Zealanders Kim Logan and Peter Hillary in an attempt to scale the West Ridge. Their schedule put them several weeks behind us, but the bad weather which had slowed our progress made it feasible that we might reach the summit on the same day, a feat we had joked about with Peter and Fred in Kathmandu the previous year. The nickname of this Australian group, a close-knit crew based in Melbourne, was the "International Turkey Patrol"

LEFT: The full moon above Pumori (behind) and Khumbutse.
ABOVE: At the Camp 1.8 site, Greg belays while Andy climbs the fixed rope.

We could see two separate camps close together on the upper lip of the Icefall, slightly below us and several kilometres away.

"They're probably there somewhere," said Andy. "Let's give them a yell."

At first we shouted Nepalese swear words, but the reply was barely audible and may even have been imagined. Again we shouted, this time a synchronised "Tur-key Pat-rol!"

That got a definite roar of recognition. Floating across the thin, cold air came the words "A-team" – the nickname we had been given somewhere along the line.

What a shock for the "Turkey Patrol" as they sat outside their tents watching avalanches pour off Nuptse, Lhotse and Everest's South West Face. Cries from another world. Our tiny figures would have been barely distinguishable against the snow slopes behind Lho La. As we skied the long gentle slope back to Camp I, I was charged with excitement. The human presence in mountains as huge as the Himalaya was never significant. Simple and shallow though it had been, our contact with the other expedition somehow helped to justify our right to be here. Proof that ours was not an isolated ambition, and the knowledge that others were risking their lives as we risked ours, made our climb seem more sane.

We judged that, unless it snowed overnight, on the following day conditions would be right for us to head up the Face again. This time it was the turn of Tim and myself to lead the way. By travelling light, we hoped to reach our previous high-point early in the day and continue up to the safe ground at the base of the main rock buttress.

Greg was keen that he, Geof and Andy should follow us up and establish a camp at the bottom of the buttress.

A small team such as ours could not afford to waste energy. Too much work low on the mountain would burn us out and leave us with no strength for a summit push. All our efforts had to be productive.

LEFT: Looking across from the Lho La into the top of the Khumbu Icefall, the camp of expeditions attempting the Nepalese side of the mountain can be seen as dots on the glacier near the centre of the picture, below the shadow at the base of the face of Nuptse.

BELOW: Tim on the Lho La, with the Khumbu Icefall and Glacier behind, and the Nepalese peaks of Taweche and Cholatse. Kalar Pattar is the extreme right.

"What if there's no camp site at the rock?" I asked Greg. "Will you carry all your gear back down again?"

"There'll be a place up there somewhere."

"And if there isn't you'll have to come all the way down, and you'll be too buggered to go up the next day. That means there'll be no one fresh and ready to go up. And that means we'll have lost a day."

"If we do manage to camp tomorrow night – which we will – we'll have gained a day," countered Greg.

"I suppose there's no harm in being optimistic," said Tim. "They should be able to find somewhere they can at least bivvy, and then move the camp up to a better site the next day."

Eventually a compromise was reached. The five of us would go up: Tim and I to make the route, Andy to carry a load, and Geof and Greg equipped to stay several days on the mountain. I admitted to myself that part of the vehemence of my argument was because I had looked forward to a day of climbing with Tim, uncomplicated by others. Tim and I had gone through so much together that climbing with him had come to be almost like being alone on a mountain; we communicated little directly but felt the reassurance of each other's strength. However, I accepted that personal whims had to take second place to the expedition consensus on strategy.

Tim and I reached the top of our fixed ropes just as the sun hit the Face. I shouted down to Greg that the kitbag had been spared by the avalanches. A whoop of joy was his answer.

The next few hundred metres we climbed as quickly as possible because the wide gully was not a safe place to be. First of all, I ran out two hundred metres of rope to the shelter of a big black rock in the centre of the gully. My difficulty then was to find a good anchor in the poor rock. With that done, Tim jumared up the rope and led out a further hundred and fifty metres to the base of the big rock buttress. But there was no suitable camp: the snow slope was steep and the snow too shallow for digging a snow cave. Both Tim and I made attempts to explore the ground higher up, but the climbing was difficult and the ice-covered rock unrelentingly steep. Added to that unsavoury combination it began to snow heavily. Soon avalanches would be pouring off the Face.

"Time to get out of here," I called down.

The others did not hear me, as they were busy digging a ledge on which to squeeze the tent. Quickly I placed an ice-screw as an anchor and abseiled back to the proposed tent site. I did not envy Geof and Greg what would undoubtedly be an uncomfortable night in an unsafe position. While Tim and Andy helped put up the tent I continued abseiling down the ropes. Luckily it stopped snowing before the slopes became too dangerous. On the glacier I watched Andy cross the dangerous 'schrund then skied down to wait in the comfort of the tent at the Stash. From there the three of us skied the good snow down to Camp I. We had been on the move for fourteen hours – a long day at these altitudes – and went to bed exhausted.

For Tim and me to be fresh enough to relieve Geof and Greg after two nights on the mountain, we needed a rest day, yet someone had to accompany Narayan and Tenzing up the ropes the next day with essential supplies for Geof and Greg. Andy was the only choice. He was probably not quite as tired as he had not broken trail or plugged any steps. We woke late in the morning several hours after Andy had left with Narayan and Tenzing. Later he said he was tempted to shout at our tent as he left to instil a little justice into the start of the day.

At last we were making real progress. Geof climbed the ice-covered cliff above their tent to reach a steep, unstable snow slope. The slope sharpened to a crest which butted onto a vertical rock cliff about twenty metres high. The first ten metres of the cliff were covered with enough snow to allow straightforward climbing. Above was a vertical ice-choked gully which took Greg two hours to climb although it was only ten metres high.

ABOVE LEFT: Howard (behind) and Lincoln at the Lho La as clouds close in.
Both are wearing harnesses improvised from webbing to replace proper harnesses lost in the bergschrund avalanches.
LEFT: Mike films on the Lho La.

ABOVE LEFT: Tim making good use of his cross-country skis on the Lho La.

LEFT: Mike looks for the perfect camera angle as he films Geof and Tim watching an avalanche fall off the face of Nuptse.

ABOVE: Fixed rope and footsteps lead up to the tent at Camp 1.8. A climber ascends the rope above.

RIGHT: Tim climbing the slope below Camp 1.8.

The rock was loose and many of the holds were frozen over so that he had to chip the ice away before he could hang on. The footholds were so small that he needed to remove one crampon from his boot. At the top of the gully the snow slope continued up steeply. He climbed until the rope which tied him to Geof became tight. Above, at least another hundred metres of steep ground remained, and where he clung to the mountainside there was no place for a camp. Because it was late in the day and Geof was unable to climb the rope up the gully with only one jumar clamp, Greg decided that the best thing to do was descend. He placed his ice-axe in the slope as an anchor then abseiled down to Geof.

Mike and Howard were filming the climbing from the glacier with Mike's huge tele-photo lens. At one stage, the snow which Greg cleared from the holds gathered loose powder as it slid down the slope below, and the small avalanche landed directly on their tent. When Andy, Tenzing and Narayan arrived at the camp (which we had named 1.8 in the hope of finding somewhere better for Camp II higher up), they found the tent flat-tened and the poles broken. They cleared the snow away but left Greg and Geof to repair it as best they could.

The two climbers reached their camp at about six o'clock. Immediately Greg radioed Camp I with news of the day's progress, not knowing that Mike and Howard had kept us well informed. We began to discuss whether they should stay there or descend, though there seemed to be no question in Geof's mind: he regarded the camp as too dangerous. A larger avalanche could sweep the tent from the mountain. Greg was keen to keep the forward momentum and was prepared to risk another night so that he could work with Tim and me on pushing the route up the mountain the next day.

Greg finished the conversation with the comment that his eyes were sore because he had climbed all day without his sunglasses. Down at Camp I we looked at each other knowingly.

"He'll probably be snow-blind tomorrow," I said.

"No probably about it," said Jim. "He won't be able to see a thing."

Back on the radio, "How did that happen, Greg?"

"I took my pack off at the bottom of the gully when we were still in the shade and it was four hours before I got back to it and put my glasses on. What does Jim suggest I do? The pain is getting worse by the minute."

Jim named the ointments in the first-aid kit he had made up for each of us. "The silly bugger should know better than that, with the amount of time he's spent in the moun-tains."

The problem was that the glare from the snow had burnt his eyes, and the result was that he would be blind for a day or two.

"Do you think we should try and talk him into coming down?" asked Howard.

"No point!" I answered "He's too stubborn. Tomorrow he'll probably try and climb with his eyes closed. As it's only temporary damage there's no real danger in him staying there. At least, no more danger than if he could see."

LEFT: Geof climbs the fixed rope in Greg's Gully as snow dislodged by a climber above catches the sunlight.

RIGHT: Mike films our progress on the mountain with an 800 mm lens on his 16 mm camera.

Sure enough, when Tim and I reached Camp 1.8 at mid-morning the next day, Greg could barely see out of one eye and was completely blind in the other. Inside the clumsily repaired tent he wore sunglasses because any light whatsoever was painful.

Tim had gone ahead with some rope and the hope of reaching a good camp site. I shouldered my heavy pack and said to Greg, "We'll be back soon to help you up to a better camp than this disaster area. How's that for optimism?"

The optimism was justified, though it was hard work plodding up the steep loose snow, and Greg's Gully (as we immediately nicknamed his solution to the vertical cliff) was a real struggle. Because Tim had moved the anchor another two hundred metres higher, the stretch in the rope rendered it not much use as an aid. I cursed Tim for adjusting the rope inconsiderately, then cursed myself for carrying such a heavy pack. Driven by my anger I puffed up the 200-metre slope above.

Tim was waiting at the top. A few words from him and my anger vanished. It was only misdirected energy. Tim had done well to fix the rope unassisted and I should have been pleased with myself for managing to carry a thirty-kilogram pack up steep ground to almost seven thousand metres. High altitude had closed my mind to the fact that I was living out every climber's ambition – a perfect day of climbing a new route on the highest mountain of them all. On an expedition, high altitude becomes the excuse for every flash of temper and mood of darkness.

Behind Tim the ridge levelled out, though both sides dropped away steeply. He pointed to a spot twenty metres further. "There's a possible site for a snow cave over there."

Walking along the crest of the rib was like being on the pointed roof of a building a kilometre high. The snow sank under our tread into definite footsteps and gave an illusion of security which walking on roofing tiles could never have done. The situation was magnificent, with the steepest part of the Face beneath us now. On one side of the rib was the Great Couloir. There was nothing to give perspective or scale. It was possible to believe that the huge ice cliffs of the Great Couloir overhung us, though logic told us that since we were to the right of the Couloir that could not be the case. On the other side of the rib it was a sheer drop to the bottom of the Face. We were higher than the peaks of Khumbutse and Lingtren so we could look over them to the peaks of Nepal's Gokyo Valley. Changtse no longer loomed above us for an impossible distance. All around, up and down, the views were spectacular. It was a great place for a camp.

RIGHT: Looking down on Tim and Andy as they climb the fixed rope between Camp 1.8 and Camp II. The dangerous slopes of the Great Couloir lie to the right.

BELOW: Greg, snowblind, in the tent at the precarious but temporary Camp 1.8. Some of the tent poles were broken by a small avalanche the previous day.

ABOVE: Howard's telephoto shot from 6400 metres on the far side of the Northern Cwm shows a figure standing on the ledge at Camp II. Fixed rope can be seen to the left then to the right of the trail of footsteps above the camp. All but the biggest avalanches were split by the prominent ridge before sweeping down both sides of the camp.

RIGHT: In this photo taken by Colin from the North Col, our route crosses the picture diagonally from near the bottom right-hand corner, up the prominent rib which casts a shadow into the Great Couloir. Greg's Gully is the first weakness at the right-hand end of the dark rockband. Camp II, with footsteps leading up and out of the picture, can be seen as a dot on the crest of the ridge above and towards the left-hand end of the rockband. The upper third of the photo shows part of White Limbo.

PRECEDING PAGES: From Camp II, less than a third of the way up Everest's North Face, the peaks in cloud-covered Nepal seem dwarfed, except for Cho Oyu and Gyachung Kang on the horizon.

"What do you think?" asked Tim.

"If the snow is good, it's fantastic. It had better be good because it doesn't look like there's anywhere else."

"We can't go any higher than this, anyway," said Tim as I unstrapped the snow-shovel from my pack, "or we'll never get here in a day from Camp I with loads."

Tim dug a metre or so into the snow then poked into the hole with his ice-axe. The snow was deep and firm, in perfect condition for a snow cave. Tim headed back down to fetch another load and to help Greg, while I set about digging the cave.

The first task was to dig a ledge across the Face, wide enough and long enough for us to sit on while we attached our crampons to our boots, and so that we could lounge about and enjoy our afternoon tea on beautiful days such as this. Having room to move around outside, unroped, did away with the feeling of being trapped by constant danger.

Once I had dug a ledge the size of a single bed, I began to tunnel into the slope at the far end. There was a lot of snow to be shifted, but with the snow-shovel I could carve large blocks which I then rolled down the slope, and so made good progress. Every half hour or so I would take a five-minute rest to have a drink, eat some chocolate and admire the incredible panorama around me. After two and a half hours I had a hole big enough to sit a couple of people. It was an awkward size because there was not enough room to wield the shovel efficiently. I was crouched inside when I heard the familiar "Whoompf!" of an avalanche.

Sounds like a big one, I thought. I'll have a look at that.

I stepped out onto my narrow ledge and looked across towards the West Shoulder where I expected to see the avalanche. There was nothing. I turned to face the North Col. Nothing there either With horror I realised the only other possibility. I jerked my head up to see the sky filled with huge clouds of snow, seconds away from sweeping me off the mountain. There was nowhere to go but into my embryo snow cave. As soon as I had flung myself inside, the avalanche hit. Thousands of tonnes of snow poured over the entrance. There seemed to be a real danger of being buried alive. I crawled out onto the ledge I had cut into the slope and pressed myself against the wall. There at least I would be buried less deeply. Snow was forced into my nostrils and my mouth as I breathed so I covered my face with my hands.

"Please don't let the whole slope be swept away," I said aloud, not so much to any-body or anything, but in the irrational hope that voicing my wish would make survival more likely.

After several minutes the slide of snow lessened and finally stopped. The air was full of snow swirling in the wake of the avalanche. The late afternoon sun glinted from the tiny flakes, reminding me of the facts which at that moment needed no further emphasis – how beautiful is the world, how good it is to be alive.

I gave a whoop of delight, then sobered with worry about the fate of Greg and Tim. I shouted and heard an answering cry. Somebody was alive at least. When I tried to hold my ice-axe I realised that my whole body was shaking with the shock. Not wanting to trust my trembling legs I crawled along our tracks to where I could peer down the steep slope. Greg was only fifty metres below.

"Are you okay?"

"Yeah!" was the feeble reply.

"What about Tim?"

"He was answering nature. His clothes are full of snow."

Greg's answer told nothing of Tim's safety but his manner implied he must be all right. I lay back in the snow and laughed hysterically. It was the biggest avalanche I had ever seen, let alone been underneath.

"Lincoln!" There was an urgency in Greg's voice.

I stood up and listened.

"I'm soaking wet and really cold. If I'm not there soon come and give me a hand."

"Do you want me to take your pack?"

"No, it's just that I'm cold."

"Okay. You're nearly at camp. Give me a yell if you need me."

The sun was sinking low in the sky. Time to return to digging that night's shelter.

Soon the cave was big enough for me to work in more quickly. When I bulldozed the accumulation of snow off the ledge with my boots Greg was just arriving. He looked worn out and was shivering violently. The snow of the avalanche had worked its way down his neck and sleeves and into his pockets so that now his clothes were quite wet.

He sat down to catch his breath while I pulled dry clothes out of his pack and listened to his story. Both he and Tim had seen the avalanche fly over the ice cliff above and had thought how impressive it would be watching it roar down the Great Couloir. As it tumbled closer and closer they realised it was too huge to be contained in the Couloir. There was nothing they could do but watch it fly over the edge of the rib and bear down on them. Tim, who was in the process of doing up his trousers, threw himself back to the fixed rope where he had attached his pack and hung on with all his might. Greg, who was firmly tied to the fixed rope a little way above, was swept off the slope. The snow poured over him, stretching the fixed rope as the force of the avalanche tried to drag him down. Then it was gone, leaving them stunned but uninjured.

"It took my mind away from my aching eyes for a while," he said in conclusion. "Pass me the radio, will you. Camp I has got to hear about this."

I continued work on the snow cave while he repeated his tale to Jim who, in a fit of conscientiousness, recorded it for the film soundtrack.

Half an hour later Tim arrived, unperturbed as usual. After a short break the three of us set to work and the snow cave grew at five times the rate. As the sun set we levelled the floor and passed our packs inside. It had been the hardest and most exacting day of the climb.

We estimated our Camp II to be at about 6900 metres. It was a long way from Camp I but the avalanche had shown that nowhere below was safe. As Tim prepared dinner we chatted about the possibility of the ropes and Camp 1.8 having been torn off the mountain. We would hear the extent of the damage when Geof and Andy came up the next day.

"Just as well it didn't happen yesterday, Greg."

An avalanche plunges over the huge ice cliffs above and to the left of Camp II and continues down the Great Couloir. The avalanche that swept over the camp was several times larger.

The first night at a significantly higher altitude is always uncomfortable, but this time our exhaustion encouraged sleep to come easily.

The next morning as breakfast was cooking we radioed Camp I. Jim had replayed Greg's description of the avalanche during dinner time with staggering effect.

"I'm not going to come up," said Geof, "because I don't want to die."

The announcement astounded us. We appreciated that we had been lucky to survive the avalanche, but now that it was over it was an incident to laugh about. Avalanches of such a huge size could not happen very often. Anyway, we reasoned that yesterday's slide would have cleaned most of the dangerously loose snow from the slope above. Certainly there was a possibility that smaller avalanches might strike us as we climbed but that was a risk we all had accepted back in Australia. Now at least the gigantic avalanche had shown that Camp II was safe.

Geof had weighed up all those factors and had come to a different conclusion. On a small, essentially leaderless expedition such as ours, each of us had to assess what was an acceptable level of risk and what was not. Geof's decision left us with less manpower but no less respect for him as a mountaineer. In fact, his reaction made me think a great deal about whether my decision to stay on the mountain was foolhardy.

The three of us talked about the risks and decided that we could continue. With Narayan and Tenzing we had shared the dangers of other mountains but now we felt the margin of safety was too small. It seemed unfair to ask them to accept risks which Geof had found unacceptable. We knew they would come up the mountain if asked, but we preferred that they restrict their energies to Camp I where cooking for both the climbers and the film crew was almost a full-time job.

The previous evening Andy and Geof had debated for hours and both spent a sleepless night of worry. In the morning Geof reaffirmed his decision to stay down, but Andy chose to take the risk of coming up.

After breakfast Greg abseiled down to Camp 1.8 to fetch another load and while Tim belayed me I ran out a couple of hundred metres of rope. I was intensely aware of the possibility of being avalanched until steeper and more demanding climbing distracted me. The ice slope which wound its way through steep rock onto the base of the huge snow slopes of White Limbo was more intimidating than difficult. So absorbed was I in the climbing that I did not notice another sizable avalanche sweep down the Great Couloir a couple of hundred metres to my left. I ran out all the rope we had at the camp then abseiled back down to Tim.

Andy and Greg arrived from below shortly after Tim and I set about enlarging the snow cave. Andy was tired but impressed with both the climbing and the site of Camp II.

Since all the avalanches of the previous days had occurred in the afternoon, the logical thing to do was to get up early and be back at camp by midday. The next morning Tim, Greg and I left the snow cave at seven o'clock. Andy stayed in his sleeping bag promising he would get up soon and fetch another load from Camp 1.8. From our high point Greg belayed while Tim climbed. It was too cold to hang around until the rope was fixed so, unroped, I followed Tim's footsteps. The surface of the snow was firm and we made quick progress until we came to the end of the rope where we waited for Greg.

"Perfect for a slab avalanche," he muttered as he arrived. "The whole lot could go."

We agreed it was foolish to spend more time up here than was necessary. Greg wanted to descend all the way to Camp I that day so Tim and I shared his load and watched him abseil down. Though we had no more rope to fix to the slope, we decided to climb another seventy metres to the shelter of one of the big rocks we had picked out from the glacier below. There we would be able to dump our gear without fear of it being avalanched. The snow was treacherously unstable, and it was with the added energy of adrenalin that we cached the gear and started down.

There were no other chores for that day, Tim and I lolled around on our "verandah" soaking up the view. Andy arrived shortly, looking very annoyed with himself.

"I dropped my pack," he growled. "It's at the bottom of the Face."

I glanced at Tim who also looked puzzled.

"Ah, Andy ... What's that on your back?"

"That's Geof's pack. I took mine off while I put on my sunglasses and it overbalanced. It fell down the Great Couloir. Geof caught up to me so I took his load."

Tim abseils down to Camp 1.8 after fixing the rope.

"Well, that's not such a major calamity. Geof will bring yours up tomorrow. It should have survived the slide down the Couloir."

"So Geof decided to come up," said Tim. "That's good news."

"He said he didn't mind so long as he could start going down by midday before it gets too dangerous. Narayan and Tenzing felt the same."

"Cheer up, Andy. Have some chocolate."

It was not a serious incident. His sleeping bag and personal gear were in the snow cave. Andy was just annoyed with himself for being so careless.

"Everything's got its bright side, Andy. Think of the good story it'll make." But he only scowled at me.

In the morning the three of us abseiled down to Camp 1.8 to fetch the loads Narayan and Tenzing had carried up. On the way down I stopped to rearrange the rope in Greg's Gully to make ascending it easier. Narayan and Tenzing arrived at Camp 1.8 just as I abseiled into view. Narayan was his usual exuberant self, even at this height, while Tenzing, also typically, was smiling gently in the background and saying little. We took their loads and jumared back up the ropes. At these altitudes every hundred metres makes a critical difference. It was noticeably easier carrying heavy loads below Camp II than it was just fixing rope above. The trend would continue until, near the summit, every step would be a tremendous, barely manageable effort.

On the bitterly cold morning of 18 September we left the snow cave half an hour before dawn. The first light of day revealed high, dark clouds across the sky from the south to the north-west. The clouds were a sure sign of bad weather and an explanation for the sudden drop in temperature. The early morning cold cut through my clothing as if it did not exist. My feet and hands, which had been warm when I left the snow cave, soon froze. All of us felt chilled to the bone. The cold tore at our lungs as we gasped for air. I burst into a fit of coughing. The cold air was more than my throat could take. It was a case of climbing up to the top of White Limbo as quickly as we could, dumping the gear

165

Tim descends the fixed rope just above Camp II.

ABOVE: Doctor Jim Duff takes Colin's blood pressure at Camp I as part of the regular check he kept on our health.

BELOW: Geof, Tim and Lincoln at breakfast in the Camp I mess tent.

and descending to the shelter of the snow cave. I cannot remember much of that morning because so much of my attention was focussed on the cold and the attempt to stop my body succumbing to it. To make matters worse, the final snow slope of White Limbo was very unsafe. A thin crust rested on deep, unconsolidated snow – perfect conditions for an avalanche. Out of habit I glanced at the weather, but my discomfort prevented me from taking in the beauty of the colours captured in the foreboding clouds.

At the top of White Limbo we anchored the rope to a large rock, cached the gear and immediately started down. For the last couple of hundred metres the sun shone and the temperature rocketed up. Suddenly life was bearable again.

Back in the snow cave we melted snow for tea and packed the few things we wanted to take down from the mountain. The time had come for us to have a good rest and wait for the best conditions to attempt the summit. We drank our tea then radioed Camp I that we were on our way, leaving a few minutes apart as only one person could descend each length of rope at a time. It made more sense to wait in the snow cave than on small stances on the mountain. I was the last to go and by the time I reached the glacier it was snowing gently. Soon it worsened to a blizzard, and once again Geof's coloured flags marking the route proved their worth.

At Camp I the three of us sat in the mess tent drinking and talking to the others for an hour or two before heading down to Advance Base Camp with Greg and Tenzing. For about the fourth time on the expedition I staggered into camp exhausted. After I sat down and drank some tea I began to feel the benefits of Advance Base. The icy bite in the air was no longer apparent and every breath felt silken to my sore throat. After four nights at almost 7000 metres the air 1500 metres lower seemed full of welcome oxygen. We slept solidly until late in the morning.

As we had expected, the weather was bad the following day. Everyone apart from Jim and Colin came down to Advance Base Camp. As competent climbers with previous Himalayan experience, Colin and Jim felt a little frustrated in their role as film-makers. In an attempt to combine their love for climbing with the job at hand they planned to go up to Camp II, dig a second snow cave, ferry supplies up there, then stay to film our return. They hoped to film the next part of the ascent by climbing with us to the top of the fixed rope at 7500 metres. It was an ambitious but possible plan.

Advance Base Camp was noticeably colder than it had been two weeks before. The grass which had once been green was now a dull brown. The flock of a dozen Tibetan snowcocks which lived around the comparative oasis of our sheltered and watered valley had retreated to lower, less hostile altitudes for the oncoming winter. Yet to us, Advance Base was a haven of comfort after our time on the mountain.

Unfortunately my cough had followed me down. The slightest effort reduced me to a fit of coughing. The rawness of my throat from the extreme cold on the mountain was compounded by a bad headcold. Now was precisely the time I needed to be fittest and strongest. Long sessions of yoga gave me some relief, but it was only with time that I would recover fully.

The bad weather passed quickly but in its wake a strong wind remained. From the summits of the mountains around us snow was blown in plumes, and of course the biggest plume was from the summit of Everest.

During our last stay at Advance Base Camp all we had to preoccupy us were thoughts of the two tentative forays we had made up the Face, and the huge amount of mountain still to be climbed. The weather and the danger had left us frustrated and concerned that we might have chosen a season of exceptionally bad weather. This time we could feel satisfied with what we had achieved. One camp was established on the mountain and well stocked with provisions, and we had gear and food cached halfway up the Face at the top of the fixed ropes. Now, at last, everything was as planned. We were poised ready for the summit.

The knowledge that the next spell of clear, windless weather would see us struggling towards the top of the world's highest mountain made us nervous with anticipation. We all knew that for a small team, unassisted by oxygen equipment, the dangers of mountaineering were doubled or trebled at extreme altitudes. The lack of oxygen made one's reactions to an accident slow, and perhaps inappropriate. Death was never very far away.

To the fear that we naturally felt was added a concern about how we would perform

ABOVE: Clouds give a halo effect to the summit of Khumbutse as seen from Camp I.
RIGHT: Strong winds blow a plume of snow and cloud from the summit of Qomolangma, as Howard, Andy and Geof watch from Camp I.

individually. If I did not recover from my cold and cough I knew that I would be unable to reach the summit. My disability was slight enough to be ignored at sea-level but at 8000 metres and above it would be crucial. An oxygenless ascent of Mt Everest is probably the hardest imaginable feat of strength and endurance, and to have any chance of success, I needed to be one hundred per cent fit.

My weakness took the edge off my spirits. Enthusiasm for the climb was replaced with depression. I kept to myself and sought distraction from my worries by reading. Tim and Greg were rearing to go and Andy was in very good spirits. Geof had reasoned that as the big snowfalls of the monsoon had ceased, the danger of avalanches was reduced sufficiently to make the level of risk acceptable.

With a small team such as ours, personal ambition had to be a secondary consideration. On every other expedition I had climbed strongly and well. Now, on the most prestigious climb of them all, I might have to force myself to take a back seat. My ego found that possibility hard to consider.

After two days the wind appeared to be easing and on the third day it was back up to Camp I for the last time. We agreed virtually without discussion that we would all attempt the summit and let the mountain choose the victors, although it was probable that one or more would turn back before our highest camp, so fickle are one's physiological responses to extreme altitude. With success or failure depending on so many things all of us had reservations about ourselves and about each other. Apart from the technical problems of the climbing, the next few days would be a continual struggle to stay aware of everything around us. The slightest miscalculation could be our last mistake. It was little wonder that as I walked up the glacier my reasons for attempting such a dangerous goal turned over and over in my head.

If I can keep control of my mind, I told myself, I'll be all right.

I looked up to the summit and tried to imagine distances, times, and the enormous space which would surround us.

CHAPTER TEN

THE WAITING GAME

WINTER had arrived at Camp I. Apparently the calm season of autumn had been overlooked. No trees existed; no disposable leaves gave advance notice of change. In Tibet, the rugged lines of the landscape suited the sudden changes in climate. The storms of the monsoon had changed to the clear, cold skies of winter.

The severity of the new season was also a surprise. We decided to leave Camp I early: the snow would be frozen firm and we would reach Camp II early enough to be well rested for the hard day's climb up to Camp III. We left Camp I before dawn, expecting the cold to be fierce but tolerable. Soon, however, my hands and feet rebelled at temperatures which must have been minus 20 degrees Celsius. The circulation in my hands and feet had never fully recovered from frostbite suffered six years before. My throat was still raw from the coughing fits which had plagued me at Camp II and contact with the cold air set me off again into paroxysms of coughing that left me breathless.

I can't climb the mountain when I'm like this, I told myself as I plodded along the glacier, cursing the pain in my fingers and the energy drain of my cough. I'll be a physical wreck before we leave Camp II. What to do, I wondered. Push on without the strength to help make the route higher up the mountain? Or stay behind? The only answer seemed the latter. A week earlier I would not have believed I could talk myself out of the summit attempt so easily; I would have given anything to be able to try. But now, with a headcold making me tired, my cough leaving me weak and breathless, and the monstrous cold nibbling my hands and feet, it was a simple choice. My body had made the decision for me.

I staggered up to the Stash. This day, unlike any other, I had fallen a long way behind my friends. Geof and Greg were still at the tent, putting on the climbing gear they had left there. Mike and Howard had risen very early to film our preparations as we arrived and left the Stash. Geof was just leaving as I dropped my pack to the ground.

"I'm not going to come up. My cough's exhausting me. And this cold!"

Geof was not surprised, because the day before at Advance Base I had confided my fears about my health.

Greg did not seem to hear, busy as he was rummaging for some misplaced equipment.

LEFT: A morning snowstorm clears at Camp I. Without Everest (to the left, out of the photo) for comparison, Khumbutse appears huge.
ABOVE: Our dome tents, pictured at Camp I, stood up well to even very heavy snowfall.

"Greg," I began. "I don't think I'll come up ... "

He was flabbergasted.

"Why not?"

"This bloody cough is burning me out down here. It will be impossible up there."

"But Lincoln," he said after a pause, "I don't think we can do it without your strength. I really don't."

His words made me realise the importance of what I had given up. The summit of the world. The goal we had been trying to reach for two months. And what was more, as our small team was dependent on each and every member, my decision to stay down might cost the expedition its prize.

I sat on my pack, head in my hands, reduced to tears which I half-heartedly attempted to conceal. Mike was quick to film and to signal Howard into position with a microphone.

"But I have no strength at the moment. I'd only be flailing along behind coughing my lungs out."

Greg and I sat and talked for half an hour. I was surprised at how much he was upset by my decision. Some of that no doubt came from an appreciation of how much each of us had put into getting this far, and therefore how much I was giving up. Of course, in my concern with my own problems I had not thought of the effect of my retirement on our chances of putting someone on top. But no amount of encouragement could cure me. Greg and I hugged each other before he shouldered his pack and plodded after the others, heavy in spirit.

I crawled into the tent to warm my numb hands and feet. In an hour the sun would arrive. I sat there waiting for it, thinking about my decision. Was it as simple as all that, or did fear colour my judgment?

I was scared. Of course I was scared. The risks were not the insinuated threats common to all mountaineering but, as our narrow escapes had shown, direct dangers with no respect for any pretensions we may have held of immortality. Some climbers seemed to operate on the premise that death was something that only happened to other people. I had been close enough to dying too many times to believe that. And now, I keenly felt how much there was to live for, how pointless it would be to die on this mountain. To stay down would ensure my survival. Were my cough and headcold an attempt by my subconscious to protect me from a fatal ambition by yielding my body to disease? It was impossible to know. My disability prohibited an attempt on the mountain, and that was all there was to it.

A couple of hours later, Mike, Howard and I sat in the sun watching the slow progress of the others up the ropes. It was the first time I had seen the Face with climbers on it from anywhere other than directly beneath. They were nothing more than tiny dots moving imperceptibly higher and higher.

"It'll be a great film, Mike," I said. "It looks so dramatic from here." And I remembered how dramatic it looked from up there, with the huge expanse of steep snow sweeping down below.

Suddenly Howard shouted.

"Mike! Quick! Over there!"

Across near the West Ridge, the North Face had avalanched. Thousands of tonnes of snow were sliding down the Face. Howard's cry had been to alert Mike to the filming possibilities, but for the first time on the trip Mike's reaction was one of panic – an entirely justifiable response. It was a huge avalanche. Mike ran towards us, but there was nowhere to go.

"Are we safe?" he asked.

Howard and I stared at the enormous cloud of snow, now almost at the bottom of the Face. Neither of us wanted to commit ourselves to an answer. Neither of us was sure.

"I think so, Mike."

But Mike was already lying on the snow filming the rapidly approaching avalanche.

"We should be all right ... "

"I'll just zip up the tent ... "

A few seconds later snow was harmlessly swirling all around us. The force of the fall had been lost as it rolled across the kilometre-wide glacier.

Howard and I laughed hysterically. What a thrill. What an amazing sight. The radio crackled to life. "Mike," it asked. "Did you like that one?" And then laughter. From up on the

An avalanche from the North Face rolls across the nevé of the Northern Cwm towards the Stash.

FOLLOWING PAGES: "Across near the West Ridge, the North Face had avalanched. Thousands of tonnes of snow were sliding down the Face... Mike ran towards us, but there was nowhere to go."

Face where Jim and Colin were waiting to film the climbers there was a good view of the avalanche, and Jim, who had the radio, had imagined the fright it would give us. He had recovered the good spirits he had lost for a while after painfully damaging a tendon in his foot on the climb up to Camp II.

The summit of Everest was a dramatic sight. Strong winds blew a huge plume of snow from the top. The three of us stayed at the Stash all day watching the climbers gradually progress and the wind continue to blow. Tim was the first to reach the snow cave, at about three in the afternoon. Immediately he spoke to us on the radio.

"It's incredibly windy up here, Lincoln. If this keeps up we'll have to come down. What do you think if we come down this evening?"

"Better to wait till morning. Remember it was at six o'clock in the evening when that huge avalanche swept over us last time. And there've been enormous avalanches at this end of the Face."

"Okay. Will you listen to the Radio Nepal weather forecast tonight and relay it to us? We'll be listening at ten, and make our decision then."

"Okay." My hopes began to rise. "Over and out."

If they came down it would be a day or two before they went up again. By then I would probably have the strength to go with them. That hope brought with it the realisation that I had felt relief not to be going to the summit. I had begun to accept that the dangerous part of the trip was over for me. Relief had filled the space where fear had been. Now I had to stem that flow, and turn the hourglass upside down again.

Back at Camp I that evening we listened to the special weather bulletin for mountaineering expeditions broadcast from Kathmandu. It was a bad forecast. At 7000 metres, about the height of the snow cave at Camp II, the temperature the following day would be minus 15 degrees Celsius and the wind twenty knots. At the top of Everest those figures were doubled. It certainly held little prospect for climbing.

"Looks like we'll be down tomorrow," said Tim over the radio.

The next morning dawned clear but still a plume of snow blew from Everest's summit.. The others decided to descend. A big advantage of our direct route up the North Face was the speed with which we could retreat. Greg was the first back to Camp I early in the afternoon, and Tim, Geof and Andy arrived not much later. Jim and Colin took some good footage of the climbing up to Camp II but were frustrated by the climbers' descent from filming anything above there. Colin arrived back late and tired. Jim did not arrive at all. He had collapsed exhausted at the Stash, having been slowed down by the pain of the injury to his foot. Two days up high had been too much time for him. The mountain was an inhospitable place. Both Jim and Colin lacked the psychological spurs which we used to drive ourselves to the summit. Their aim was to film, and at 7000 metres it was one of the toughest jobs in the world.

From Camp I to Camp II there was a total height gain of a thousand metres prefaced by a three-kilometre trudge up the glacier. At this altitude it was a hard day's exercise even without the extra demands put upon us by the danger. At this stage of the climb, each time we climbed up and retreated we were using strength we needed to save for the summit attempt. Now we were as acclimatised as we would ever be. Excess body weight, both fat and unused muscle, had been burnt off by our exertions over the past weeks. We were trim and fit but with no strength to waste. We could not afford the effort of another fruitless climb up to Camp II and down again. The next time we would have to continue to the summit. The problem was to judge whether a spell of fine windless weather would last long enough for our climb. To be able to succeed we needed at least four good days.

The monsoon had definitely finished and the winter weather pattern of clear days and strong winds was firmly established. All we needed was for the wind to drop, and that was most likely to occur when the dying monsoon interfered with the constant windy weather. Such a break would last only a few days. When the conditions were right precious time could not be wasted by the whole team waiting at Camp I if I felt unfit.

It was back to playing the waiting game again. With every day that passed the others became increasingly frustrated. For me, each day gave more time to recover my strength. Failure to climb a mountain because it was technically too difficult, or because one's reserves of strength were inadequate, was acceptable. But to return home without making a solid attempt for the top because the weather conditions did not allow it was intolerable.

The cloud over the summit of Qomolangma is distorted into a hat-like shape by the ferocious winter winds.

That outcome would teach us patience and remind us of our insignificance before the mountain. However, thoughts of such lessons in virtue were little solace as we sat and watched the wind blow.

Rather than dying, the wind picked up. Fantastic clouds blew past the summit, changing their shapes like swirling foam in a rockpool. For hours clouds continued to boil up from behind the West Ridge and accelerate over the summit before being blown to nothingness in the sky beyond. The mixture of airborne moisture and snow was a magnificent sight but frightening and frustrating to our mountaineers' eyes.

It was a difficult few days. We had passed the point of optimum fitness and now the altitude was beginning to eat away at our reserves. The psychological pressure of not knowing when our chance would come, if it came at all, increased our restlessness.

After our third day of waiting the wind lessened considerably. Greg arrived at our tent door in the morning urging us to leap out of our sleeping bags and head up the mountain. Our sleeping bags were warm and cozy; outside, with the sun hours away, the morning seemed unbearably cold.

"Better to go back to bed, Greg, and if it's still good tomorrow we'll go up then."

We wanted to be sure that the fine weather was a lasting spell and not just a temporary easing of the wind.

Greg was not sure whether common-sense or laziness was the stronger force in our argument. At any rate, he reluctantly agreed.

Everest did not bother to obey weather forecasts. The strong winds predicted for the following day did not arrive. As soon as it was light enough to see that no snow was being blown from Everest's summit – a sure sign that the winds were gentle at the top of the world – we began to get ready to leave.

An hour later we were trudging slowly up the glacier in the bitter cold of the early morning. At the Stash we strapped our crampons to our boots, warmed our fingers, and plodded on across the upper névé to the foot of the Face. We travelled at different speeds. Some were impatient to tackle the problem before them. Others walked slowly with their thoughts, saving strength for high on the mountain when every ounce of energy would be needed. There was a great deal to think about – so much that Andy had lain awake half the night in nervous anticipation. Finally, at 2 a.m. he took a sleeping pill which kept him dopey until about ten in the morning. He wandered along in a daze behind the rest of us.

"An hour later we were trudging slowly up the glacier in the bitter cold of the early morning."

LEFT: Jim and Colin near Camp II. Their plan to film above the snow cave was frustrated when strong winds forced the climbers back to Camp I.
ABOVE: The climbing above the old site of Camp 1.8 was steep and strenuous.
FOLLOWING PAGES: Greg arrives at Camp II 900 metres above the Rongbuk nevé.

By contrast I felt wide awake. My feelings about the climb were all positive. The dangers had not diminished but my attitude had changed. I felt strong and aware, and secure in my ability to survive. I was ready. All that we needed was luck with the weather. Without that, no matter how strong we felt, the climb would be impossible.

Since little film had been taken above Camp II, Colin came with us to record our departure from the snow cave and the first few hours of climbing above. To make things easier for the climbers he broke the trail up the Face. It was a slow process since he had to kick new steps in the snow and free the rope where it had frozen to the slope. For the rest of us the lower ropes, which had been such an effort to climb a month before, seemed easy now. That comparative easiness – exaggerated by our slow climbing pace – was very welcome because the next few days were sure to be amongst the most demanding of our lives.

As it happened, the demands of the following day were intense but of an entirely unexpected nature. We woke before dawn to an impossibly cold and windy morning. At first we hoped the wind would die as the sun rose. When that did not happen we accepted that we would have to wait till tomorrow. Foremost in all our minds was the worry that the wind might not stop for days. Should we descend if the wind continued the next day or should we sit it out here in the snow cave?

"We have to decide whether we lose more strength by going down and coming back up, or by wasting away here because of lack of oxygen," said Greg.

"And lack of proper sleep," I added.

"There's no point worrying too much about it," said Geof. "We're committed to staying here today, and tomorrow hopefully we'll go up."

In the morning the wind was still blowing strongly. It was another day of lying in our sleeping bags, eating, drinking, dozing. I read stories to the others from an anthology of fantastic literature. This luxury which Andy had carried up was proving worthwhile. Living

ABOVE: Afternoon tea is brewing as Greg and Andy arrive after carrying loads up to Camp II.

RIGHT: Colin films our activities at Camp II. Above his head on the skyline is Cho Oyu. The prominent triangular peak to the left is Pumori.

PRECEDING PAGES: After arriving at Camp II, Greg sits down to remove his crampons from his boots. Changtse is in the background.

as we were in a world of our own imaginations were very receptive to worlds created in other people's minds.

Colin had been pessimistic and had descended the previous afternoon. He and Andy had shared the second snow cave which Colin had dug close to ours. Over the past few years we had spent a lot of time sitting out bad weather in tents and snow caves. Andy's method of coping with days of forced inactivity was to drift into slumber almost as deep as hibernation. Alone in the second cave without a watch, he posed a problem.

"How will we wake you in the morning?"

"I'll leave the radio on in my sleeping bag where the batteries won't freeze, so you can call me. I probably won't sleep very well."

"That's because you've been asleep all day."

The irony was that Andy had no difficulty in spending whole days asleep to pass time, but here and at Camp I worry and nervousness cost him many sleepless nights.

The next day the wind blew less fiercely but it was still too strong to allow even vaguely comfortable climbing.

Each of us coped with our confinement to the snow cave in different ways. Nobody quite had Andy's knack for sleeping, though Greg could sometimes manage a good imitation. Once we had accepted our immobility, passing the time was not a big problem. Time operates in a different gear at high altitude. The lack of oxygen slows one's thinking. With every thought taking twice as long there was effectively half as much time in the day. Meals took a long time to prepare as did the many drinks we needed to combat dehydration. With the hours spent melting snow, cooking and eating, only a few hours of the day remained for dozing and talking and listening to stories.

Greg decided he had tired of my monotone, so he grabbed the book of stories and gleefully cut it up into sections. His joy came not from the destruction but from the feeling of performing a definite act, however minor, instead of lying there bored.

"After all," Tim rationalised "Andy bought the library with expedition funds so it's appropriate that we share the book like this."

Andy himself was depressed, not about his book, but by the situation.

"Another day of this and I'll go mad," he said. "You'll have to improvise a strait-jacket out of my down suit."

The stove on the left boils water, while Geof, cosy in his sleeping bag in the Camp II snow cave, signals how many sugars he would like in his tea.

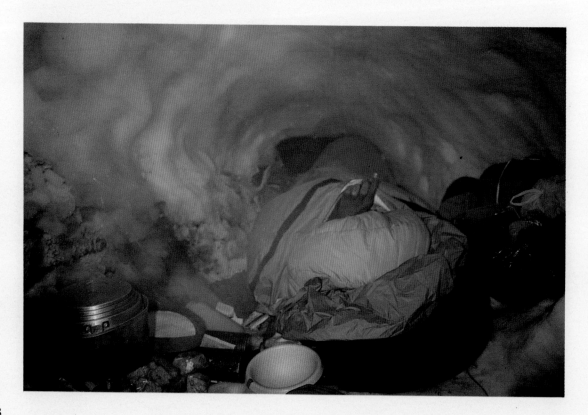

ABOVE: Sunset colours clouds on the peaks of the West Rongbuk.

BELOW: Ice-axes pin our helmets, harnesses and crampons to the wall above our open-style verandah at Camp II. To the right, the space blanket which acts as a door to the snow cave is rolled up on this comparatively windless evening.

LEFT: At mealtime in the snow cave there is little room to move amongst the cheese, biscuits and pots full of soup and tea.
ABOVE: The last sun touches the tip of the Nuptse Ridge. Qomolangma's West Ridge is in the foreground.

"We'll just seal up the door of your snow cave and open it when the weather improves."

Tim and Greg remained determined to climb the mountain, even if it meant returning to Camp I and waiting another week for the wind to stop. Neither Geof nor I relished that prospect.

"When I go down from here," Geof said, "that's it. I'm not coming up again. We've been here for two months, and that's enough. It's time for me to get on with the other things in my life."

"But think of the incredible effort, not to mention expense, of getting ourselves into this position," replied Tim. "All we need is a few good days."

"Starting tomorrow," pleaded Andy, hoping that some higher power was listening.

It may well have been, for the next day we were given our chance. The night had led us to fear the worst. The strongest winds we had yet experienced blew a continual stream of spindrift snow in the door until we had to block the entrance with our packs. It was a reluctant move, since there was little enough oxygen at that height without compounding the problem by blocking the door.

We expected the winds to continue through the day so we were delighted when Greg crawled outside and shouted back immediately that it was almost calm.

"But still really cold," he added.

We immediately began the lengthy process of making breakfast and packing up. There was excitement in my haste and a tightness in my guts. The tightness was the embryo of fear which would remain with me now until I stood safely at the bottom of the mountain again. The sun reached the door of the snow cave and we were ready to leave.

ABOVE: As the sun rises, the shadows of Everest and Changtse are cast onto Cho Oyu, Gyachung Kang and smaller peaks further west.
LEFT: Preparations at Camp II. Lincoln adjusts his boots as Tim comes out of the snow cave.

CHAPTER ELEVEN

QOMOLANGMA

GREG, who was always quick to organise himself, was away first. He had the un-enviable task of breaking the trail up the soft snow of the rib leading to White Limbo. The snow on White Limbo itself was in much better condition – firm and far less prone to avalanche than when we had last climbed it, two weeks before. Towards the middle of the giant snow slab I took over from Greg the task of plugging the steps and freeing the ropes which here and there had been buried under a few centimetres of snow. The last hundred metres to the big rock, where we had deposited our gear during our first sortie up the slabs, was hard going. With every step I broke through the crust into deep white powder which had not consolidated enough to take firm footsteps. Each step collapsed into the one below it, making the climbing slow and frustratingly tiring. Above the rock, on solid snow again, I relinquished the lead to Greg and Tim.

I kicked a ledge to sit on and rested for a while. Here at 7300 metres, Everest's North and West Ridges no longer provided shelter from the wind. With each gust the cold forced me to turn my face because of the pain and the fear of frostbite. Luckily the gusts were infrequent. Every movement at that altitude was a great effort, seemingly greater after our days of inactivity in the snow cave. Nevertheless, it was a relief to be climbing upwards again, making positive progress towards our goal.

Geof and Andy appeared around the halfway rock. It was time to move on to avoid congesting the ropes. The firm snow was much easier to climb. Every couple of minutes I would stop to catch my breath for thirty seconds, then stagger on. What lay above and beneath, and the magnificent panorama of the mountains and hills of Tibet were forgotten as I concentrated on gulping in air.

Fifty metres below Geof stopped and shouted that he was coming no further.

"I'm dizzy and I can't see properly, and my legs have gone weak. I'll have to go down."

He described the symptoms of cerebral oedema – fluid retention in the brain – one of the most serious ways in which high altitude interferes with human metabolism. The

LEFT: Clouds driven by winds of fifty to a hundred knots leave strange shadows across White Limbo and the upper part of Qomolangma.

ABOVE: Lincoln wears a face mask as protection from the bitterly cold wind and to help warm the air as he breathes.

The last thousand metres of the Face, seen from the North Col. The solid line shows the route of ascent, and the broken line the route of descent. Camp IV is marked by the triangle to the left of the photo. "A" marks Andy's high point and "B" Lincoln's.

only cure was to descend, for to continue up would cause the condition to worsen and almost certainly result in death. A rescue operation by a small team such as ours would be a difficult, dangerous affair so Geof had to descend while he was still capable of looking after himself.

Later, back at Camp I, I talked to him about his decision to turn back.

"Of course, I was disappointed. That morning was the first time I felt strong enough to have a chance of reaching the summit. But certainly I made the right decision. Even back down at Camp II, I had a hard time. My vision was blurred and I had a dreadful headache. I didn't sleep at all because I was frightened I'd die. It was the worst night I've ever spent."

Andy, who was only a few metres above him, took the communal gear he had been carrying. I watched Geof descend to the halfway rock and abseil out of sight.

His retreat was a sobering reminder of the dangerous situation we were in. Apart from the dangers presented by the mountain we needed to be constantly aware of the insidious effects of high altitude. The highest Geof had climbed was to the summit of Pumori, across the valley in Nepal. It was now a few hundred metres below us. Geof had broken his personal altitude record – a feat which would give him some satisfaction at least. How would the rest of us cope when we passed 8000 metres, the height of Annapurna II's summit? The only way to tell was to climb on.

I pulled my ice-axe out of the snow and plodded slowly to the top of the fixed rope. Our cache of food and equipment was safe. When I reached the rock which had sheltered our gear, Tim was transferring his share of food into his pack and Greg had already begun the long traverse left to the Great Couloir. Somewhere in the Couloir we would have to find a camp site, hopefully a sheltered one, for the gusts of wind were becoming increasingly frequent. With sunset approaching there was no time to spare, yet it was cold enough for me to waste precious minutes putting on my down suit. Tim, Andy and Geof had been wearing theirs all day. The bitter wind blew away our doubts about the need for clothing which was a great deal more elaborate than we had used on any other climb. Manipulating the zippers on my suit numbed my fingers, and while I warmed my hands by putting them under my armpits, I rested and soaked in the beauty of the view. The lengthening shadows cast by the peaks beneath made a jagged pattern on the glacier. Harmless clouds drifted over the passes from Nepal emphasising our distance above the rest of the world. Evil and ugliness did not seem to exist up here: to experience a world without them was sufficient reason to climb mountains.

Andy reached me.

"How's it going?"

"Okay," he puffed. "Except I'm exhausted."

"Needless to say," I commented, standing up to make room for him on the small ledge. "I'll keep going. See you at Camp III, we'll have to make that really soon because the sun will be gone in an hour."

I set off. No longer did any effort have to be expended lifting my body up step by step. Now it was a simple matter of traversing. At 7500 metres nothing is easy, but it was a relief not to be dragging myself upwards. The excitement of new ground brought an extra burst of energy. Tim and Greg had already disappeared out of sight in the Couloir.

Moving "across" rather than "up" meant turning side-on to the slope instead of facing into it. I became much more aware of the huge drop below. The snow-covered slabs of White Limbo opened out beneath me and the bottom third of the Face, being steeper than White Limbo, was hidden from view. Over one and a half vertical kilometres below lay the glacier. Almost the same distance above was the summit. Whatever lay between me and the top was unknown territory. For the next few days we would be totally on our own. It was a good feeling. Whatever the final result, we would push ourselves to our physical and mental limits, and in the process redefine the boundaries of our spirits. The hardship and the danger seemed worthwhile.

Greg and Tim had found a perfect camp site inside a deep crevasse with an entrance where the crevasse gaped open. To the right, the roof had closed over, forming a perfect natural snow cave. A short shuffle along the inside downhill wall led to the completely sheltered and comfortable ledge they had dug in less than an hour.

"What a great spot!" I said, as I peered into the icy chamber. "And we won't have the

Seen from the start of White Limbo, Geof, Andy, Tim and Lincoln have just left Camp II.
The ledge outside the snow cave is visible near the bottom figure.

ABOVE: Climbing up White Limbo en route to Camp III.
RIGHT: Andy on top of the halfway rock at 7300 metres on White Limbo.

BELOW: Looking down to Lincoln at the start of White Limbo. Tracks leading to and from Camp II can be seen on the spur to the left. Behind and below is the icefall at the bottom of the South Face of Changtse.
RIGHT: "The snow-covered slabs of White Limbo opened out beneath me and the bottom third of the Face, being steeper than White Limbo, was hidden from view." Tim near Camp III.

FOLLOWING PAGES: Greg and Tim climb the last few hundred metres to the top of White Limbo before making the long traverse to Camp III, off the picture to the left.

torture of pulling down a frozen tent in the morning."

Small benefits such as these become major issues in extreme cold, especially when under the influence of high altitude-induced lethargy.

"It's fantastic, isn't it?" agreed Greg.

Tim, the perfectionist, was shovelling a few final lumps of snow from the wall.

Andy arrived a little too exhausted to express his admiration. Sunset was only minutes away so we hurried to settle ourselves into our sleeping bags. The ledge was just large enough to fit all of us. We knew that once the sun had gone the temperature would plunge twenty degrees within a few minutes.

Set up with stoves, and cozy in our sleeping bags, we radioed Geof. He was safe at Camp II but sounded in a great deal of pain from headaches. The altitude drop of five hundred metres would be enough to relieve his symptoms. All we could do was tell him he would feel better in the morning. Small comfort.

The low atmospheric pressure at high altitude means that every part of one's body is starved of oxygen. Oxygen-deprived minds become slow and unreliable, and soon one learns to think every decision through a few times to search for forgotten considerations and errors of logic. In order to keep vital tissues supplied, the flow of blood (and hence oxygen) to one's extremities is severely reduced. A legacy of bad frostbite suffered in the past was poor circulation to my feet and hands. My feet had been numb since I had put them in my frozen boots that morning and, here at an altitude of 7500 metres, they did not want to warm of their own accord.

I accepted Andy's offer to use his stomach as the equivalent of a hot-water bottle. For a couple of hours I sat with my feet tucked inside Andy's sleeping bag. Six years before Tim and I had spent a night out at almost 7000 metres without sleeping bags. We warmed each other's feet in our armpits, but neither of us had much heat to spare. My feet did not thaw out till two days later (after our climb to the summit) by which time they were severely frostbitten, to the extent that parts of my toes had to be amputated. This time I was going to do everything in my power to avoid the pain, frustration and permanent

Tim and Greg check for camp sites in the Great Couloir, eventually discovering a perfect spot in a crevasse immediately behind and to the right of Greg. The high peaks on the central skyline are Menlungtse and Gaurishankar.

incapacitation of being frostbitten again. With fourteen hundred metres of mountain still to be climbed it would be a difficult task.

Tim cooked a simple but magnificent meal of soup, followed by cheese and noodles. We chatted optimistically about our chances of success then settled down to sleep. After several nights at 6900 metres, sleeping six hundred metres higher was not as difficult as we had feared.

We woke in the morning well rested and reluctant to relinquish our warm sleeping bags. Over the radio Geof spoke of the dreadful night he had spent, but was confident of being able to descend safely. Once again Greg was the first to leave, followed by Andy, Tim and finally, as the sun reached our crevasse, by me.

It was another brilliant day. The wind continued to blow but the gusts were infrequent and comparatively gentle. Higher up, where the Couloir narrowed, we hoped to be more sheltered from the wind.

The climbing conditions were perfect. The surface of the snow had frozen hard so that our boots did not sink in and our crampons bit firmly into the slope. The only problem was that a fall would certainly be fatal as it was impossible to stop a slip on the ice. A hundred metres below Camp III, the Great Couloir plunged over a huge ice cliff, the most prominent feature of the North Face, then continued in an unbroken sweep to the bottom of the mountain. For the sake of speed we climbed unroped, though each of us was very much aware of how serious a fall would be.

Andy gave himself a considerable fright when, a short way above Camp III, he shoved his ice-axe into the snow as a handhold. The unexpected result was a loud crack as a narrow fissure snapped open across the width of the Couloir. Andy was frightened that the whole slope was about to slip, carrying away not only himself but also Tim and I who were beneath. Nothing happened after the initial shock. Below, Tim and I remained happily oblivious of the new potential danger.

After half an hour's climbing I traversed to the edge of the Couloir in search of a place where I could remove my pack. Having done so, I radioed Camp I to let them know how we felt and what the conditions were like. It was strange talking to people who were safe and secure on the glacier below. The problems of their existence were so different from ours, almost as if we lived in different dimensions.

I put the radio away and began to climb again. Half my mind concentrated on keeping my balance and on other fine points of not falling off. The rest of my mind devoted itself to the mechanical movements of climbing. There was not enough oxygen for my mind to cope with more than those few thoughts.

Shortly, the angle of the slope eased to about forty degrees. Looking up, the snow slope seemed endless. Somewhere above the Couloir merged into steep rock, but that was too far away to worry about. All I could do was to take one step and make sure it was followed by another. Twenty steps then a rest, then twenty steps again.

Every now and then I used the view as an excuse for a longer rest. It was heartening to see the enormous bulk of Changtse fall further and further beneath my feet. My slow pace was getting me somewhere after all. Andy, whom I had passed earlier, was catching up. Above, Tim was now ahead of Greg but overall there was not much difference in our speeds. We were all climbing well and felt as strong as one could hope to feel at almost 8000 metres.

The walls of rock flanking the Couloir began to close in, bringing with them a feeling of hostility. It was no place for humans. There was no air, no water, no hope. I shook my head and fought away the pressure of those negative thoughts. It's just another mountain, I told myself. It's just another climb.

By early afternoon the cliffs on the right of the Couloir were shading our route. The hostility of the mountain was now reflected by the cold and the wind which blew almost continuously. At the first sheltered spot I stopped to warm my hands. Tim and Greg had stopped here and moved on because the spot was not big enough for a tent, and at any rate, we needed the camp to be higher to give the best chance of reaching the summit the next day. I unzipped my down suit and shoved my hands under my armpits. Andy plodded up to me and continued past without a word. There was no spare breath for smalltalk up here. My hands warmed up after about fifteen minutes, the longest rest I'd had since leaving Camp III, and long enough to muster some reserves of energy. I set off

ABOVE LEFT and ABOVE: Evening sun on Changtse and the North Col from the Camp III crevasse.

LEFT: Lincoln, Greg and Tim (and Andy behind the camera) celebrate settling into Camp III at 7500 metres with a drink of water and a block of chocolate.

again. A hundred metres or so above, Tim had crossed the Couloir and climbed up a snowy ramp on the left wall. It was the wrong direction for the summit so he could only be in search of a camp site. He was in the sun again, and I envied him its warmth. After twenty minutes of slow but exhausting climbing my hands were getting cold again so I had to stop and warm them. I lay on my pack in the snow to keep the wind out of my down suit while my hands were stuffed under my armpits once more. It was frighteningly cold. Another twenty minutes, I told myself, and you'll be back in the sun at the camp site. Only another twenty minutes.

Somebody shouted down to me, worried that I had collapsed from exhaustion. I hollered back, nothing in particular, just acknowledgment that I was okay. By the time I had put my gloved hands back in their over-gloves and over-mitts they were cold again. It was a losing battle, but at least so long as I warmed my hands frequently frostbite was not a danger. I staggered on across the Couloir, a little alarmed by the many hairline cracks in the slope. Each crack was a promise of an avalanche to come – only small ones but enough to send me tumbling down the slope. I reassured myself with the thought that it was so cold that everything would be frozen in place at least until tomorrow's sun. At the edge of the Couloir I left the shadow behind. Thirty metres above, the others were digging a ledge for the tent. A short way above them were the distinctive yellow cliffs of the Yellow Band which we would have to climb the next day. My hands were painfully cold again but my wish to stay ahead of the shadow kept me moving.

Basketball-sized blocks of snow came bouncing down the slope from the ledge the others were digging. If I followed their footsteps I would be hit by the barrage. To be safe I plugged my own steps up the soft wall of the gully. With every step I cursed my "friends" for forcing me to break my own trail when good steps already existed. I soon realised it was an irrational anger. The extra effort of the diversion I had made was a small price to pay for being able to pitch the tent before the sun set on our slope. Fiddling with the tent poles and guys, jobs which required removing our outer mittens, would be much more unpleasant once the sun had set.

Though the slope was not sheer it was steep enough to fall from. Because there was little room on the ledge for more than Greg, Tim, Andy and the tent, I stood a few metres below contributing nothing but a few sighs of exhaustion as they pitched the tent. In order to look busy I took some photographs. My grunts were enough to lead Greg to suggest that I be the first to crawl inside.

Once in the tent it was possible to forget that a 2000-metre drop fell away immediately outside the door. The tent was home. Our worries now were to make ourselves comfortable and to eat and drink enough. The difficulties which lay between our camp and the summit were worries for tomorrow.

Though the tent was cramped with four people inside, the bliss of being able to relax at last obscured the inconvenience. The melting of snow was an extended process because of the extreme cold and, even with two stoves and four bodies in the tent, the moisture from our breath formed frost on the walls. Every few minutes windblown snow which had accumulated on the slope above slid down in minute avalanches.

"Wouldn't this be miserable if we didn't have the tent?" commented Andy.

"Sure would," said Tim. "Just like when you two guys sat above Lincoln and me on the Annapurna II bivvy and knocked snow down on us every time you moved."

"Well it was certainly worth the effort of carrying the tent up," I said. "It's so bloody cold out there." After a pause I added, "It's so bloody cold in here." I was trying to warm my feet without much success.

For the whole time we were at that altitude we were suffering mental and physical deterioration. Our appetites were small but we forced ourselves to eat. We needed all the nourishment we could get. Hours passed as we melted snow for drinks. When we radioed Howard at Camp I the weather report was not encouraging.

"There hasn't been much correlation between the forecast and actuality before now," said Andy.

ABOVE: From Camp IV we could see into the East Rongbuk Valley.
BELOW: "There was little room on the ledge for more than Greg, Tim, Andy and the tent."
Camp IV at 8150 metres.
PRECEDING PAGES: Above Camp III in the Great Couloir "the only problem was that a fall would certainly be·fatal, as it was impossible to stop a slip on the ice."

"It'll be a perfect day tomorrow," said Greg, the optimist.

"Oh, will it?" I asked, "I'll sleep well now that we're sure of that."

Unfortunately, sleep did not come easily. The snow under the floor was uneven and uncomfortable. With four people there was no room to lie around the hollows and lumps; we had to tolerate them. The problem was compounded by the lack of oxygen. There was not enough of the life-giving gas to sustain someone who was breathing normally. One's breathing slowed down during the gradual drift to sleep until a point was reached where a simple reflex made one gasp for breath. Finally, though, tiredness over-rode the panic of suffocating and a restless sleep followed. We woke unrefreshed, but at least our minds had been free of worry and fear for a few hours.

The weather was perfect, not a cloud in the sky and only a slight wind. A radio call to Howard confirmed that no snow was being blown from the summit. The conditions were ideal. Now it was up to us.

We wasted little time getting ready, only the standard two and a half to three hours needed at high altitude to make breakfast, pack up, and put our boots and crampons on. At least today we did not need to carry much, just cameras and minimal survival gear. It was too cold at night to contemplate a forced bivouac, and anyone who could not descend if darkness fell would certainly suffer severe frostbite. The key to success was to carry as little as possible: every extra ounce would count against us. Tim decided to leave his pack behind and take only his cameras, tape-recorder, headlight and water-bottle to the summit – things he could fit in his pockets or stuff down the front of his down suit.

I radioed Camp I to tell them we were on our way. Their excitement bubbled through the radio – "Good luck!", "Go for it!", "Take care!"

Their enthusiasm reminded me of the import of what we hoped to do. Our oxygen-starved minds could not spare the space for excitement. Today was the day. Now it was a matter of determination and keeping ourselves under control. The effort of thinking clearly was draining up here, but the ability to concentrate was vital to our survival.

Greg was the first to leave, at about eleven. Tim and Andy left next. Fear and nervousness stimulated my bowels in a way I could not ignore. I undid all the relevant zips on my several layers of clothing before stepping out of the tent. When I returned a few minutes later I was chilled to the core, and my hands were too numb to undo the zip on the tent door. I collapsed inside, stunned by the cold.

"Madness," I said aloud, though the others had left, then decided to wait for the arrival of the sun. At noon the first rays hit the walls of the tent, making an instantly noticeable difference.

Outside, the others were disappointingly close. An hour of climbing and only a few hundred metres away. We would have to speed up if we were to reach the top.

The first part of the climb involved a long traverse to the middle of the Couloir. A couple of hundred metres above, the Couloir ran out into steep rock walls. As I started the traverse, Tim and Greg were just beginning to climb the rock barrier known as the Yellow Band which ran diagonally upwards from near Camp IV. The route they had chosen did not look easy but was perhaps the best option. After two hundred metres it gave way to more straightforward ground. Photographs, our map, and hours of peering through telephoto lenses led us to think that the climbing above would be technically easy. The problem there would be the almost superhuman effort needed to climb without oxygen.

Andy was about a hundred metres from the top of the Couloir. All three were still in the shade. The cold would be eating away at their spirit. How good it felt to be in the sunshine.

Here at 8150 metres the Couloir was much narrower than it had been the day before. I climbed across to the middle and began to follow the crampon prints the others had left on the firm snow. I was a few steps up from the traverse when a barrage of ice bounced down and whistled by on either side of me. Looking up I could see that as Tim and Greg climbed diagonally right across the cliff, they were dislodging ice and snow from the holds. I was directly in the fall-line, and as I watched another volley came down. Time to move away from here, I thought.

The only safe place to be was on the right-hand edge of the Couloir. There the snow proved to be deep and unstable, and it was slow and tiring work plugging knee-deep

steps. The looseness of the snow kept me very much aware of the danger of the slope avalanching from beneath me. Almost an hour later I had gained enough height to move safely back to the solid snow in the middle of the Couloir.

"Lincoln!" Andy shouted from a short way up the Yellow Band. "I've broken a crampon. Can you ask the others to drop me a rope?"

From where he stood the others would not hear his cry. Since I was in sight of them I relayed his request. No reply. I yelled again.

"Not possible," came back the answer from Greg. "He's too far below us."

Our rope was thirty metres long and Tim, who had the rope, was more than twice that distance above Andy.

"No go, Andy," I called. "You'll have to manage on your own."

Tim emerged on the skyline, the difficulties beneath him now. A wave of triumph swept through me. Tim was still a long way from the summit, but I knew he would reach it. During the years we had climbed together his stamina and determination carried him through the toughest situations. Nothing would turn him back now. The only questions were how long it would take, and which of us would stand up there with him.

I checked my watch. It was two-thirty. In two and a half hours I had made the long traverse and climbed up a little under two hundred metres. There was not enough oxygen in my system to allow me to climb and think at the same time. I covered a few more metres to where I could kick good steps in which to rest and let my mind struggle with the calculations of how long it would take to reach the summit, 500-odd metres above, at my present speed. To my crippled brain the simple sums were as complex as Einstein's algebra. The answer came eventually and remained the same when I checked it. Six hours. That would put me on the summit an hour after dark. Frostbite would be a certainty on the descent, and the prospect of that was too awful to consider. The only other option was to descend. Now? Or higher up from somewhere which would still allow me to reach the tent before dark? I stared at the obstacle of the Yellow Band. Climbing that would be okay but descending alone, exhausted, would be unjustifiably dangerous. The safe way to come down this cliff was to abseil, and with only one rope between the four of us, we would all have to descend together. If I climbed up now I would have to wait till the others descended, probably in the dark. That alternative spelt frostbite as well.

Descent, then. Retreat without the prize. The others would take it for me – for us – and that was enough. Or almost enough. There were too many things to worry about for me to waste time contemplating the disappointment which would come later, and the envy I would feel because Tim, Greg and Andy managed what I could not.

Before heading down I decided I would stagger up the last few metres to the rock of the Yellow Band. I could manage only half a dozen steps at a time before I was forced to stop and gasp for breath. Any more than that and I burst into a coughing fit which almost suffocated me. There was no way I could climb faster than this. There was no way I could climb to the summit and return unscathed. Go down while you are still ahead, I told myself. The summit was not everything. Survival was.

I turned around to admire the view, and to lock it into my memory. Eight thousand, three hundred metres of air and earth beneath me. Clouds and mountains cluttered the small kingdom of Nepal. The brown hills of Tibet stretched for eternity to the north. Here and there a distant, snow-capped peak emphasised the enormity of the land. Over the top of Changtse I could make out the hollow which held Advance Base, and further down the valley – twenty kilometres away – was Base Camp. Strange to think of the others there waiting for news. Should I radio? I should, but it seemed too much effort to take the radio from my pack.

My daydreaming was interrupted by the familiar and frightening whir of ice ricocheting down the gully above me. Cricket-ball-sized pieces of ice flew past me on the way to the bottom of the Face. It was time to be gone.

Once I had traversed across to the left side of the Couloir I shouted to Andy that I was going down. There was a pause. I guessed he was summoning the breath to make a reply.

"Okay," he yelled back.

The others were out of sight. I decided to cross at this height then drop straight down to the tent so that I would get a good view of Andy, Tim and Greg, and be able to peer over the North Ridge into the East Rongbuk. After fifty metres I was forced to change my plan,

PRECEDING PAGES: Looking up the West Rongbuk to Cho Oyu from inside the Camp IV tent.

BELOW: Looking down the Rongbuk Valley from the top of the Great Couloir at 8300 metres. Advance Base is on the right near the top of the "S" of white ice where the Middle Rongbuk joins the main valley. Base Camp, twenty kilometres away, is near the tear-shaped pattern of moraine in the centre of the picture.

as the snow was dangerously unstable, waiting for an excuse to avalanche. Quickly I descended until I could cut back across into my ascent tracks. From there it was simply a matter of following my footsteps down, but even that was hard work in the thin air.

Back at the tent I shrugged my pack from my shoulders and sat on it. It was four o'clock. Looking up I could see that Andy had just reached the top of the Yellow Band. Tim and Greg did not seem to be far ahead of him. I radioed Camp I, sure that they would be eager for news. Through the huge telephoto of Mike's 16 mm camera they had watched my descent and would also be able to follow the others on their way to the summit. I talked to Geof who had recovered completely from his cerebral oedema.

"Only a catastrophe will stop Tim getting to the top," I said. "And hopefully the others will make it too. But it's so hard and the descent will be torture. I found it exhausting enough to descend the few hundred metres I climbed."

The angle of the sun made it difficult for me to see, so I relied on events being relayed to me via radio from Camp I. Later I listened to Tim's impressions of the climbing through the Yellow Band which he recorded with his miniature tape-recorder. His speech was prefaced by tremendous gasps for breath.

"... It almost seems impossible that we can go any further. We've just climbed out of the Great Couloir in a very, ah, unusual way ... not that it's been done very often .. but I suppose the need to get into the sun, more than anything else, forced us to choose this route – very, very steep for this altitude and very broken.

"At one point I thought I was going to fall, and a fall there would mean, well, you'd go to the bottom of the Face. Then above there was some quite loose slabs. Now we're hopefully above the difficult ground ... we've just got those 1500 feet to go.

"You do six steps and you're totally exhausted ... Breath just can't come out any faster. Your whole being is just absorbed in the task of breathing.

"It's a beautiful day, a perfect day. Not a breath of wind, a little bit of high cloud. I suppose it's getting on in the day ... must be about three o'clock. Plenty of puffy clouds all over Nepal, 1500 feet to go and it's three o'clock – can we make it in time? Who knows ... watching the sun, since my watch is covered up by clothing, the sun is the only way of telling. Anyway, that's the 'real' time."

He burst into a fit of coughing and switched off the recorder.

Meanwhile back at Camp IV, I sat absorbed in the view as the radio crackled with the noise of a conversation between Geof at Camp I and Simon at Advance Base.

Suddenly above me I spotted a bird, then another one. Within moments, soaring together on the updraft was a flock of a dozen or more.

Excitedly I grabbed the radio to tell whoever was listening.

"It's amazing! There's a dozen choughs up here. At twenty-seven thousand feet! Amazing!"

Perhaps below they thought I was hallucinating and no doubt found my excitement unexpected. But for me to see other creatures so jubilantly alive at this incredible altitude was proof of the worth of being in such an inhospitable environment.

I decided to make the tent more comfortable by building up the snow under the floor until it was level. That kept me busy for a couple of hours. Occasionally I would ask for progress reports over the radio. Everyone's speed had decreased markedly, but they continued to struggle on towards the summit. I began to worry. Even if they turned back now a large part of their descent to me in Camp IV would be in the dark.

There was nothing to be done but let the time pass. Geof had asked me to collect some rock samples for him from the Yellow Band. I was on my way to do so when an unexpected gust of wind picked up the tent. The rope-guys held it to the slope but for one horrific moment I imagined it breaking free and being blown across Tibet. Frail shelter though it was, its slight protection and the sleeping bags inside meant the difference between living and dying. In a panic I hurried back as quickly as the steep terrain would allow. I pegged it out more securely and crawled inside.

"Sorry about your rocks, Geof," I radioed. "But I have to stay inside to stop the tent blowing away." There was no need to add that none of us would get down if the tent with our sleeping bags disappeared.

Geof agreed that I had my priorities right, and told me that up near the summit the figure in front seemed to have stopped moving.

Greg reaches the top of the Yellow Band at 8500 metres, happy to emerge from the shaded steep ground into the sun, and to have the security of the rope dropped to him by Tim. Below, tracks lead to the red tent at Camp IV.

"Mind you they are only tiny dots, even through Mike's giant lens, so it's hard to know what's going on."

It turned out that Tim had stopped to wait for Greg, catch his breath and record more of what was happening. Again, as he tried to slow down his gasping for breath so that he could speak, he would lose control and cough violently. Each fit ended with frantic gulps for the oxygen he had been deprived of while he coughed. At last he was able to talk.

"This ... is going to be ... the hardest day of my life ... physically ... and mentally ... The summit is somewhere up there ... How far? I'm not quite sure ... but the sun is sinking fast and we've got to make it before sunset otherwise ... we'll miss out on the view ... and we won't be able to do any filming for Mr Hill either, will we? Greg is about ..., oh, ... 400 yards behind me, ... and Andy's coming up too, it seems ... From time to time we catch a glimpse of him.

"The view up here is absolutely just incredible. It's hard to believe I'm near the top of Mt Everest ... Two to four steps and you're exhausted ... but couldn't have asked for a more perfect day ... the odd gust comes through ... which, of course, is cold ... but it's just perfect compared to what it has been."

His speech was interrupted by another fit of coughing and he turned off his machine.

At 7.45 p.m. Tim and Greg reached the West Ridge. A couple of apparently insignificant rock bands had given more involved climbing than planned and that had slowed them down. But now the North Face had been climbed. The final snow slope to the summit took another half an hour. Just on sunset, shortly after eight o'clock, Greg and Tim stood on top of the world. I could not see them, but a jubilant Geof radioed from Camp I three thousand metres below.

"They're on the top! I can see two figures on the top!"

We had done it. Three years of planning, three months of climbing. Tears of anguish and joy; fears of death and of a more harmless failure. And so much more besides.

For Tim and Greg it was too soon for elation. That would come after the descent. The immediate feeling was of immense relief. The "up" was over. For a few minutes the top of the world was theirs. And for the first time I felt a twinge of disappointment that the events of this one vital day had made my share in the success so much less. Until now everything had been equal between us – the fear, the cold, the exhaustion, the magnificence of the mountains, the intense satisfaction of living and working together. All of us had known the same joy, the same suffering. But now the summit divided us into two categories: Tim, Greg and Andy who had proved themselves equal to the challenge, and Geof and I who had been beaten back. The summit was ours, the expedition combined had won it, but more particularly it was Tim's and Greg's, and very soon it seemed it would be Andy's as well.

The summit of Everest was such a special place that every action seemed steeped in ceremony. Greg held up an Australian republican flag, a Wilderness Society banner, and a Buddhist prayer flag, all tied to a string, while Tim took a photograph in the last of the light. Tim switched on his tape-recorder to capture the culmination of all our struggles. His attempts to speak were frustrated by coughs and the need to concentrate fully on breathing. Eventually he was able to say a few words on each out-breath and so gasp enough air to speak coherently.

"Well, this is the summit of Mt Everest ... Qomolangma ... Mother Goddess of the Earth. It's the most beautiful sunset I've ever seen ... and I'd like to thank everyone involved in making this expedition successful. Firstly, my parents, for giving me an organic upbringing ... Hello Dad, I didn't think I'd see you here ... and everyone else on the expedition who couldn't make it here this evening – our success is due to them as much as anyone else. And Narayan and Tenzing for looking after us so well down at Camp I and at Advance Base. And, of course, there's all the sponsors of the expedition ... I'd like to thank Sam Chisholm for believing we could do it.

"Everest ... is probably one of the wildest places on earth, yet I know at this moment there's four other expeditions attempting to climb the mountain ... The world's getting a small place. In Australia, we are lucky enough to have lots of space, and many beautiful wilderness areas ... but I wish Australians would take more care of their natural heritage. There are places right at this very moment that are threatened by despoliation and for no real, long-term reason. Places like South-West Tasmania, Cape Tribulation. These are very valuable parts of our natural heritage and will be considered even more valuable by future generations. If there is one thing that makes Australia Australian then it's the landscape, and I think every Australian should respect their landscape.

"The sun has set on every other peak apart from Everest, and it's just about to set on us. We've got a long way to go down tonight, but hopefully it's going to be okay ... going down a different way ... we'll avoid the steep rock band which we climbed this morning ... took so long ... we'll have a short abseil to do near the end. That's going to be interesting, 'cos we don't have much in the way of anchors to anchor the rope ... anyway, we'll sort that one out when we get to it ...

"Doesn't look like Andy's going to make it. He wasn't very far behind ... maybe half an hour or so. It's very hard to believe this is the summit of Everest, but it must be because as I said before there isn't any sun anywhere else ... Once again I'd like to thank everyone else on the expedition who couldn't make it here this evening, for helping get us here, and our success is every bit theirs.

"The world is absolutely staggeringly beautiful from up here. In fact, it's beyond superlatives. It seems so stupid that there are people out there engaged in contemplating things like nuclear war and I feel ashamed, as an Australian, that Australia has a part in the nuclear fuel cycle. A country such as Australia endowed with so many natural resources should devote more of its time to researching things like solar power, and certainly shouldn't endeavour to get a petty amount of money from selling a product like uranium. One thing's for sure ... if there ever is a nuclear war ... then Everest will certainly remain the wilderness that is."

He paused for breath, then added, perhaps as an afterthought, "I'm sorry you couldn't make it up here Lincoln ... but I know you're here in spirit."

Geof's announcement of the success sent a wave of triumph through the whole expedition which was reflected in the excited chatter on the radio between Camp I and Advance Base.

I interrupted to ask about Andy, and Geof replied.

"He's right on the West Ridge. That puts him about fifty vertical metres below the summit. From here it looks so bloody close. He seems to have stopped ... it looks as though he may have turned back ... but the light is really bad; it's hard to tell ..."

That is what happened. Andy had stopped to repair his broken crampon and had dropped further behind Tim and Greg. The ground immediately beneath his high point would be dangerous to descend at night, and as darkness fell he turned back. He was temptingly close to the summit but his priority was to survive.

Tim and Greg began their descent after twenty minutes on the top. They soon reached Andy who had slipped, stopped his fall, and sat recovering his strength. With only one headtorch between them they needed to stay close together. It was a dangerous time. Darkness and exhaustion exaggerated the already considerable difficulties. Instead of descending the route they had climbed, they came down the obvious continuation of the Couloir above the rock band, which would have been the best way up had the bottom thirty metres not been prohibitively steep. The steepness was not a problem on the way down because they could abseil. The only difficulty was in finding an anchor which was strong enough to hold someone's weight as he abseiled down the rope. In the end they buried one of the aluminium stiffening bars from Greg's pack in the slope and tied the rope to that.

Meanwhile, back at Camp IV, I waited. Both billies were full of water and simmering on the stoves. There was nothing more for me to do but relax and try not to worry. The weather report from Howard was as dismal as usual, so as usual I ignored it. At half past eleven I looked outside and saw, still above the abseil point, a lonely pinprick of light – their headlamp.

With great relief I radioed Howard. It was little news, but it ended our directionless speculation. It would be a few hours yet before they arrived back. I turned off the stoves and lay back to doze.

Some time later Tim called out. My immediate thought was that they needed help, but he was just establishing contact. I lay in my sleeping bag watching the candle burn down. The stub was all I could offer when, three hours later, Greg called out for light. He needed to work out where on the slope the tent was pitched. The candle was so far gone that it burnt itself out as I held it up to the slightly open door. It would have to do. I lit the stoves in preparation for their arrival.

Greg was first. I unzipped the door and he collapsed into the tent and lay sprawled across my legs.

"The others are okay?" I asked nervously as he lay there panting.

"... Yeah ..."

I hugged him and wept.

For a few minutes he could say nothing.

"It was hard ... so hard."

"But you did it, you clever bastards!"

"Yeah ... But what happened to you?"

I shrugged, "Too much of a body whip for a sane man like me."

Tim arrived next, so I hugged him as well. There was no need for words, emotion was enough.

And at last Andy staggered down absolutely exhausted. He could not find the breath to speak.

Tim spoke for him. "Andy's got frostbite ..."

The mountain had taken its price.

RIGHT: "On the summit of Qomolangma Greg held up an Australian republican flag, a Wilderness Society banner and a Buddhist prayer flag while Tim took a photograph in the last of the light."

FOLLOWING PAGES: From 8840 metres, Ama Dablam (in the foreground), Mera Peak and the peaks of the Hinku Valley break through the sea of cloud over Nepal.

BELOW: Looking south-west across the clouds and peaks of Nepal from the summit.

CHAPTER TWELVE

RETURN TO EARTH

I TOOK OFF Andy's gloves and looked at his fingers. The tips of all but his right-hand thumb felt wooden. The tissue was frozen, and thus destroyed. Some regeneration would occur, but at this stage it was impossible to judge the severity of the damage. Certainly we had no idea of the grim eventuality; a few months later parts of all his fingers would be surgically removed.

The issue at the moment was to decide the best treatment. It was not possible for us to lower him down or even hold him in balance with a rope, simply because the only rope we had carried up to this height had been unavoidably left behind on the abseil down the Yellow Band. Consequently Andy would have to climb down. During the return from the summit he had continually used his ice-axe so his hands were frozen into appropriately shaped "claws". His hands would have to remain frozen until he had made the 2000-metre descent to the glacier. If his fingers thawed now they would be unusable, and his attempts to climb down would increase the damage and probably result in further frostbite. It was so cold in the tent that keeping Andy's hands frozen was a simple matter of leaving them ungloved at the mouth of his sleeping bag. I radioed Camp I with the suggestion that Geof climb up to Camp II to meet us. It was unlikely we would be able to descend further than that on our first day.

The next priority was to make sure Tim, Greg and Andy drank as much as they could to offset the dehydration of their exhausting high-altitude push. All the pots and water-bottles we had with us were full of the water I had melted. The atmospheric pressure at 8150 metres was so low that the water boiled at a much lower temperature, and consequently our hot drinks cooled quickly. No one had any appetite so we lay down to sleep.

At that height I found the dark claustrophobic. Sleep was supposed to be a state of rest but instead, as I dozed and my respiratory rate dropped, I plunged into a frightening world of suffocation. Opening my eyes did not relieve the panic because the darkness continued. There was nothing for my mind to hang on to in the swirling blackness; I breathed violently and deeply until at last I calmed down. Sleep was impossible so I lay in my sleeping bag and considered our situation.

LEFT: An evening storm in the West Rongbuk.
ABOVE: "It was time for joy to begin to surface, and to start to wallow in the delights of being alive."
Stream detail, Nepal.

A photograph taken in Lhasa shows the extent of Andy's frostbite. In February 1985 his fingers were amputated near the first knuckle.

My three friends seemed to be able to sleep. Exhaustion ruled them completely. Greg in particular had not moved since crawling into his sleeping bag. In a few hours it would be dawn. Hopefully Andy would be able to descend without assistance; if he could not the descent would be doubly difficult and dangerous. It was ludicrous to be near the top of the highest mountain in the world with no rope at all, but for our small team, everything we carried had to be justified. With forty-five years of climbing experience between the four of us we felt confident we could climb most obstacles safely without a rope. The extra speed from having light loads gave a greater safety factor than the inherent security of slower roped climbing. Now we faced the consequences of our decision.

With the first light I was able to sleep. When the panic of suffocation overcame me I could stop it by opening my eyes, and thus see I was still safe in the tent. Being able to make that orientation was sufficient to allow me to overcome the panic and drift into sleep.

At ten o'clock I awoke. It was time to get ready to leave. The first chore was to stock up on fluid so I roused everyone and cleared a space on the floor for the stoves. Greg remained virtually unconscious; grunts were his only answers to questions. For an hour or more we lay there as I piled snow in the billies to make a continual relay of hot drinks. Tim and I talked while the others dozed.

"Okay," I said at last. "Let's get ourselves organised and out of here."

Being fonder of bed than of anywhere else it was most unusual for me to make the morning's first move. Today, though, as the person with the most strength and the clearest head, I needed to set the example. When I had put on my down suit and packed I helped Andy. With frozen hands he could not put on his harness, boots, crampons, nor his clothing. Tim meanwhile had got ready and began to pack Andy's rucksack. Everything except Andy's survival gear was left for the rest of us to share. The easier it was for Andy to balance, the safer he would be. Some of his fingers had blistered already which meant I had to slit his gloves before his fingers would fit inside.

He talked of what had happened. "Above the Yellow Band I stopped to fix my crampon. I took off my gloves except for the last layer, and because I was working with metal my fingers got incredibly cold. I suppose that was when I got frostbitten. I managed to put on my fibre-pile gloves but I couldn't pull my overmitts on again, so I kept going without them."

"But surely Tim or Greg would have put them on for you."

"Yes ...," and he paused to think "It was dark when they reached me and, well, I forgot. You know what your mind is like up here when all your energy goes into physical effort."

Andy tested his grip on his ice-axe. It was secure. I unzipped the door and helped him outside.

"We'll catch you up soon," I said as he started climbing down.

"He doesn't seem to be having too much trouble," said Tim. "Thank God for that."

I turned to Greg who was still in his sleeping bag. "Come on, you lazy bugger."

He groaned and sat up.

I warmed my fingers in my crutch and watched Greg. He was usually quick to get ready and sometimes irritated at having to wait. Tim and I assumed he had been lying there until Andy's departure left some space in the cramped tent. It was soon apparent that his slowness was due to something more serious than that. His movements were awkward and slow and his attempts to put his crampons on were very clumsy. Though I had wanted to keep my fingers warm I grabbed his crampon and fastened it to his boot.

"Thanks," he muttered.

"Here, give me the other one."

Tim, meanwhile, stuffed away the few odds and ends that Greg had neglected to pack.

"Pass me your sleeping mat," said Tim.

Greg moved from a sitting position onto his knees. The sharp points of his crampons tore the floor of the tent as if he had forgotten they were on his feet. He rolled up the thin foam pad to where his knees pinned it down, and seemed annoyed that it would not continue to roll. It was as if his knees, pressing into the middle of the mat, did not exist. I shot a horrified glance at Tim. He was watching in glum amazement.

"Here, Greg. Get off it," I said. "Let me do it."

Greg sat on the floor, his crampons tearing the fabric again.

Tim and I had a major problem on our hands. At best, severe exhaustion had left Greg in a sleepy stupor; at worst he had cerebral oedema. Many climbers had died of that illness at these altitudes because their companions did not have the strength to help them down. We did not even have a rope.

Tim radioed Jim at Camp I to say that we were on our way down, and to ask advice about Greg's condition.

"Bring him down! Just get the hell out of there! Get down or he'll die."

It was hardly the message of reassurance we needed.

I immediately started off with Greg. There was no time to strike the tent, and no energy to carry the extra weight. The next bout of strong winds would blow it to shreds. The time was four o'clock, four hours after I had hoped to leave. Andy was just a tiny spot near the bottom of the main part of the Couloir. Looking up I could see that Greg was following me very slowly. Tim was still in the tent, having remained behind for reasons I did not commit to memory.

My mind was filled with more important things, such as the incredible urgency that had come with the realisation that Greg was no longer able to look after himself. At any minute I expected him to topple over and plunge to the bottom of the Face, but I had forgotten to take into account his exceptional abilities as a climber. Over the years his climbing had become as automatic as reflexes. Now, he was moving slowly but with a confidence which belied his mental state.

We climbed down to the Couloir, out of the sun and into the cold. A stiff breeze swirled across the wide gully. Though the avalanche danger was greater I moved back to the edge of the Couloir where the snow was softer but still in the sun. Greg was frustratingly slow. I hurried ahead to where I could shelter from the wind beside a rock. Tim was coming down now, and soon overtook Greg.

He reached me and stopped to talk. "Greg's really slow."

"I know."

"I need to get down. I don't want to spend another night up here."

I knew what he was saying. I sighed inwardly then said, "Okay, you go down, and I'll stay with Greg."

If Greg fell, that was the end of it. Otherwise, one of us could look after him as well as two. I well understood Tim's desire to get off the mountain. I felt the same, but since my early retreat had left me with greater reserves of strength it made sense that I should stay with Greg.

"You've got to hurry, Greg!" Tim shouted up to him.

"See you when it's all over," I said.

Tim smiled and started down, his determination and strength showing with every step. His endurance never ceased to amaze me. The man had just climbed Everest without oxygen and now, the following day, planned to descend all the way to Camp I. And I knew he would do it.

Greg drew level.

"How's it going?"

"Okay," he mumbled.

"Well, let's keep going. We really have to hurry."

Greg nodded but continued at the same slow pace.

A few hundred metres lower we escaped from the worst of the wind. I sat and stared at the panorama. At last I viewed the magnificence of the mountains with acceptance rather than awe. Greg caught up and stopped a short way above me. We had been descending for over an hour but were not even halfway to Camp III. What a huge mountain this was.

From there Greg and I moved down at almost the same speed. He had little energy to spare but now seemed to be much more alert, a fact which gave me hope that his problem was exhaustion rather than deadly cerebral oedema. Tim was out of sight, but far below we could see Andy abseiling the ropes down White Limbo. At least he and Tim would reach Camp II that night. As the sun sank lower in the sky it was looking more and more likely that Greg and I would not make it past Camp III. Even so, the 700-metre altitude drop from Camp IV would make a great deal of difference to how well we rested.

About a hundred metres above Camp III I tended too far to the left, onto hard, icy snow. On such ground it is much easier to over-balance, and to stop a fall would be almost impossible. Consequently I halved my speed, then decided it was not worth the risk, and traversed the fifty metres back to easier ground.

Meanwhile Greg, who had remained on the softer snow, overtook me so I continued down about ten metres behind him. The slope steepened for the last hundred metres down to the crevasse where we had made Camp III a few days earlier. We had climbed down this far facing out from the slope, heels dug in and using an ice-axe in the fashion of a walking stick. There was a point where the slope was too steep to allow that technique, and one needed to take the slower option of kicking toes into the snow, and jabbing an ice-axe into the slope as a handhold. As the slope reaches the crucial angle, facing outwards becomes increasingly insecure.

Greg was moving steadily and apparently quite under control when suddenly he caught his right crampon on his left boot and tripped, falling forward and somersaulting down the slope. Horror-struck, I stopped and stared. There was nothing I could do but watch him slide towards the edge of the huge ice cliffs and certain death below. After a couple of somersaults he managed to roll onto his stomach and dig into the snow with the pick of his ice-axe. It pulled through without slowing him down at all. In desperation he used the shaft of his ice-axe and finally managed to stop. He lay motionless against the slope.

"Are you okay?"

"Yeah," came the shaky reply.

This is too much, I told myself, we are getting too close to the edge. As Greg slowly began to move again, I swung my pack off my shoulders and unstrapped my ice-hammer. It was time for caution. Although only a spectator I trembled from Greg's tumble. The sun had set just as Greg fell. It was as if the two most important things in my life at that instant had fallen away from me. Greg had been reprieved; but the sun had gone. Thoughts of how close I had come to spending a night alone on the mountain were put aside as I began to concentrate on climbing down. I faced into the slope with an ice-tool in each hand. It was much slower and needed more energy, but the extra safety of the technique made me feel immeasurably more secure.

The sunset was incredibly beautiful. The rugged skyline was softened by clouds crowding the lower peaks in Nepal. It grew dark quickly. I did not want to stop and replace my prescription sunglasses with my spectacles since the effort of kicking a ledge and removing my mittens so that I could rummage for my glasses was too great. It was better to continue as fast as I could and hope to reach camp while I could still see. Unfortunately it was further to our crevasse than I had remembered. I took off my sunglasses and let them hang around my neck. Short-sighted in the semi-darkness I found it impossible to judge the size of the ice cliffs around the crevassed area. My memory could not tell me much; either the cliffs were very small and close at hand or large and further away. My concern was because I was at the top of a steep section which would be okay to descend if short, but dangerously tiring if long. I took the safest option of climbing back up and across, then dropping down on easier-angled ground. I had enough spare energy for a smile when I realised from below that the steep part had been only three metres high. I had guessed thirty!

I began to wonder about Greg. Had he gone ahead, missing our crevasse in the bad light, or had he fallen, this time unable to stop? I was saved the agony of worry by his shout, which was alarmingly close.

There he was, only ten metres away standing on the lip of the crevasse. "I thought maybe you'd try to reach Camp II tonight," he said.

I bent over my ice-axe to gather some breath to speak. "Not today. Not in the dark. It's too cold, too far, and I'm too buggered."

"Yeah, so am I."

Behind him the snow was glowing from the diffused light of the candle he had lit in the crevasse.

"Not much of a beacon, is it?"

We crawled inside and lay back exhausted until, after only a minute or two, the cold prompted us to unpack our sleeping bags. We stretched out on the ledge we had dug three days before. Greg seemed very much more aware and in control of himself as we set up the stoves in the space between us, and began the long process of melting snow.

It was about ten o'clock by the time we were sufficiently organised to sit back and radio the others.

From Camp II Geof joked with us that the meal he had prepared for us would now be wasted.

"Just bring it up the ropes, Geof," I said in reply.

Andy had abseiled down to Camp II and was firmly ensconced in his sleeping bag being waited upon by Geof. Tim had reached the base of the Face and was about to ski down the glacier to Camp I with Howard. Everything had gone according to plan apart from the fact that Greg and I were six hundred metres above the snow cave in a much less comfortable camp.

After our cramped tent at Camp IV, our four-person-sized ledge in the crevasse at Camp III seemed luxurious. Greg soon dozed off to sleep. The wall to my left was of ice, so I had to disturb Greg and ask him to dig some snow from the wall on his side. He grunted then went back to sleep. Five minutes of cajoling culminating in persistent prodding with the snow-shovel was needed before Greg sat up and dug snow for our drinks. In the process he knocked one stove over. The lukewarm water poured down my arm and froze almost instantly on the outside of the sleeve of my down suit. I said nothing. Clumsiness was easy when exhausted at this altitude. As he settled in his sleeping bag again he knocked over the second pot, this time onto my sleeping bag.

I could not help but curse him, especially when he was reluctant to sit up and get more snow to replace the wasted water.

Having assured Jim at Camp I by radio that Greg was almost his normal self, I began to doubt my judgment. In a situation such as our descent from Camp IV, where a lapse of concentration could be fatal, Greg had held himself together. Now, when the demands upon him were less immediately directed to his survival, he had no energy to spare for them. It was good that he rested. Tomorrow he would need all of his reserves.

We both slept well that night though my cold feet did not warm up at all. When I had finished cooking our basic meal at one in the morning, Greg straight away vomited his onto the snow. My patience ran out, even for the important task of warming my feet.

At 6900 metres in the snow cave at Camp II we had slept well, but above that height, lack of oxygen prevented proper sleep. For the last three nights we had done no more than doze, and though our bodies relaxed they did not gather strength. Each day it was harder to overcome lethargy and marshall some momentum. The end was close; one more demanding day and we would be down.

I was woken shortly before dawn by Greg preparing to light the stoves. My first thought was that my feet were still numb. I had been stupid not to warm them the night before. At worst, I would have minor frostbite which would not inconvenience me until we were off the mountain, and that was not an issue to worry about right now. Greg could not remember where he had put the cigarette lighter so we dozed again until first light when I found another lighter in my pack.

Thirsty though he was, that morning it was even more difficult to rouse Greg into shoveling snow into the "kitchen" space between us. As I prepared breakfast, I radioed Camp II where Geof was cooking and Andy was fast asleep. Geof would descend with Andy to help at those places on the fixed ropes where he needed to use his hands. Jim and Colin would come up to the bottom of the Face with Colin's sled and our one oxygen set, since immediate treatment might help save Andy's fingers.

Breakfast made Greg nauseous again. He leant his head over the crevasse, ready to vomit but trying desperately to keep the small amount of food down. Being short of oxygen, sleep and food for several days, left us dangerously weak. It was important that we take as much nourishment as our bodies would accept, and that was a miserably small amount.

Shortly before the sun reached the crevasse at midday, we began to descend. Greg had been slow but had managed to dress and pack without assistance. Now he climbed down slightly ahead of me, no doubt keenly aware of how close he had come to death the previous evening.

The sun shone but it was bitterly cold. It seemed that we had made our summit bid at exactly the right time. The strong winds which had begun to blow again gave us added incentive to descend as quickly as possible. First of all we had to make the long traverse across the top of White Limbo to the fixed ropes. The ropes had become frozen into the slope again, and neither of us wished to expend the energy needed to pry them out. We had been climbing ropeless for over three days now, so having a rope nearby offered a security greater than we were accustomed to. Just the same, it was a great relief, a short distance below, to be able to clip into the rope halfway down White Limbo. The rope would catch us if we fell. Now we were safe, so long as we continued to exercise the same caution and attention to detail which had become second nature to us over the last two months. The problem was to prevent our tiredness interfering with our common-sense.

Our plan had been to take all our equipment down from the mountain. It was obvious we did not have the strength for that, but we did manage to retrieve the three hundred metres of rope which ran up the slope above Camp II. At the snow cave, Greg sat inside with the stove, thawing the frozen pot of tea Geof had made for us before he had descended with Andy. I sat outside coiling endless lengths of rope and stuffing them into a kitbag. I stuffed our down suits in as well, bound the bag firmly, then called Greg outside onto the narrow ledge so he could share in the ceremony of throwing the kitbag down the remaining thousand metres of the Great Couloir. Since Andy's pack had survived being dropped from almost this height a few weeks before, and Jim had repeated the act through exhaustion rather than accident, it now seemed the logical way to clear Camp II. That morning Geof had packed up and thrown off everything at Camp II apart from the stove and the frozen pot of tea, leaving only the rope and the non-essential climbing gear we had carried down for us to jettison. The kitbag bounced down the slope then disappeared over a cliff in a frightening imitation of a falling person. At least that was the image which came to my mind. Carefully I stepped back from the edge and clipped onto the rope.

"Okay Greg," I said. "Are you ready to go?"

He nodded.

"I'll go ahead and see you at the bottom of the Face. Is that okay?"

"Sure," he replied.

"Just make sure you start as soon as I'm off this rope. It's four o'clock now and we are both going really slowly. Okay?"

"Okay."

My main worry was that he would sit down here and go to sleep until the cold of the sunset woke him. If he began the descent now I was confident the abseiling would keep him alert.

"See you down there," I said, and quickly abseiled over the edge.

It was good to be going down over familiar ground where the dangers and difficulties were known. Also good, was the capability to abseil and at the same time think clearly and quickly. The few hours' descent from Camp III to Camp II had brought us to air which, though hardly rich in oxygen, offered enough of the vital gas to allow me to feel approximately normal again. Looking up, I could see that Greg was following me as planned, so there was no need to wait.

Despite my wish to hurry, my muscles did not have enough strength left for me to move quickly. I was content to go down slowly. There was time on the long abseils between anchors to think about our feat. We had done it, climbed a new route on Mt Everest without oxygen; a first, a real mountaineering coup. But of more importance in my mind was the thought that this was our last day on the mountain. No more painful load-carrying up the fixed ropes, no more cold feet and hands, no more worrying about the fickle mountain weather. From now on, back in Australia or away in the mountains, Mt Everest would never be the same. Gone was the air of mystery which had surrounded the mountain during our years of planning. Gone were the doubts of whether our small team was equal to the challenge. Gone was the fear that I might not return from the largest, most impersonal, but somehow most inviting graveyard of all.

At each of the anchor points I needed to interrupt my train of thought to swap my abseiling tool from one rope to the next. I remembered only too clearly the descent Tim, Andy and I had made from the summit of Ama Dablam in Nepal, where in the dark I had not noticed my waist karabiner undone. Only luck had saved me from falling to my death. Luck cannot be taken for granted. More than a fair share of it had come my way in the mountains. Nowadays I expected a run of bad luck, so I acted with an appropriate excess of caution.

An exception came at the large crevasse at the bottom of the Face. Our rope led down and across a flimsy snow bridge. A quicker and more exciting alternative would be to jump the gap. I edged towards the lip and peered into the bottomless chasm. It looked considerably less inviting a prospect from close up. I could retrace my steps, but there would be no other opportunity to regain the self-respect I would lose by backing out. It would be like climbing down the ladder from the high diving board. So I jumped. I landed with my ice-axe in the steep downhill slope but my feet did not grip on the ice, and shot out from underneath me. I was left hanging by one hand from my ice-axe. Quickly, I pulled up and carefully climbed across to easier ground. My heart was full of laughter as I descended the avalanche cone to the glacier. One last thrill. Silly perhaps, but what the heck?

What I thought to be several people sitting in a bunch on the glacier, turned out to be Colin waiting with the pile of gear that had been thrown down from Camp II.

He walked towards me and hugged me. Another down alive. "Well done! Welcome back!"

Back to the world of the living, to the world of people beyond our small expedition, to the beginning of the rest of my life. At last I could afford to relax my concentration enough to think about those things. There was no rush but it would be good to get home.

But meanwhile we had to wait for Greg who was still several hundred metres up the Face. I sat on my pack and drank lukewarm tea from Colin's thermos.

"How's Greg?" he asked.

"Okay when he's climbing, except really slow. But in camp he's been really vague. I think he is so burnt out that he doesn't have any energy left to think."

I considered my words and realised I had painted a very gloomy portrait.

"He's all right, really," I qualified. "He just needs a couple of weeks on the beach."

Back down on the glacier below the Face, Lincoln talks to Tim about the last part of the descent with Greg.

Colin nodded and stared up at the small dot slowly following the ropes down.

Tim arrived from Camp I on skis looking a little weary but in great shape considering the rigours of the last few days. We sat and talked for a while as shadows crept up the mountain. Soon it would be dark, and there remained the few kilometres to Camp I. Colin had brought my skis up from the Stash. Gratefully I changed into my ski-boots and stepped onto my skis. Tim, Colin and Mike (who waited at the Stash) would escort Greg down. I needed to get to Camp I where I could lie down and drink my fill of whatever Narayan and Tenzing could give me.

Directly below the Stash was the steepest part of the glacier. Normally I tried to ski it, often falling on the turns as I zig-zagged down between the crevasses. Today I was too exhausted to want to pick myself out of the snow, and my legs felt as if they would buckle under the strain of carving the turns. I removed my skis and walked down the slope to where the angle eased again. By then it was completely dark, and already the peaks of Lingtren and Khumbutse were lit with moonlight. I remembered that today or tomorrow was the night of the full moon. Tim, Colin and Greg would have good light to travel by. Meanwhile I skied along slowly, all my tired muscles tensed to absorb the bumps as I tried to judge the angle and my speed over the ice in the darkness. I slid to a stop as I crested a small rise. The snow around me was rapidly losing its blackness. The distinct line between the mountain's shadow and the white light of the moon seemed to sweep towards me as I stared. I turned around in time to see the tip of the full moon rise directly over Everest's summit.

I could not believe my eyes, yet the unbelievable was definitely happening. The moon rose huge and bright over the apex of the mountain we had just climbed. The snow around me glistened as particles of ice threw the light up at me. The irritability which had been growing with my tiredness disappeared. How could anything be wrong in this most magnificent of settings? Awe filled my being, not with fear or insignificance, but with the warmth of belonging, of being a part of something so beautiful.

I turned around and skied along the well-lit slope. The moonrise could not have been better timed, nor could I have been better placed to appreciate it. The coincidence of those events left me feeling privileged, because I had survived the impersonal strength of the mountain, and had been given such a breathtakingly beautiful scene for my farewell. No longer did my weariness annoy me. The short rests I took every few minutes were not merely delays between me and the comfort of Camp I, but chances to admire the perfection of the night.

At nine o'clock I reached Camp I exhausted. Tenzing heard me take off my skis so he came to carry my pack the last fifty metres to the camp.

"Congratulations," he muttered in the soft voice he reserved for speaking English.

I thumped him on the back a little powerlessly and laughed.

At the camp I collapsed into the mess tent. The tea Narayan immediately gave me was frustratingly too hot to drink. Having smelt its steam I could hardly bear to wait till it cooled.

"It's all over now, youth," said Jim with a huge grin as he and Geof crawled into the tent.

"It sure is."

"Sounded hard up there," said Geof. "It was more than hard enough where I got to."

"How's Andy?" I asked.

"Sleeping like a log," said Jim. "It's difficult to know about his hands for a while yet, but they're pretty bad."

We sprawled in the tent and drank endless cups of tea while we talked about what had happened. Narayan and Tenzing produced a marvellous meal, but my only appetite was for sleep, and to see Mike, Colin, Tim and Greg return to camp. They staggered in at about eleven o'clock. Greg could barely stand, but found the breath to joke about what an epic it had been.

It was eight days since we had left this camp for the summit. During that time, keeping alive our faith in our ability to succeed and survive had been an enormous psychological drain. The sheer physical effort had almost crippled us. It was time for the joy to begin to surface, and to start to wallow in the delights of being alive.

The first real pleasure was to become familiar again with the feeling of good solid sleep. In the tent which I shared with Tim, I could barely summon the strength to undress and crawl into my sleeping bag. The ground was flat and the air was smooth to breath; sleep came at once.

The next thing I knew, Tim was shaking me awake. Narayan was crouched in the doorway with the kettle and behind him was the soft, blue light of morning.

Tim poked a steaming cup of black, honey-sweetened tea at me. I sat up and shook my head.

"Where did the night go?" I grumbled, "I could sleep for days."

Tim laughed softly and put his arm around me.

"There'll be plenty more nights."

PRECEDING PAGES: Andy, Geof, Jim and Mike walk back down to Camp I after the climb. The late afternoon sun highlights the crevasses and our ski tracks.
FOLLOWING PAGES: The truck loaded with our gear follows as we drive away from Base Camp. Though Qomolangma dominates the skyline it no longer rules our lives.

Memories feed nostalgia but not the soul. Everest is not the ultimate: other mountains await; life goes on.

EPILOGUE

"Why on earth do you climb mountains?" People ask me so often that the question now rings unspoken in my ears. I look at my shoes or out of the window and wonder why I cannot reply. Only today, sitting here while the rain falls, do I appreciate the reason for my inability to explain: now is afterwards, and so my hunger has gone. Today a photograph of a mountain leads my practised eye to pick out a route, but there is no quickening of my heart as I imagine climbing the steep ice-face.

Comfortably alive and back in Australia, I ask myself why I spent two months of my life risking storms, rockfalls and avalanches while, on the Nepalese side of the mountain, five people from three expeditions died attempting the same feat. The secret of survival is to be able to judge precisely what one's limits are, and to have the determination and discipline to push oneself that far and no further. The temptation to reach just a little beyond one's ability is great, but the penalty is final. Though I shall never see the summit panorama other than through the eyes and hearts of Tim and Greg, I know that no view is worth that price.

The history books will remember our climb because two of our team stood on the top of the world. As with every expedition our overt goal was to reach the summit. Yet as each climb progresses I realise that it is not the summit that brings me to the Himalaya but the need to relearn the value and beauty of existence. Not only my existence, but that of the mountains, the sky, the friendship with my companions. But those rewards do not come from simply looking at the mountains. One must accept their challenge and try to touch their peaks. During the attempt, danger and hardship strip away all pretence and self-delusion. And the realisation grows that the only thing which keeps one alive is the strength of one's spirit.

When I have the time to be alone with my thoughts I can understand why I climb. But what can I say to the person who expects the answer in a single phrase? How do I tell someone who expects me to speak of fame and glory that it is really a trip into myself? How do I explain that sometimes there needs to be more to life than comfort and pleasure, that fear and suffering can reveal another dimension? And, hardest of all, how do I explain the reason for two deaths which in no way seem warranted?

Less than a week after the first Australians trod Everest's summit Craig Nottle and Fred From fell to their deaths from high on the West Ridge. As we left the mountain we had hoped that their expedition would echo our success. Now the echo rings hollow and horrific.

The mountain had cast the same spell on climbers from both teams. It had given existence a purpose. At the time when life meant most it was taken away. In its place is a vacuum and the unforgettable grief of loved ones who stayed at home. For Fred and Craig life was not muffled by fear but enhanced by it. Their final expedition gave them feelings and experiences of an intensity that few people who live to three times their age will know.

High on Everest, the line between success and tragic failure is very fine. As it was, three of our team of five climbed the mountain (Andy will not be recorded in the statistics of Summiteers but, to our minds, fifty metres from the top of the 8848-metre peak is good enough) and we all survived. The loss of Andy's fingers seriously mars our triumph, and shows again just how small are the margins between the completely unscathed, the incapacitated and the dead.

So now I feel like a survivor. The clearest view in the world is when your head is on the block, and once your head has been there the view stays in your mind for a long time. Friendships are deeper, the sunshine warmer, there is value in everything. As I sit here the rain is not spoiling the weekend but dancing across the road to nourish the grass and shrubs in the park. Being alive has never felt so good, though all I do is sit and watch the rain.

Lincoln Hall Manly, 26 October 1984

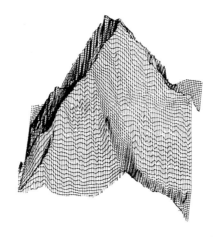

BIOGRAPHIES OF EXPEDITION MEMBERS

CLIMBING TEAM

GEOF BARTRAM (33), born in Port Augusta, South Australia, but latterly of Queanbeyan, New South Wales, works as a mountain guide and climbing instructor in New Zealand, the United States, Nepal, India and (his second home) the Peruvian, Bolivian and Ecuadorean Andes. He has completed difficult ascents in all these countries. He was a member of the 1980 Australian Annapurna III Expedition (Nepal), the 1981 Australian Mt Anyemaqen Expedition (China), co-leader of the 1982 Australian-American Expedition to Trisul (India), and leader of the remarkably successful Andean Pumori Expedition (Nepal) when all seven members reached the summit of the peak.

LINCOLN HALL (28) was born in Canberra. In 1976 he completed a B.Sc. degree in Zoology at the Australian National University. Rather than following a career in that field, his love of mountains and climbing led him to work as a mountaineering and trekking guide. He has rockclimbed in Australia for the past thirteen years; mountaineered in New Zealand and South America; and taken part in expeditions to India (Dunagiri, 1978; Kulu Himal, 1979; Trisul, 1982), Nepal (Ama Dablam, 1981; Annapurna II, 1983) and China (Mt Anyemaqen, 1981).

ANDREW HENDERSON (28) of Sydney is a computer engineer, a graduate of the University of New South Wales, whose most recent work was for CSIRO at the radio telescope in Parkes, New South Wales. His climbing experience includes rockclimbing in Australia and Britain, mountaineering in the New Zealand and European Alps, and expeditions to Changabang in India (1977), Mt Anyemaqen in China (1981), Ama Dablam (1981) and Annapurna II (1983) in Nepal.

TIM MACARTNEY-SNAPE (28) of Greta, Victoria, is a director of the adventure travel company Wilderness Expeditions. He was born and spent the first twelve years of his life in Tanzania and graduated from the Australian National University in 1979 with a degree in Biological Sciences. Since then he has worked on his family farm in Victoria, and as a mountaineering, skiing and trekking guide. Rockclimbing in Australia and mountaineering in New Zealand provided the background that was needed for the expeditions he has made to Dunagiri (1978), Kulu Himal (1979), Ama Dablam (1981), Mt Anyemaqen (1981), Trisul (1982) and Annapurna II (1983).

GREG MORTIMER (32), from Sydney, is a geologist whose work since his graduation from Macquarie University has led him to many remote places in Australia and into the mountains of New Zealand and Antarctica. His dedication to climbing has taken him all over the world. He has made difficult climbs in Australia, New Zealand, Africa, Britain, Europe, Nepal, North and South America. Most impressive are ascents of Yerupaja and Pyramide in the Peruvian Andes, Mt Kenya's Diamond Couloir, and the South Spur of Annapurna II with the 1983 Australian Expedition.

LOBSANG TENZING SHERPA (24) is from the Helambu region of Nepal where he spent nine years in a monastery studying Tibetan Buddhism. Since then he has worked in Nepal's thriving tourist industry both as a guide and as a cook. He has taken part in the Australian expeditions to Ama Dablam (1981) and Annapurna II (1983).

NARAYAN SHRESTA (24) was born near the town of Dhulikel in Nepal's Kathmandu Valley. His profession as a trekking sirdar (foreman) and high-altitude guide has taken him throughout the Himalaya; to the summits of Mrigthuni and Devistan in India; and high on the slopes of Trisul and Sudershan in India, Gaurishankar, Himalchuli, Ama Dablam and Annapurna III in Nepal. He reached the summit of Pumori, an outlier of Everest, as a member of the 1984 Andean Expedition.

247

FILM CREW

MICHAEL DILLON, film producer and cameraman, was born and raised in Sydney. He studied Arts at Sydney University while working part-time for a film company. He shot his first film in Timor in 1972, which was followed in 1973 by the very successful "A Himalayan Journey", shot in Nepal. Since then he has worked as a freelance cameraman, specialising in filming adventurous activities such as swimming the English Channel and hang-gliding from the summit of Kilimanjaro. His particular love is the Himalaya, where he has shot eleven films. He has worked with Sir Edmund Hillary to produce four films: "The Ocean to the Sky" in India, "Return to Everest" and "Beyond Everest" in Nepal, and "A Journey to the Dawning of the Day" in Fiji. He is undoubtedly Australia's most accomplished cinematographer in the field of adventure film-making.

JIM DUFF (39) is from Kendal in the United Kingdom. He began rockclimbing at the age of fourteen, and since then he has climbed widely in Britain, Norway, the European Alps, North America, New Zealand and Australia. He has taken part in several expeditions, most notably to Changabang in the India Himalaya, K2 (the world's second highest peak) in the Karakoram in Pakistan, and was a climbing doctor on the South-West Face of Everest when it was first climbed in 1975. He studied medicine at Liverpool University and has practised in Britain, Nepal and Australia. He has travelled widely but now lives in Hobart with his wife and daughter where he practises naturopathic medicine.

COLIN MONTEATH (35) spent his early childhood in Glasgow, Scotland, where he was born, moving to Australia with his parents at the age of nine. In 1972 he graduated from Sydney University with a B.Sc. in Agriculture. He has worked as a Soil Conservation Officer in Australia and as a National Park worker and mountain guide at Mt Cook in New Zealand. For the ten years preceding the Everest Expedition he worked for the New Zealand DSIR Antarctic Division, mostly as Field Operations Officer, based in Christ- church but with many trips to Antarctica. He has been a climber for nineteen years, first rockclimbing in Australia, then mountaineering at a high standard in New Zealand, Peru, Canada and Antarctica. In 1980 he was climbing leader on the Australian Annapurna III Expedition, and in 1982 took part in a smaller, more adventurous expedition to the Garhwal Himalaya in India. He lives with his wife and two daughters in Christchurch, where he works as a free-lance writer and photographer.

HOWARD WHELAN (31) grew up in Bountiful, Utah, where he began skiing at an early age. He skied professionally for twelve years, racing in the United States, competing in freestyle events in the United States, Canada, and Europe, and skiing the Haute Route in Europe. His climbing experience was gained on mountains in the United States and Mexico. In 1973, he and two companions became the second party to walk the 4200-kilometre Pacific Crest Trail from Canada to Mexico, a feat which took five months. He has worked as an avalanche controller in Utah, a freelance writer and photographer, and an adventure sports writer for a Seattle newspaper. More recently he has worked in the television and film industry as a commentator and cameraman. For the last few years he has been living in Sydney with his Australian wife and their daughter.

JOURNALIST

SIMON BALDERSTONE (30) grew up in Victoria's Western District. He studied Arts at Monash University before joining the "Age" as a reporter. After an apprenticeship in Melbourne he headed the "Age" Bureau in Sydney for two years, then worked in Canberra for five years as a political correspondent. He is now back in Melbourne writing a sports column. The Expedition was well pleased with the accuracy and sensitivity of his report, and we were delighted when, after the climb, he came runner-up (to his boss!) in the Journalist of the Year awards. With a strong sporting and walking background, he also works as a part-time trekking guide, having visited the Kashmir Himalaya every year since 1980.

EQUIPMENT

One of the most important considerations for any Himalayan expedition is careful selection of equipment, from simple things like pots and stoves to the most sophisticated climbing gadgetry. As a small team attempting a new route on Mt Everest, our preparation needed to be particularly thorough. We did not have the resources to carry more than essentials on the mountain, so each item had to be foolproof, lightweight and as versatile as possible. Nevertheless we needed to equip ourselves well enough to be able to deal with every imaginable type of climbing obstacle, since once we left Australia we would not be able to buy any climbing gear at all. At least one of us had climbed before with virtually every item we took. We were reluctant to take anything solely on someone else's recommendation.

Our clothing was made to our specifications by Verglas, the manufacturing label for Mountain Designs. After our climb of Annapurna II we made many alterations, mostly to reduce the total weight of what we carried. A hundred grams here and there added up to a worthwhile saving.

Our principle of dress was to have many layers in order to be as versatile as possible. Next to our skin we wore thermal underwear made by North Cape, Peter Storm or Damart, depending upon personal preference. The difference between Peter Storm and North Cape was mostly in cut rather than performance. Damart, on the other hand, was much warmer (though heavier), so most of us wore Damart for the summit push.

The next layer was a full fibre-pile suit made by Mountain Designs. The suit had full-length arms and legs, and a semi-circular zip in the seat. Handwarming pockets with openings on the side were sewn on the chest, so that they could be used while wearing a harness. The suits were not personally tailored and were a trifle large for everyone but me. Tim found the best solution to the loose fit was to cut off the arms. Either over or under the suit we wore light Helly Hansen pile jackets, which all of us found to be very warm for their weight.

Over the pile suit we wore a Goretex-covered down-filled suit with a detachable hood and a zip from the neck down through the crotch up to the middle of the back. The zip was in two sections to avoid having the slider sit uncomfortably on one's back. Zips also ran down the side from the armpit to the ankle so that the suit could be put on while wearing boots and crampons. This time the handwarming pockets at chest level had closable pockets on top of them.

The final layer was a light (two-laminate) Goretex windsuit. I tested a prototype of this suit on Anyemaqen in 1981, and with further refinements after that climb and Annapurna II, Mountain Designs came up with a superb weatherproof garment. The zip configuration matched the down suit except for the cut of the hood (which was not detachable).

Low on the mountain we wore the windsuit over underwear or the pile suit. Higher up, the down suit replaced the windsuit as our outer layer except for the coldest conditions, such as the descent from the summit in the dark, when the windsuit was worn over the down suit. That was considerably warmer but the abundance of zips made access to one's body a frustratingly difficult procedure, especially since gloved unmittened fingers immediately became numb.

On our hands we wore Damart gloves underneath woollen or fibre-pile gloves, which in turn were underneath Dachstein mittens. The final layer was Thinsulate-filled overmits made for us by High Tops. They were warm but difficult to put on with cold unmittened hands. In extreme cold there was an inevitable compromise between warmth and retaining an element of usability in our hands — too many layers and we could not hold onto our ice-axes or anything else.

Our boots were Koflach Ultra Extreme doubles — a plastic shell with Aveolite inner boots. We had Super-gaiters glued and stapled to the welt. We wore thermalactyl socks underneath woollen ones. Geof wore vapour barrier socks, which he found good. I used Serval Thinsulate overboots which were very warm but had the disadvantage of not being able to hold cable crampons. The boots which I lost in the bergschrund were large Ultra Extremes with Super-gaiters. I had transformed them into triple boots by having the plastic shell heat-stretched and wearing a felt inner between the shell and a smaller Aveolite inner. Since my frostbite in 1978, cold feet had always been a problem. It seemed that these triples were the solution until the avalanche stole them.

We had Chouinard-Salewa non-rigid crampons and Lowe Footfangs. The Chouinard-Salewas worked better for the small amount of rockclimbing we did, but were less secure on ice. The disadvanatage of Footfangs was their weight — a factor not quite compensated for by the ease of fastening and removing them, and their superior holding power. On low-altitude mountains weight is not the major consideration; it is, however, when climbing Everest without oxygen. The crampon which Andy broke on the Yellow Band was one of a pair of old-style Salewas I had bought ten years before and brought along as spares. Ironically, I had not worn these cram-

pons since I was frostbitten on Dunagiri.

On our heads we wore balaclavas of silk, wool, fibre-pile or Damart thermalactyl, depending on personal choice. Helmets (made by Daylite in New Zealand) were essential protection from the ice which fell down the lower part of the Face. At that time of year the danger from rockfall was minimal. To cut down the weight we carried, none of us wore helmets above Camp III.

In the selection of our climbing equipment weight was again a very important consideration. Our harnesses were the lightest available, made by Aspiring in New Zealand. Greg had unintentionally tested the strength of these by falling 100 metres while wearing one in South America in 1980. The ice-axes lost in the bergschrund were of titanium alloy. During the short time we used them we found their only drawback (a minor one) to be the extra effort needed when using one to deball snowed-up crampons by tapping them. After their loss we used Chouinard axes with carbon fibre or bamboo handles. Our North-wall hammers were Lowe Hummingbirds which we found to be very good indeed in spite of their weight — very secure and easy to use. Their sliding wrist loop system would probably be valuable on steep frozen waterfalls, but for our purpose it was only a nuisance.

Our other ice-climbing equipment was fairly standard — snow stakes of different lengths; and an assortment of ice-screws, mostly Chouinard, Snarg and a few Warthogs. Our small rack of rock gear consisted of a few blade pitons, a few nuts and several Friends. We had found the Friends to be very good on the appallingly bad rock of Annapurna II, and the same applied on Everest.

All our rope was manufactured by Beal. Our lead ropes were 50-metre lengths of 8.8 mm Everdry, and the fixed rope reels of 7 mm static. Past experience had shown that while 7 mm rope is adequate for fixing ice and snow, thicker rope is preferable for rocky ground. On the whole, the Petzl ascenders we used were good, though slightly small for mittened hands. Towards the end of the trip one of Greg's jammed and was useless. We chose figure-of-eights as our descenders because they are foolproof — an important consideration for oxygen-starved minds.

For stocking camps up to Camp II we carried our loads in Lowe Expedition packs. They were very comfortable but the shoulder straps had the annoying habit of slipping through their buckles when the pack contained a heavy load. For climbing above Camp III we had special lightweight packs made to my specifications by the New Zealand company, Macpac. Both of these packs were excellent for their different purposes.

Each of the climbers had two sleeping bags. For use up to Camp I we took Verglas Eggerlite bags from off the rack. On the mountain we had the special bags which we tested on Annapurna II. The shell was made of very lightweight ripstop cut widely (for wearing a down suit inside) and very long with a reinforced foot section (which provided space for keeping our boots and water bottles unfrozen in extreme cold without tearing the lighter fabric of the rest of the bag). The hood was large and the quality of down very high. There was no zip, in the interests of warmth and weight. The filling of down was less than factory textbooks would suggest, but when used in combination with a very light, close-fitting Goretex bivvy bag, extra air was trapped, and it was a very warm place to sleep for a combined weight of 2.4 kilos. Only at

Camp IV did we need to sleep in our down suits.

When we slept on snow or ice – that is, Camp I and above – most of us used two full-length closed-cell-foam Karrimats to sleep on. The extra warmth of two was very noticeable.

Lowe Super Diamond dome tents provided our shelter from Base Camp to Camp IV. As extra insurance against Everest's gale-force winds we added four extra guys at the points where the poles crossed. A velcro tab on the inside of the fly held the fly to the crossed poles. On other dome tents the metal poles had occasionally broken at these points in exceptionally strong winds. We also used two Wild Country Quasar tents – it was one of these that was avalanched at Camp 1.8. The other we reserved for high on the mountain, but when Geof turned back, we decided to cram the four remaining people into a single dome and thus save weight. The Lowe Alaska tents which we used up to Camp I proved unsuitable for heavy snowfall.

The large car-camping tent given to us by the Sydney firm of Goodearl and Bailey proved to be weathertight even when collapsed under thirty centimetres of snow. The giant pyramid tent which was our kitchen and mess tent at Advance Base weighed several yak-loads but was very strong and weatherproof, and roomy enough to provide a comfortable refuge for all of us on bleak days. At Camp I the North Face North Star which we used as a mess tent was cramped with twelve people inside, but very cosy and strong.

For cooking we used large kerosene stoves at Base and Advance Base. At Camp I we used kerosene in Optimus and MSR stoves, and at Camp II MSRs. The kerosene provided by the C.M.A. was of high quality and we had few of the problems caused by dirty fuel which were familiar to us from Nepal and India. At Camp II and Camp IV we cooked with Camping Gaz stoves (Bluet 200S) with special high-altitude cartridges containing a 60/40 mix of propane and butane. Having used these stoves on Annapurna II, we knew that they had a number of limitations. No other available propane fuel stoves were light enough, and we soon learnt that industrial safety regulations prevented other brands of stoves or cylinders from being altered. We took the French Gaz stoves because they were the only stoves which came close to fitting our needs. Having accepted their limitations, we used them satisfactorily at Camps III and IV. When our stoves had difficulty operating because of lack of oxygen, we felt better about not firing on all cylinders ourselves.

For travel on the snow-covered sections of the glacier we had a choice of cross-country skis and snowshoes. Most of us used skis – metal-edged Kharhu Bearclaw stepped skis with Telemark bindings and Asolo double boots. The worth of the boots was demonstrated when Tim wore them to the summit, having lost his Koflachs in the bergschrund. Equipped with lined Forrest overboots for extra warmth, and Footfangs to provide rigidity, they were a workable solution. Our ski stocks were Raimer Extendables, which could be joined together to make avalanche probes. Because the extended pole tapered at each end and was thick in the middle, it was not easy to probe with – it either jammed or froze if left deep in the snow.

Our Bollé glacier glasses were excellent in both sun and storms. The leather nose guards were used by some, but were found to be a nuisance by others. High on the mountain we replaced our glasses with goggles to provide protection from the cold as well as the glare. Both Andy and I had prescription lenses made for our glacier glasses. I managed to find a cheap pair of goggles which took prescription lenses – these were not very comfortable, and one of the lenses popped out and rolled down the mountain.

To send our gear to China we packed breakables in plastic barrels and non-breakables such as tinned food, tents, rope and clothing in kitbags or polyhessian sacks. Everything was first put in plastic garbage bags. Our skis were bundled together and sheathed in kitbags, and these were the only things to suffer more than superficial damage during the long journey to Tibet.

FOOD

TIM MACARTNEY-SNAPE

On a mountain, even more than in normal life, food becomes central to one's existence. There, one's supplies must satisfy both psychological and nutritional needs. Food surreptitiously rules one's life and becomes the raison d' etre for all feelings, negative and positive. High altitude also breeds a serious disinclination to eat, and fussiness about what is eaten increases in direct proportion to the altitude. Not only must food be good nutritionally; more importantly, the climbers must believe it to be good. Any doubts about a food's worth will render it unappetising to the point of inedibility at high altitude. On a high-altitude climb, food can therefore make the difference between success and failure.

Our main ethic regarding food was that it should be as natural as possible. Excessively processed, preserved and coloured foods have no place in the diet needed for prolonged periods of constant exertion and mental anxiety that are so much a part of Himalayan climbing. Luckily, the Expedition as a whole had homogeneous tastes and it was not difficult to persuade those who were not vegetarian to become so for the duration of the climb. The difficulty of digesting meat is exacerbated at high altitude and my belief is that it decreases the general efficiency of one's digestion. Meat also needs more time to cook, so more fuel must be carried; it is difficult to preserve and, if not dehydrated, it is heavy.

I believe that, from a humanitarian and environmental viewpoint, modern meat production is one of the most deplorable aspects of human development. The Expedition's success is definitive proof that vegetarianism works in the toughest imaginable conditions.

Proteins were provided in our diet by cheese, milk powder, a varied selection of nuts, legumes and other seeds, egg powder, and to a lesser extent by grains such as wheat, rice and oats.

In terms of quantity, carbohydrate was the most important item in our diet, and we relied heavily on sugar, muesli, dried biscuits, chapattis, pasta and potato powder. Rice was the dominant carbohydrate lower down but, because it required pressure-cooking, we did not use it above Camp I.

Fats were less obvious in our diet but, contrary to popular belief, I believe they have an important role in the perfect high-altitude diet. The fats from nuts, cheese, chocolate and butter act as long-term sources of energy during periods of continuous climbing. Marine lipids, which we took as a dietary supplement, dissolve fats in the bloodstream with the result that blood flow, particularly cardiovascular, is improved.

An important role was also played by other dietary supplements in the form of organically bound minerals and vitamins, garlic oil and herbal extracts. We are indebted to Bioglan Pty Ltd for providing the Expedition with these supplements.

Last but not least in our diet was water. Survival at high altitude depends on a high intake of fluids. A minimum of five litres per day is essential, but more is preferable. The main problem is that all water must be melted from snow, an endless and tedious task since snow occupies six to ten times more space than the same weight of water. To entice ourselves to drink more we had a range of beverages: coffee, chocolate powder, soya milk, orange and lemon powder and a variety of teas (of which the tangy ones were most popular high up).

The form that our food took was determined largely by cost and weight. Weight is critical in the mountains as all supplies have to be carried. Wherever possible, therefore, we used dehydrated food. Freeze-drying preserves food quality best, but on previous expeditions we found that pre-prepared freeze-dried dishes soon became unappetising. On Everest we chose individual products such as vegetables and fruit, and combined them with our own spices and carbohydrate base such as rice or noodles. We found this system to work very well, as we could cater to our varying tastes rather than being forced to eat the unvarying flavours of packaged meals.

Air-dried foods were cheaper, so we used many of them lower down the mountain. We are grateful to Sanitarium Health Foods for providing us with ample quantities of dried fruit and nuts.

Fresh food is always best but its availability is limited in the Everest region. The high points of our diet were the fresh vegetables — potatoes, cabbages, carrots, cauliflowers and onions — that we brought with us from Lhasa. The supply ran out towards the middle of the Expedition and only a small quantity of potatoes were available locally.

We took a few luxury items for boosting morale and stimulating our altitude-jaded tastebuds. Delicacies such as tinned fruit, cream, plum puddings, muesli slices (four hundred of which were generously donated by Buttercup), lots of chocolate and even humble mayonnaise kept us healthily salivating.

Typical menu for one day at low camps

(Base Camp, Advance Base, Camp I)

Awakener	Milky sweetened tea
Breakfast	Porridge and muesli
	Cheese omelette
	Tea, herb tea, chocolate drink
	or instant coffee
Lunch	Milky sweetened tea
	Flat bread — chapattis, parathas or
	puris
	Potato and pea curry
	Peanut butter, honey, tahina, jam
	Roasted nuts, cheese
	Teas or coffee
Afternoon Tea	Sweet biscuits and tea
Dinner	Soup — dehydrated packet soup
	without preservatives
	Rice or noodles with potatoes,
	cabbage, onions, garlic, ginger,
	dried peas or beans
	Tinned or dried fruit with custard
	Hot drinks

Typical menu above Camp I

Breakfast	Tea
	Porridge or muesli
	Tea, herb tea, soya milk or hot
	powdered-orange drink
Lunch	Chocolate, nuts, muesli slices
	Water or fruit drink
Dinner	Tea and biscuits
	Soup with quick-cooking noodles and
	onions, spices, dried mushroom,
	peas, beans or parmesan cheese
	Stewed dried fruit
	Hot chocolate drink

HEALTH AND MEDICAL CONSIDERATIONS

DR JIM DUFF

The Expedition's health was approached in a variety of ways. A sufficient supply of drugs and surgical equipment was carried to treat most medical and a number of surgical problems (Appendix A). As well, acupuncture needles and homoeopathic remedies were used to treat illness in the early stages to reduce the need to resort to possibly debilitating drugs.

The climbers were nourished by an essentially vegetarian diet which proved acceptable to all. Dietary supplements were taken regularly by all the team. These were chosen for the following reasons and taken in high dosage.

Vitamin C: Non-healing cuts and abrasions. Cracks at corner of mouth. Cracked lips. Fatigue. Viral infections.
B complex: Stress. Insomnia. Increased haemopoeisis.
Evening primrose oil and **Marine lipid:** Increased blood coagulation.
Iron: Increased red cell production.
Calcium: Osteoporosis.
Various minerals: Decreased immune response. Increased red cell production. Fatigue. Insomnia.

Acupuncture was used for muscle injuries, back strain, sinus catarrh, headache, cold feet, haemorrhoids and cough.

Homoeopathic remedies included: arnica for strains and bruises; bryonia for bronchitis; coca for altitude headache; drosera for cough; pulsatilla for catarrh; staphysagnia for infection; and rhus. tox. for strains.

Prior to the Expedition everyone was asked about his previous medical history and allergies to drugs. Blood count, group and antibody testing were performed in order to facilitate blood transfusion between members of the Expedition.

Eleven Expeditioners spent 65 days at Advance Base Camp (5400 metres) or above. Most of the time was spent at Camp I (5700 metres). At first the weather was mild with heavy snowfall, gradually becoming colder with less snowfall but more wind. The clement temperatures during the monsoon were a very helpful factor in acclimatising without losing fitness due to cold and wind stress.

Weight loss varied from three to nine kilograms. Only two of the eleven did not suffer from one or more symptoms of mountain sickness (headache, nausea, insomnia, shortness of breath) on flying from sea-level to Lhasa (3500 metres). (While we were in Lhasa a tourist died of acute mountain sickness following this abrupt ascent.)

Three people (at least) suffered further symptoms of mountain sickness at Base Camp (5200 metres) after a four-day ascent from Lhasa.

Colds and diarrhoeas settled soon after achieving the isolation of the mountain.

Minor ailments included insomnia, diarrhoea, bronchitis, headache, sunburn, rampant dandruff, snow-blindness, cough, back injury, haemorrhoids, cold sores and cold feet.

Serious illnesses were pulmonary oedema (Expedition interpreter), cerebral oedema (Geof Bartram), frostbite (Andy Henderson) and retinal haemorrhage (Tim Macartney-Snape).

A case of cerebral oedema (a type of acute mountain sickness) occurred above Camp II at 7300 metres. Symptoms started abruptly and consisted of severe headache, nausea (followed by vomiting), dizziness and mild visual disturbance. All symptoms cleared rapidly on supplementary oxygen at Camp I.

Equipment failure (metal fatigue, probably cold-induced, in a crampon) necessitated a climber removing his outer gloves at 8500 metres in the shadow of the mountain. Frostbite occurred to most digits but was not recognised immediately and the climber continued to 8800 metres. Rewarming was purposely delayed till the climber had descended the Face. Oxygen, intravenous fluids and large doses of Vitamin C were given. An antibiotic was commenced for the journey home and oxygen administered on the high passes traversed by truck between Base Camp and Lhasa.

Despite a severe cough starting at 8000 metres another climber reached the summit and descended to Camp IV where he was seen to be exhausted. He was very slow descending and went into a state of near-hibernation for several days. The main worry was of possible brain damage due to cerebral anoxia but, apart from a rapidly disappearing short-term memory dysfunction, all seems to be well.

Finally the other summiteer developed a retinal haemorrhage the day after reaching Camp I on the descent. This was close to the macula and produced visual problems especially with close work. Taking aspirin as an anticoagulant may have contributed.

Practically all the team members have experienced some degree of "culture shock" or distancing from their surroundings since return.

Special thanks to Dr Peter Gormley ANARE, Dr Ian Young, Hobart Red Cross, and Dr Paul Taylor for advice and dental supplies.

Most of the medicines were left in Lhasa for the 1985 New Zealand Everest Expedition with the request that they be donated to the local hospital on its return.

APPENDIX A:
MEDICAL EQUIPMENT

Intravenous giving sets
Intravenous fluid
Chest drain
Scalpels
Artery forceps
Needle holders
Sutures
Laryingoscope
Endotracheal tubes
Tracheostomy tube
Retractors, forceps,
scissors
Dental forceps/syringes
Opthalmoscope/
  auroscope
Sphygmomanometer
Inflatable splints
Plaster of Paris

Traction kit
Blood collecting bags
Cross matching kit
Syringes and needles
Rectal tubing
Nasogastric tubing
Urinary catheter
Oxygen cylinders (6) and
  mask
Subnormal thermometers
Nebuliser
Antibiotics
Analgesics
Antidiarrhoeals
Antacids
Anti-inflammatories —
local and general
Anticonvulsants

Anaesthetic — local and
general
Antinauseants
Antifungals
Aunty Maude
Sleeping preparations
Laxatives
Cough suppressants
Diuretics
Tranquillisers
Dressings
Bandages
Elastoplast
Emergency resuscitation
  drugs
Eye and ear preparations
Sterilising tablets
Sun screen

APPENDIX B:
PERSONAL FIRST-AID KIT

Morphine, 2 ampoules
Diuretic, 2 ampoules
Antinauseant, 1 ampoule
Syringe and needle

Anti-inflammatory for
snowblindness
Gauze pad
Roll of tape

Antidiarrhoeal, 10
Codeine tablets, 10
Sleeping tablets, 4

APPENDIX C

Thanks are due to the following companies who donated their products:

Abbot Australasia
Astra Pharmaceuticals
Beecham Research
Laboratories
Bioglan
Bristol Laboratories
Commonwealth Serum
Laboratories

D.L.C.
Du Pont
Ethicon
Hamilton Laboratories
Knoll A.G.
Roche Products
Sandoz Products
Schering

Smith, Kline and French
Laboratories
Smith and Nephew,
Australia
Tupperware
Upjohn
Wander Australia
Winthrop Laboratories

STILL PHOTOGRAPHY

Mt Everest is a tough place not only for climbers but also for their equipment, particularly delicate machines like cameras. Meltingly hot days on the glacier, freezing dawns, wet snow and the insidious dust of Tibet were all conditions which our cameras had to tolerate. Ideally, they would not only operate perfectly in these varying conditions but would be robust enough to survive a fall down the mountain, photograph low-light telephoto shots of sunsets and close-ups of snowflakes, and weigh no more than matchboxes.

Of course this was not the case, and once again it was a matter of compromising weight with versatility and strength. Each of us compromised in different ways. Andy restricted himself to using only a small Rollei 35 mm fixed-lens camera. Everyone else used 35 mm SLR cameras of different brands and with varying quantities of accessories.

Most of us chose as our standard lens a middle-range zoom lens (spanning somewhere between 30 mm and 105 mm focal length depending on the particular lens). The advantage of this was that the same scene could be photographed at different focal lengths without changing the lens. If one wore mittens or several layers of gloves there was a constant danger of dropping the lens or of getting fluff or snow inside the camera; if barehanded, fingers became painfully cold and hence clumsy. Climbing shots often require quick framing and focussing, allowing no time for changing lenses, especially when one is trying to pay out the climbing rope at the same time. A zoom lens, though heavier than a lens of fixed focal length, is much lighter than two or three such lenses which together cover the same range as the zoom. The only disadvantage is that zoom lenses have a larger minimum aperture and are therefore slower than fixed lenses. However, we found that the loss in clarity of high-quality zooms was not considerable enough to outweigh their other advantages.

We all had telephoto lenses of focal lengths from 135 mm to 500 mm (the 500 mm being mirror lenses). Several people had two camera bodies. My own experience indicates that the camera to take on a mountain should be one with a mechanical shutter that operates even without batteries. There is nothing more frustrating than a camera which has become useless because the temperature is too cold for the batteries to work.

During difficult climbing, or on the push to the summit of a peak, I usually carry only a small Rollei 35 in order to save weight. The results from this camera are invariably excellent, provided that my oxygen-deprived mind remembers to make all the necessary adjustments. Tim took an Olympus XA to the summit of Everest and was very pleased with the results. Other advantages of small cameras such as these are that they fit into a pocket so they do not freeze up, and that they are always at hand when a good photo presents itself. Many of the climbing photos in this book were taken by the Rolleis belonging to Andy and me, or by Tim's Olympus XA.

We made no attempt to organise compatibility with accessories by selecting a particular brand of SLR because some of us had firm but differing personal preferences. Canon, Nikon, Pentax, Olympus and Ricoh were all represented.

I used a Nikon FE2 and an FM2, and found both to be excellent. Lighter cameras do exist but I have found none robust enough to withstand the knocks and shakes of climbing. Canon lent to the expedition two F1 bodies and a selection of lenses and other accessories. Howard, who used this equipment, was very pleased with its performance, but found it prohibitively heavy for use on the mountain.

Most of the film we shot was Kodachrome, a mixture of 25 and 64 ASA. While climbing it was usual to carry one still camera and one Super 8 movie camera. It therefore made sense to have the still camera loaded with the most versatile film. For our purposes, this was Kodachrome 64, which reproduces both bright snowy landscapes and darker scenes such as the inside of tents and snow caves. Kodachrome 25 is probably better for snow shots: it captures detail in people or other comparatively dark objects without washing out the bright background. However, it is too slow for dawns, sunsets or hand-held shots in camps. Most of our 25 ASA film was shot on the glacier when we had access to tripods or other cameras loaded with faster film.

Ektachrome 400 was good for photographs in dark monasteries and for hand-held telephoto shots of people, but was of limited use once we reached regions of snow and ice. The extra graininess of this fast film also limited its popularity.

Most of us kept UV filters on our lenses to protect them from scratches, dust and snow. Polarising filters were very useful in the glary conditions, though they can make the sky look unrealistically dark. A problem occurs when using a polarising filter while wearing polaroid sunglasses. When the lenses are orthogonal the viewfinder goes black, not necessarily at the point where the filter is aligned to the correct angle for the desired photographic effect. In addition, hands covered with mittens and gloves are often too clumsy to control the adjustment of a polarising lens.

All sorts of restrictions limit one's photographic capability during a high-altitude climb. Changing film while unroped on a steep face can be a delicate process, especially when one must prevent light from leaking into the film cassette in the extremely bright conditions. Beautiful dawns and sunsets are photographed at the cost of numb fingers. In extreme cold film must be rewound slowly, otherwise sparks of static electricity leave blue dots in every photo. The burden of photography, in terms of both the effort needed and the weight of the equipment, increases the higher one heads into the earth's atmosphere. To compensate, the scenery is often so magnificent that the simplest snap can yield a stunning result. The spurs that photos dig into one's memory, as well as the appreciation the photos bring to non-climbers, make the effort of mountaineering photography worthwhile.

CINEMATOGRAPHY

Michael Dillon

More vital than equipment choice is the choice of the film crew, and immediately things augured well: firstly, the Expedition climbers wanted a film crew with them, and secondly they chose the film crew. They chose friends, people they knew they could get along with. They chose people who, with the exception of myself, were good climbers in their own right, people with excellent still photography backgrounds but not necessarily with any film-making background. It was simpler and safer, everyone agreed, to teach a good climber how to film than to teach an experienced cameraman how to climb.

As an added bonus the five climbers were themselves to be an integral part of the film crew. They joined the pre-departure film training programme and all of them filmed on the mountain, Tim and Greg even filming from the summit. Andy might have been there with them had he not been weighed down by the tape recorder he used so effectively on the ascent.

So it was quite a team effort! I know of no other Everest expedition where every single person (including Tenzing and Narayan who cooked and carried for us) was so fully and harmoniously involved in the film-making process and all deserve tremendous thanks. So do those who took the financial risks: Channel Nine's Kerry Packer, Sam Chisholm and David Hill.

With the film team settled, other questions arose. What cameras, what general equipment to use? How best to cope with the thick humid air at one end of the trip, the great scarcity of air at the other, the oven-like heat of the high glaciers, the sub-zero cold of the summit?

The lower two-thirds of the Expedition we filmed in the conventional way, using 16 mm Eastman 7291 and 7294 negative film in a nickel cadmium battery-powered Aaton camera and a Nagra III quarter-inch crystal sync tape recorder. But from Base Camp on, we abandoned all but one 16 mm camera – the ever-reliable Arriflex ST, its variable speed motor powered by a nickel cadmium battery and a back-up arrangement of alkaline batteries wired in series/parallel. Lenses used were an Angenieux 12-120 mm and a Canon 800 mm extreme telephoto. The latter, mounted on a heavy-duty tripod, gave excellent results provided there was absolutely no wind buffeting and this we achieved by filming from a protective screen of skis and space blankets, and sometimes by filming from the bottom of a crevasse.

But primarily, from Base Camp upwards, we filmed in Super 8. Super 8 has its disadvantages: scratches and hairs in the gate look four times as large as they do on 16 mm film; the reversal film stocks allow less exposure latitude; and high-contrast situations (people in snow etc.) require careful handling (best achieved by using the camera's zoom lens and automatic exposure system like a spot meter, then setting the chosen exposure manually). But against these disadvantages (all, with care, surmountable) Super 8 offers tremendous advantages. The cameras are light, compact enough to fit in a waist pouch, quickly and easily loaded, quick to bring into operation, easy to use, cheap and unobtrusive. Super 8 Kodachrome 40 film and its magnetic sound stripe, when transferred to video, are both virtually indistinguishable in quality from video transfers of 16 mm film and quarter-inch sound.

For general use and, we hoped, for summit use as well, we took nine Canon 514XL Super 8 cameras with 9-45 mm zooms and 5.9 mm wide angle attachments. Percy Jones of Motion Picture Services, Sydney, extended their zoom handles, their on-off switches and battery check buttons so they could be operated wearing three pairs of gloves. For added power in cold conditions, he made up separate "D" size battery packs for each camera. We gaffa taped the eye-piece diopters which otherwise tended to work loose and for general protection Anthony Hardy of Pigeon Bone made neoprene jackets for each camera.

The Super 8 sound cameras used were robust Canon 1014 XLs with 6.5-65 mm 200 m lenses and 4.3 mm wide angle attachments. We used professional quality microphones plugged directly into the camera and took plenty of spare microphone-to-camera leads. Camera noise was virtually eliminated by using the camera's base cut and limiter facilities; holding the Sennheiser 416 directional microphone in front and to one side of the camera; and placing a lead-lined camera jacket or the hood of a down jacket over the camera.

We used tripods whenever possible because the alternative, handholding, involves breathholding and that, at altitude, is almost impossible. Our tripods ranged from Miller Super 8 fluid heads to ice-axes fitted with tripod screws.

In all, we shot some sixteen hours of film using the excellent Kodachrome 40 and when necessary, the grainy high-speed Ektachrome 160. The latter should never be used out of doors unless you are filming snow storms you want to look impressive. Using Ektachrome 160 instantly doubles the amount of snow.

For "wild" sound such as interviews we had two Sony TCD5 Pro Cassette recorders and five Sony WM D6C Professional Walkmans. The latter, stuffed in a pocket, and used in conjunction with tiny Sony Electret ECM 150T or ECM 30 neck microphones, gave wonderful sound high on the mountain, including good sound of walkie-talkie conversations. Our nine walkie-talkies were Shinwa SH 404 KGs, their range further extended by high-gain antennae at the three lower camps.

Our cameras, walkie-talkies, headlamps and tape recorders were all amply powered by Duracell Alkaline batteries. We used almost two thousand of them, half of which were kindly donated by Duracell.

To help contain and protect film, cameras and recorders within rucksacks, Mike Law made padded vinyl stuff-sacks and on the journey in by plane, bus, truck and yak all equipment was packed in foam inside Willow-ware holidaymaker coolers. Painstakingly developed for the safe transportation of cold beer to football matches, these sturdy containers defied all attempts by airline baggage handlers to smash them to smithereens. Field tests we carried out on 14 August 1984 proved that when they fall from a medium-sized yak, tumble 110 metres down a 65 degree slope and hit a rock at the bottom, they still won't break.

PHOTO CREDITS

All uncredited photos by the author.

Tim Macartney-Snape: Back Jacket Flap, page 58, 59, 113, 156, 163, 188, 189 Below, 202, 206, 221, 224, 225-226, 227-28-29, 238-239
Andy Henderson: p 12, 54, 71, 175, 180. 187, 192, 208 Below, 210
Geof Bartram: p 43, 80, 98 Above, 142, 168 Above, 195, 200, 201, 242-43
Howard Whelan: p 6-7, 155, 160, 177
Mike Dillon: p 37, 143 Above, 150 Above, 171, 173
Colin Monteath: p 161, 196, 240
Greg Mortimer: p 198-99
Helen Flanders: p 45

SPONSORSHIP

To approach Mt Everest from the north involves much more overland travel than from the south. Services in Nepal are a fraction of the cost of those in China and Tibet, where rates comparable to those in Australia apply for transport, accommodation and food. Consequently, the budget for our climb from Tibet was many times larger than any of our previous climbs. The Expedition would not have been possible without the support of the following sponsors. But first I would like to thank the people who helped us find our feet in the world of high finance, and who devoted their time and energy to the Everest Expedition while we were climbing Annapurna II. Our special thanks to John Allen, Ross Martin, Kevin Weldon and the firm Burston Marsteller.

Channel Nine "Wide World of Sports" was the major sponsor of the Expedition. Sam Chisholm, the president and director of TCN Nine, and Kerry Packer, owner of the Channel, had the imagination to back a venture which was just as likely to fail as to succeed. David Hill, the executive producer of the documentary, after throwing his hands in the air at the complexity of the task, did a remarkable job of organising the film project while avoiding intrusion on the mechanics of the climb. Channel Nine's dynamism in the television industry well matched our determination to climb Everest.

The Australia-China Council, part of the Department of Foreign Affairs, provided advice and a generous grant. Dr Jocelyn Chey and Richard Johnson of the Council, and Sam Gerovitch of the Australian Embassy in Beijing did their best to help the Expedition become a minor but successful part of the continuing co-operation between Australia and China.

Mountain Designs not only continually made alterations and refinements to the equipment it made for the Expedition under its Verglas trademark, but also imported the specialised gear we needed at cost if it could not convince the suppliers to sponsor the Expedition. Without the patience and perseverance of the staff, both in the factory and in the Sydney store, the climb would have taken another six months to organise.

The Age bought the newspaper rights from the Expedition and through its journalist, Simon Balderstone, provided an important means of communication from Base Camp to Beijing and Australia.

Asia-Australia Express shipped our equipment from Hong Kong to Beijing, then back to Sydney after the climb. Our thanks to Stuart Young in Sydney and Robert Cutler in Hong Kong for their enthusiasm and support.

Benalla Fund Raising Committee. In the early stages of planning the Expedition, fund raising in Tim's home district by Mrs Pat Gardiner, Mrs Hélen Dennett and the committee they organised enabled us to print brochures and letterhead, and so approach potential sponsors in a professional manner.

B.R. Converters, through director Brian Ingham-Rhodes, made a sizable donation to the Expedition at a time when our administrative costs exceeded our bank balance.

Canon kindly lent the Expedition two F1 bodies and a variety of accessories. Everything worked well in the tough conditions of Tibet. The Super 8 cameras which we used from Base Camp to the summit were also made by Canon, strength and versatility being their big advantages.

Cathay Pacific flew the Expedition to and from Hong Kong in great comfort, and arranged for the airlifting of our not inconsiderable amounts of luggage. Its familiarity with the South-East Asian arena made Cathay the obvious choice. Our thanks to Jim MacDougall and Alister Blount.

Citizen provided watches which could withstand the extreme environment of Everest. Its alarms (though we cursed them) woke us from our exhausted slumber at all camps when we needed to rise early to make the most of the day.

Clayton Utz provided we rather naive mountaineers with legal advice. Our thanks to James Gibb.

Peat, Marwick, Mitchell and Company handled the Expedition accounts and provided office space and secretarial services. Our thanks to the ever-patient Ezikiel Elias who kept our erratic methods of accounting in some sort of order, and to Larry Smith and John Cherry.

Radio 3AW bought the radio broadcasting rights from the Expedition.

Sanitarium Health Foods provided the Expedition with all its needs in dried fruit, nuts and other specialist health foods.

Storage Technology made the Expedition a donation of money and a loan of some "thin film read/write heads for high technology disk drives". We spent the money before we reached Base Camp, but Tim took the minute computer components to the summit and back.

The Hong Kong Shanghai Bank, the first company to support the Expedition financially, offered indispensable advice about the business of sponsorship and gave valuable introductions to other firms. Our special thanks to John Allen, Gordon Snowdon and Richard Joynt.

Wilderness Expeditions, of which Tim Macartney-Snape is a director, donated much of Tim's office time to the Expedition, and provided secretarial services and the use of audio-visual equipment for promotions.

Wild Magazine, a valuable forum for environmental issues and outdoor activities, featured stories about the Annapurna II climb and Mt Everest.

As the preparations for our climb progressed our sponsors were kept informed about the Expedition planning by our managers, Graham Lovett and Karen Scott of Proserve, who also helped with the negotiation of terms with several of our sponsors (including Channel Nine). Others who provided their support to the Expedition were Buttercup, Bollé, Damart, John Leckenby of Hong Kong Oxygen, Lowe Alpine Systems, Macpac, Scotpac, Dick Smith, Sheldon and Hammond, Ross McCleary of CIG, Jim Morrison of Companion, David Goodearl of Goodearl and Bailey and Belview Hosiery.

ACKNOWLEDGMENTS

There is a great deal more to producing a book than sitting down with a pen, a few exercise books, a pile of photos and the address of an interested publisher. I have learnt that discipline and persistence are needed to write a book as well as to climb mountains. It is unlikely that this would have reached the bookshelves if not for the encouragement of Kevin Weldon, Iain Finlay and Trish Sheppard, and my parents. This encouragement inspired me to start work on the book even before we left for China. Kevin Weldon supported both the Everest Expedition and the idea of a book well over a year before the climb; my friends Iain and Trish made me believe that I could write if I applied myself to the task; and my parents have always encouraged me to write and to accept all criticism as constructive. Since my return from Tibet the project has kept its momentum thanks to Cecille Weldon's dedication and Tony Gordon's willingness to do more than his job as designer required. My thanks to all these people and also to Sheena Coupe for dealing with the hyphens and commas and other editorial headaches, and to Patricia Wilkins for typing the manuscript from a dozen tatty exercise books.

"White Limbo" lyrics by Simon Binks and James Reyne are reproduced by permission of Wheatley Music.

And of course, without Tim, Andy, Greg, Geof, Tenzing and Narayan there would have been no Expedition, and hence no book. My thanks to them for their unbending support while I wrote, and for some of the best experiences of my life.

GLOSSARY

ABSEIL Method of descent by sliding down a rope. The amount of friction between the climber and the rope determines the speed of the descent. If the rope is doubled it can be retrieved after the abseil by pulling one of the ends. Longer abseils can be made if two ropes are tied together.

ANCHOR A climber attaches himself or the rope to the mountain by an anchor. It may be a natural feature, such as a spike of rock round which the rope is tied, or a man-made device such as a PITON.

ANOXIA The state of being deprived of oxygen.

ARETE A sharp narrow ridge.

BELAY see CLIMBING SEQUENCE.

BERGSCHRUND (abbr. 'schrund) The crevasse which separates the NEVÉ from the face of the mountain.

BIVOUAC (abbr. Bivvy) A night spent on a mountain without a proper camp, i.e. no tents or Dylan tapes.

BOLLARD Spike or lump of rock which can be used as an anchor.

BOOKING OF PEAK Permission to climb Himalayan peaks must be obtained from the government of the relevant country. An application is submitted by the expedition and a booking fee is paid. The mountain is then reserved for that particular expedition. Some mountains, such as Everest, are booked many years in advance.

CEREBRAL OEDEMA Retention of fluid in the brain, an often fatal malfunction of the metabolism due to the lack of oxygen and low air pressure at high altitude. Can generally be avoided by careful, gradual acclimatisation.

CIRQUE An amphitheatre formed by mountains.

CLIMBING SEQUENCE At the bottom of a cliff or particular section of mountain the two climbers each tie on to an end of the climbing rope. One man also ties himself to an ANCHOR. He is called the BELAYER. The other person, called the LEADER, begins to climb the rock face while the belayer pays out the rope and makes sure it does not snag. Once over five metres above the ground, the leader faces serious injury if he falls. In order to safeguard himself he places protection; he finds or arranges an anchor and clips the rope to it with a KARABINER. The rope can run freely through the karabiner, as if through a pulley. The anchor may be connected to the karabiner with a SLING. The anchor/sling/karabiner set-up is called a RUNNER. If the leader slips when he is six metres above the ground and 1.5 metres above the runner, the rope held by the belayer will arrest his fall after only three metres. The leader climbs up the cliff placing runners at regular intervals, the actual interval depending on the difficulty of the climbing and the availability of anchors. When all the rope between the leader and his belayer has been paid out the leader looks for a suitable ledge to use as a BELAY STANCE. There he ties the rope to one or more anchors. Then it is his turn to belay. As his partner climbs he takes in the rope. The second man unclips the rope from the runners as he climbs. If the second man slips he is safeguarded by the rope from above. Because the leader (now the belayer) is tied to anchors he is not pulled off the cliff by such a fall. Once the pair are together on the belay stance the whole sequence can begin again. A rope length climbed by this method is called a PITCH. A different system is sometimes used when climbing snow. Often the snow is soft enough for an instant belay to be arranged by plunging the ice-axe shaft into the snow. On such terrain the two climbers are tied together but do not place runners or belays. When a climber slips his partner rams his axe into the snow, and this anchors both climbers to the mountain.

COL A high pass.

CORNICE An overhanging lip of ice which is formed by wind on the crest of a ridge.

COULOIR A major mountain gully, usually with a base of snow or ice, and often providing the easiest route through steep rock.

CRAMPONS Lightweight alloy frames with twelve spikes that are strapped to mountaineering boots to enable the boots to grip on ice. Two points protruding horizontally from the front of the boot make climbing steep ice possible.

CWM   A valley on the flank of a mountain.

DESCENDEUR   A device for steep abseiling. The descendeur regulates the speed of the slide by increasing the friction between the climber and the rope.

DOUBLE BOOTS   For extremely cold conditions a light felt or synthetic boot is worn inside a large outer boot.

FIXED ROPE   Fixing rope on a mountain can be compared to building a railway line. It permits quick and safe ascents and descents between camps on the mountain. The different sections of the route need only be climbed once – after that they are surmounted by ascending the fixed rope. Rope fixing is a laborious and expensive procedure so the method is usually restricted to big mountains, mainly those of the Himalaya.

FOAM SLEEPING MATS   Used as insulation when camping on snow. They are warmer and lighter than air-beds.

FRIABLE (of rock)   Easily crumbled.

HARNESS   In the event of a fall a waist harness (to which the climbing rope is tied) is much safer and more comfortable than a rope around the waist.

HYPOTHERMIA   Subnormal body temperature. When exposed to extreme cold, the human body cannot maintain a constant core temperature. The hypothermia which occurs is fatal unless the person is rapidly rewarmed.

ICE-AXE   The essential mountaineering tool, used for climbing and belaying, and as a brake when a climber slips.

ICE-HAMMER   Instead of a claw to draw out nails, an ice-hammer has a pick for climbing ice. The hammer head is used for placing PITONS or SNOW-STAKES.

ICE-SCREW   A short metal shaft screwed or hammered into hard ice and used as an anchor.

JUMAR   A metal clamp used for climbing fixed ropes. It can be slid up the rope, but as soon as weight is applied it locks in position.

KARABINER   A strong oval snap-link used to clip the climber or the rope to an anchor or a runner.

LAMA   A Tibetan Buddhist monk.

LEADER   see CLIMBING SEQUENCE.

LIAISON OFFICER   Himalayan expeditions are required by the local government to take a liaison officer with them. His job is to ensure that the expedition does not exploit the people or climb the wrong mountain. He also helps with buying supplies and organising the porters.

MORAINE   Mass of boulders, gravel, sand and clay carried on or deposited by a glacier.

NEVÉ   Area of accumulated snow at the head of a glacier.

PEE BOTTLE   Urine receptacle. A real convenience in cramped bivouacs when it is not always practical to walk to the nearest bush or rock.

PITCH   see CLIMBING SEQUENCE.

PITON   Metal spike which is hammered into a crack in the rock to provide an anchor. Each piton has an eye to which karabiners can be clipped.

PROTECTION   see CLIMBING SEQUENCE.

ROPE   Climbing rope is used most frequently in lengths of fifty metres. Modern rope is designed to stretch to absorb the force generated by a falling climber.

RUNNER   see CLIMBING SEQUENCE.

SCREE   Steep mass of broken rock on the side of a mountain.

SIRDAR   A Nepalese word meaning "boss", applied to the foreman, guide and employer of a group of porters.

SLING   A loop of strong nylon webbing which can be draped around a bollard to provide a runner.

SNOW-STAKE   A piece of angular aluminium about sixty centimetres in length which is hammered into hard snow to provide an anchor.

INDEX

The Prologue, Epilogue and appendices have been included
in the index. Alphabetical arrangement is letter-by-letter. Italic
numerals refer to an illustration; those in bold type indicate
the main body of information on a subject.

In Chinese, the letter "Q" is pronounced "ch" and "X" is pronounced "sh"